MW00416671

High

Down the river
Slowly
Blue sky
Narrowed by trees
Immersed cool
Drifting softly
Shade and sun
Alternating
Still air
Only a whisper
Moving in treetops
Rippling water
Singing deep
Murmuring quiet
Gazing high
Higher than mountains
Listening deep
Deeper than oceans
Osprey soaring
Arching smoothly
My heart blending
Mind peaceful
But sadly knowing
Rapids ahead

Dedication
To my family, Carol, Sky, Brook and Jade.

OREGON's
Swimming Holes

Relan Colley

WILDERNESS PRESS
BERKELEY

Copyright © 1995 by Relan Colley
Photos by the author unless otherwise specified
Maps by Relan Colley and Kathy Morey
Design by Kathy Morey and Thomas Winnett
Cover design by Larry Van Dyke

Library of Congress Card Number 94-28360
ISBN 0-89997-169-5

Manufactured in the United States of America
Published by **Wilderness Press**
       2440 Bancroft Way
       Berkeley, CA 94704
       Phone: (510) 843-8080 FAX: (510) 548-1355

       Write for free catalog

Library of Congress Cataloging-in-Publication Data
Colley, Relan, 1948—
   Oregon swimming holes / Relan Colley.
      p.   cm.
   Includes index.
   ISBN 0-89997-169-5
   1. Swimming--Oregon--Guidebooks. 2. Lakes--Oregon--Recreational use--
Guidebooks. 3. Rivers--Oregon--Recreational use--Guidebooks.
I. Title.
GV838.4.U6C65 1994
797.21'09795--dc20   94-28360
                                              CIP

WARNING

Neither the author nor Wilderness Press assumes responsibility for the safety of the users of this book. There are inherent dangers in swimming in natural waters and in outdoor recreation and travel. Swimming and travel conditions undergo constant change that no one can foresee. The user of this book must assume responsibility for himself or herself.

Gentle reader: I have striven for accuracy in my descriptions. However, I am sure, due to the great bulk of descriptive data that there may be some errors, for whatever reason. If you find any, please grit your teeth, curse me and forgive me, then let me know. Write to me in care of Wilderness Press. You can write me with any other comments, too. If there are places omitted that should have been included, and which you are willing to share, let me know that as well.

Acknowledgments

All the folks who allowed pictures to be taken of them

All those who gave me directions and information along the way

Andy and Alison Moldenke

Anne Fairbrother, Environmental Protection Agency (EPA)

Bernie Smith, Forest Service

Bill Keene, MD, Communicable Diseases Epidemiologist, Oregon Health Division

Bill Veley

Bret Nyden

Brook Colley

Bureau of Land Management (BLM)

Carol Colley

Chamber of Commerce, regional information centers statewide

Chris Brashear and Betsy Krause

Cindy and Charlie Bruce

Cindy Fisher, Biochemistry Department, Oregon State University

Citizen's Lake Watch and Steve Dagget, Coordinator

Corvallis Public Library

Dave Hopkins, Oregon State Center for Health Statistics

Dave Jaret, Doug Drake, Greg McMurray and Larry Caton, DEQ

Don Nelson

Ed Fischler, Oregon State Parks

Elaine Larson, Forest Service

Eric Paterson

Gary Arnold, Surface Water Monitoring Coordinator (Storet), DEQ

George and Nancy Barker

Jade Colley

Jeep Hancock

Jerry Day, Bureau of Land Management

Jim Good, Oceanographic Extension, Oregon State University

Jim and John Kirk, and Jenny

Jim Schaad

Jo Miller, US Geological Survey

John Davenport, Mapping Division, Department of Transportation

John and Linda Myers

John Tappon

Jon Croghan

Jon Kimerling, Cartography Department, Oregon State University

Kathy Morey and Wilderness Press

Ken Clegg

Kerr Library, Oregon State University

Kevin Boyle

Lance Bruce

Liz and Jim Owens and Adam, Aaron and Bryant

Lloyd Musser, Forest Service

Lorinda Macomber

Mark McKay

Nancy Rosenberger and Clint Morrison

Oregon Department of Environmental Quality (DEQ)

Oregon Department of Forestry

Oregon Department of Tourism

Oregon Fish and Wildlife Service

Oregon Marine Board

Oregon State Parks and Recreation Department

Rich and Ori Polly

Pete Bond, Oregon State Parks and Recreation Department

Pete and Elaine Roth

Phil Paterno, Bureau of Land Management

Ren Mellinger and Stefanie and Cody

Rich Holt and Steve Mamoyac, Oregon Fish and Wildlife Service

Richard Colley

Richard Petersen

Ron Mellinger and Stefanie and Cody

Sky Colley

Steve Rowland, who was of special help

Steve Stratton

Stewart Wershow

Susan Unger and Susan Gilmont, Hatfield Marine Science Center

Uaea Satele

United States Army Corps of Engineers

United States Forest Service

United States Geological Survey

Velma Stewart

Wayne Elliot, Bureau of Land Management

Contents

(**Region**, *County*, Swimming Hole, *Point of Interest,* **Other**)

Map Legend

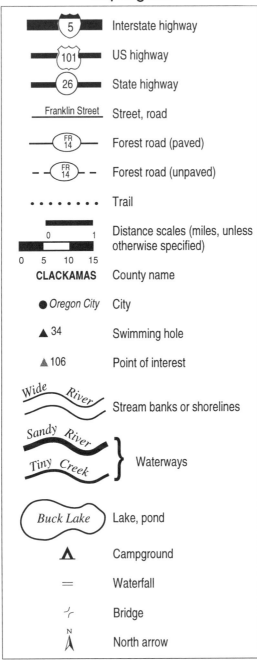

5	Interstate highway
101	US highway
26	State highway
Franklin Street	Street, road
FR 14	Forest road (paved)
FR 14	Forest road (unpaved)
· · · · · · ·	Trail
0 1 / 0 5 10 15	Distance scales (miles, unless otherwise specified)
CLACKAMAS	County name
● *Oregon City*	City
▲ 34	Swimming hole
▲ 106	Point of interest
Wide River	Stream banks or shorelines
Sandy River / *Tiny Creek* }	Waterways
Buck Lake	Lake, pond
▲	Campground
=	Waterfall
⌐	Bridge
N ⋀	North arrow

Note

If a place is readily located by use of the Official Map and my directions, no more specific map is furnished.

Preface

Few experiences in life offer the exquisite pleasure of swimming. I don't mean the fungus-infected, chlorine-filled, lap-paddling variety of swimming that requires a thorough bath to get the slime off when through. That kind of swimming often comes with a set of leaky goggles or a case of pink eyes. No, I mean the kind of swimming where the body is invited to rejoice in the natural current of a clean river, or to float with the gently undulating rhythm of a mountain lake.

There are those who think the real pleasures of natural waters yield themselves through fishing or in barging up and down with a motorboat full of beer. Frankly, I have gotten tangled up in enough lost fishing line and swallowed enough oil-scummed water to wish that the anglers and the boaters would get lost. Of course this sentiment does not apply to those fisherfolk who can hang on to most of their line and who do not leave rotting piles of styrofoam-encased worms behind. Further, these comments do not apply to the quiet boaters who can manage, without motors, to enjoy the backwaters of our land and who keep their beer cans to themselves.

I am convinced that a sure-fire cure for the ills of modern society is swimming in natural waters. We can shed the tensions of daily living by immersing ourselves in free-flowing waters that drown out extraneous noise and allow our bodies to tune in to themselves. In free waters there is an element of surprise that is exhilarating.

The United States enjoys an abundance of great swimming holes, the greatest of which is the Pacific Ocean. Swimming at Laguna Beach or San Diego is a real pleasure. If it were not for heavy dumping of waste, which makes some of its waters seem like open sewers, Southern California would be a superb swimming hole.

Ocean swimming illustrates the difference between swimming in natural waters and swimming in concrete swimming pools. The power and rhythm of the ocean vibrate right through the swimmer. While making him or her feel small, the ocean's swells, paradoxically, give the swimmer a sense of strength and grandeur. No artificial pool in the world can do that for a body! And the feeling is the same whether one is swimming off the coasts of California, Maine, or Hawaii.

Wonderful inland waters also abound. There are some fine swimming holes outside the Pacific Northwest. The Great Lakes, for example, undulate and taste like the ocean. Even a trip to bustling Chicago can be brightened by a swim in Lake Michigan. And the natural freshwater springs of northern Florida create some of the loveliest swimming holes anywhere.

This book is meant to help the swimming enthusiast find and appreciate a few of the many swimming holes in Oregon. It arises out of my own deep love for swimming in the outdoors and my quests for places to swim wherever I have traveled. I can recall several times having been on the road and hot, pulling into a gas station or market and asking where the nearest good swimming hole was. Usually, I was met with a blank look by people who wanted to help but who did not have the foggiest notion where or how to direct me. This is my attempt to help folks find and enjoy one of the best pleasures of life with minimum waste of time, energy and resources. (See Appendix A for numbers and addresses of agencies that may be able to provide useful information about many of the places in this book.)

I should mention a few things.

I do not much like reservoirs. I have included very few reservoir-connected spots, despite the fact that many reservoirs are billed as swimming locations. They lack intimacy, and they attract people in droves, particularly boaters. The reservoirs are easy to locate for those who want them.

Motorboats are anathema to me. I hope for most of them to be in the reservoirs, though they are not required to be. If a particular body of water is not protected by state law or regulation, or by federal wilderness designation, motors may be used on it. Fortunately, many places are protected by their lack of access or of suitability for boating.

I like hot springs, though they are not the major focus of my interest. Non-commercial hot springs are particularly rewarding. There are several commercial ones which I have not included in the text. They may be found listed in Appendix B, along with the names of hot springs which are not presently open to the public. (Nudity is practiced at nearly every natural hot spring and is also an occasional feature of outdoor swimming.)

I have included a few spots that are privately owned or access to which is privately owned. These places bear all the indicia of being dedicated to public use. They all clearly show that either by permit or easement, they are traditionally open to and frequently used by the public at large. I have scrupulously avoided including any places plainly marked against trespassing.

People fish at many of the places listed in this book. I have found very little friction between anglers and swimmers (except for all the lost line and litter that some anglers leave). I suppose that is at least partly because the optimum times for swimming and fishing are at different times of the day, and partly because of a mutual respect for each other's chosen recreation.

I have experienced every single swimming hole listed in this work at least once within the past two years. That means I have swum every stream and every lake, and toasted in every natural hot spring. I have toured all of the points of interest, nearly all within the same time frame. I have sampled most of the swimming holes in two different years, the first a dry year and the second a wet year.

Introduction

About Oregon

With deference to the rest of the country, there is no place like Oregon. Swimming holes are abundant and the beauty and variety of the surrounding countryside are unmatched. To the west there is ocean, to the east, desert. There are high mountain lakes in the Cascades, which stretch from California to Washington. Lovely rivers have created beautiful lowland valleys. With the exception of southeast Oregon, there is likely to be a decent swimming hole within half an hour's drive from any place in the state.

There are 2,856,000 people in Oregon, according to the 1990 census. Its 97,073 square miles (measuring roughly 375 by 275 miles) make it the tenth largest state. Oregon's landscape is dominated by the effects of volcanic buildup and of the sculpting power of water. There are over 100,000 miles of rivers, and more than 6,000 lakes exceeding one acre in size.

With few exceptions, Oregon law protects the public's, and hence the swimmer's, right and access to the vast bulk of the state's fresh and salt water. The Oregon Supreme Court has recognized the public's right, through the doctrine of custom, to unencumbered recreational access to the coastal shoreline, from the vegetation line to the ocean. Nearly all of the waters of the state, at least to the extent that they are "navigable," are preserved for public, including recreational, use. This body of law, combined with the fact that over 55% of the state is publicly (mostly federally) owned, makes it a recreational and swimmer's heaven.

There are a couple of drawbacks to swimming in Oregon.

First, ocean swimming is limited. On-shore coastal waters are often as cold in the summer as in the winter, and are colder than waters farther out to sea. This is due to the combination of steady north winds and the Coriolis effect, which causes warmer surface water to be deflected clockwise offshore, so that cold water upwells to replace it. Summer water temperatures along the Oregon Coast seldom exceed 60° F and more often hover in the low 50s, particularly toward the south. Rip currents and undertow may also occur in summer, though they are more frequent in winter. So, only a few strictly ocean spots are suggested in this book, and they are cool.

Second, Oregon freshwater swimming is mostly seasonal, from June through September. From July to mid-September is usually best. Lower elevations generally warm up quicker than higher ones, but it can remain chilly near the coast when it is warm everywhere else. Waters in Oregon may be nippy, though I have taken care to include only a handful of places that dip below 65° F in the heat of summer. Most swimmers will find water above that temperature comfortable.

Health and Safety

Nearly all waters in the United States are contaminated to a greater or lesser extent, but swimming in Oregon is neither a major source of contamination nor a particular health risk. To the extent that there is risk, it is similar to other risks faced in daily living, such as crossing the street, working in the yard, playing an outdoor game, or swimming in the local pool. According to the Department of Environmental Quality's 305(b) Report, 90–100% of river miles in each of Oregon's major drainage basins (not fully including the Columbia or the Snake) meet the Clean Water Act swimming goal (waters that do not show severe bacteria or excessive weed growth problems). All of Oregon's lakes are classified as meeting the swimming goal. I do not mention swimming holes in stream stretches that the 305(b) Report says do not support water contact during the summer. I have flagged those which are "partially" water-quality limited.

This is not to say that there are no disease risks associated with natural waters, though problems in Oregon have been rare. The parasites *Giardia* and *Cryptosporidium* can cause gastrointestinal illness. The bacterium *Leptospira* may cause fever, rashes and aches. However, no outbreaks of infection from these sources have been linked to swimming in natural waters in the Northwest. In warm, brackish water live tiny flukes that can cause a rash known as "swimmer's itch." Other bacteria and viruses may be present, but these hazards are simply things to be aware of, more potential nuisances than causes for serious concern.

A swimmer must be aware of his or her own limitations. The swimmer must recognize that natural waters change from day to day and year to year, and he or she must be prepared to adapt to the changes. In no other context is the adage "Go with the flow" more meaningful. Each year Oregon averages twenty drownings that occur during non-boating outdoor recreation.

Swimming in natural waters requires precaution:

1) Calibrate swimming to one's level of ability, conditioning and emotional comfort;
2) Learn to swim in the current—with or across it, not against it;
3) Unless a strong swimmer, avoid swift currents and large expanses of deep water;
4) Know a variety of strokes, including ways to rest in the water;
5) Take into account the dangers of heat and sun and their effect on judgment;
6) Forgo the use of alcohol and drugs when in and around the water;
7) Never dive head first into natural waters, and jump in feet first only when absolutely sure it is safe;
8) Be alert to the possibility of muscle cramps from rapid cooling in cold water;
9) Swim only with someone else—solitary swimming can be exquis-

ite but dangerous;

10) To minimize health risks, avoid swallowing water by keeping the mouth shut while swimming;

11) Do not use natural waters as a toilet and stay away from those who do;

12) Leave pets at home, both for their own good and for the health and enjoyment of people;

13) Fully supervise children;

14) Cross any rock abutting natural waters with prudence, as it is probably slippery;

15) Watch out for fish hooks and line;

16) Avoid breathing in power-boat exhaust and swallowing the oily scum on the surface of waters where boats are allowed;

17) Watch for water-borne debris, logs and the like;

18) Wear aqua socks or an old pair of tennis shoes where rocks may be encountered;

19) Learn to recognize poison oak in the lowland valleys;

20) Bring insect repellent, particularly for mountain lakes;

21) For the protection of the environment, leave no trace.

Above all, avoid panic. There is a mysterious and disorienting quality about natural pools and streams, particularly when one is alone or nearly so. When breezes blow, be aware of the unease they may engender. There is an eeriness caused when water distorts tree shadows, fallen trees and rocks. The swimmer's own monster shadow can seem strange and frightening. If, for whatever reason, it does not feel comfortable to swim, do not swim.

Natural waters are gloriously wild places and are not to be taken for granted. But, for the person who takes reasonable care, there is a joy and exhilaration in swimming in natural waters that is to be found nowhere else.

How to Use This Book

This book is intended to be used with the Official Highway Map of Oregon, which is available free at tourist centers and attractions all over the state. Entries are organized by region (see following map) and then by counties within a region. Each swimming hole and each point of interest appears on a county map by number. Detail maps are provided where more assistance may be needed (see the map legend on page xvi). With a couple of exceptions, they are based on either United States Geological Survey or Forest Service maps, with occasional not-to-scale details provided from my observations.

All measurements are given in English units. For users from the rest of the world, a simple-to-use set of conversions is included in Appendix C.

The miles specified in the driving instructions for each spot are as measured with my car's odometer, except where words of equivocation appear (such as "about" or "approximately"). In that case, the measure-

Oregon Divided Into Regions

ment is taken from a map. Hiking distances are based on my average pace through many trials on level ground. No entries are included where the hike exceeds five miles. I have inserted milepost designations where I believed them to be both useful and reliable. There are occasions where the mileposts are missing or are difficult to see, so it is necessary to stay alert. Within a county, all directions start from the same specified location.

Be aware that all data entries are a one-shot snapshot of conditions at any location, representative only, and not a definitive picture of conditions at other specific times. I have selected all data from summertime conditions, generally August. But, when it comes to natural waters, there is no such thing as "normal," and conditions have to be flexibly accepted as they are found. Streams and reservoirs, particularly, may experience great fluctuation in water level from month to month and year to year.

Each swimming entry includes a tabular listing of descriptive information, a set of driving directions, hiking instructions if needed, and a general narrative description. The tabular information listings include the following:

Rating—a subjective assessment of the swimming hole on a scale of 0 to 10, where 10 is the best and anything below 5 is not included;

Location—the land ownership unit (national, state, municipal or private) where the swimming hole is located;

Water quality—a thumbnail water description (fair, good, excellent) based on visual observations and published data, and including transparency, the single most useful gauge of water quality;

Vital statistics—includes the approximate maximum width or acreage of the swimming hole, approximate maximum depth, current speed (light, moderate, swift), summer temperature reading, amount of aquatic growth, bottom composition and an estimate of use (light, moderate, heavy);

Setting—a characterization of the terrain, vegetation, elevation, and amount of litter in the area of the swimming hole;

Minimum swimming skill ("Swim skill")—a rough suggestion of the level of swimming skill required to safely enjoy the swimming hole in the following terms: low (okay for kids who can swim a little and for other weak swimmers), moderate (for competent swimmers who may not be fully comfortable with all outdoor swimming hazards), strong (for highly skilled and conditioned swimmers able to cope comfortably with all hazards associated with rapid current, cross current, turbulence, cold, size and the like);

Amenities—includes the availability of established camping, drinking water and toilets close to the swimming hole;

Entry fee—indicates whether there is an entry or parking fee or not;

Topo(s)—the United States Geological Survey 7½' topographic map on which the swimming hole is located.

Some of the swimming holes are located in parks with nominal entry or parking fees. This is true of a few of the state parks during the summer. The state park system offers a seasonal pass.

Points of interest

I have included points of interest for those times when swimming needs a counterbalancing activity or when the weather or mood requires doing something else. Nearly all of these attractions are free or inexpensive. Hours and prices can change, so it is often a good idea to call ahead.

Conclusion

So, what makes a good swimming hole? Personally, I look for sand and well-placed rocks that provide both for easy access to the water and for comfortable lounging. I look for clear water, or at least water that seems clean even if it carries a load. The water needs to be swimmable—deep enough and large enough, without so much turbulence or current as to make it feel uncomfortable. Both shady areas and openings for the sun to get in are nice. And the surrounding area should be free of litter and pleasing to the eye.

All the places included in this book meet these requirements to a greater or lesser extent. They are all places of unique grandeur. They are to be cared for and preserved, to be savored and remembered. They are some of the most beautiful spots on earth. They are places where the heart can sing.

Upper Northwest

Rich in water and densely vegetated beauty, the Upper Northwest is dominated by the Columbia and Willamette rivers. Cool and rainy for most of the year, the region has a long summer of drought, ideal for the outdoor swimmer. Look for Douglas fir and hemlock forests, and for cottonwood trees in the low valleys.

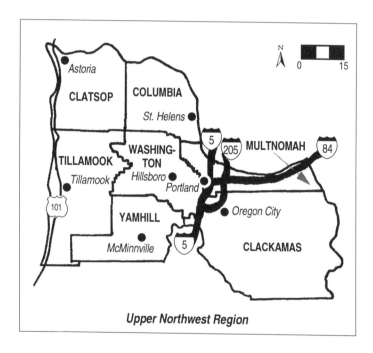

Upper Northwest Region

Clackamas County
(County Seat: Oregon City)

Clackamas County offers considerable variety to the swimming-hole world. Driving instructions begin in Oregon City at the intersection of I-205 (Exit 9) and Highway 99E.

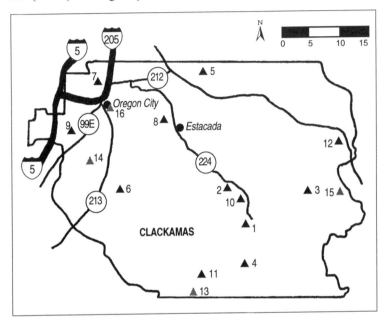

Clackamas County Swimming Holes

1. Alder Flat on Clackamas River
2. Big Eddy on Clackamas River
3. Buck Lake
4. Collawash River confluence of East and Hot Springs Forks
5. Dodge Park on Sandy River
6. Feyrer Park on Molalla River
7. High Rocks on Clackamas River
8. McIver Park on Clackamas River
9. Molalla River Park
10. The Narrows on Clackamas River
11. Pegleg Falls on Hot Springs Fork Collawash River
12. Trillium Lake

Clackamas County Points of Interest

13. Bagby Hot Springs
14. Hart's Reptile World
15. Little Crater Lake
16. McLoughlin House National Historic Site

Clackamas County Swimming Holes

1. Alder Flat on Clackamas River •••••••••••

Rating: 6
Location: Mount Hood National Forest
Water quality: Excellent; transparent to bottom
Vital statistics: 90' wide; at least 9' deep; light current; 61° F (August); light algae; rock and boulder bottom; light to moderate use
Setting: Forested valley at 1280'; light litter
Swim skill: Moderate to strong
Amenities: No-fee camping; no drinking water; pit toilets
Entry fee: No
Topo: Fish Creek Mountain 7½'

Driving Instructions: Alder Flat is 46.9 miles southeast of Oregon City. From the intersection of I-205 (Exit 9) and Highway 99E in Oregon City, head northeast on I-205 to Exit 12, the exit for the town of Estacada and for Highways 224 and 212, 3.2 miles. Take the exit and follow it to a stoplight, 0.2 mile. Turn right onto Highways 224 and 212 and drive to the point where they split, 3.2 miles. Take the right fork at this split, Highway 224, to its intersection with Highway 211 in Estacada, 15.4 miles. Stay straight on Highway 224 and continue to the turnoff for Alder Flat, 24.9 miles, just past milepost 49, on the right. (See detail map.)

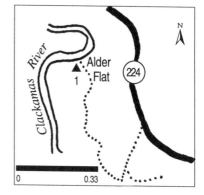

Hiking Instructions: Hike to the river on a gently descending trail through mixed old-growth forest, 0.8 mile (bear right at 0.2 mile).

Comments: The hole is nicely secluded from the bustle experienced at many other Clackamas River locations. The current is definite but manageable as far as the

downstream rapids. There are some shallows. A 40-foot sandy beach abuts
a backwater at the most logical swimming area. The camping spots along
the river are very nice. Portland General Electric Company warns of
fluctuating water levels at all Clackamas River locations.

2. Big Eddy on Clackamas River • • • • • • • • • • • • •

Rating: 6
Location: Mount Hood National Forest
Water quality: Excellent, transparent to bottom
Vital statistics: 180' wide; at least 18' deep; moderate current; 61° F
(August); moderate algae; rocks and pebbles on bed-
rock bottom; moderate use
Setting: Forested valley at 800'; moderate litter
Swim skill: Moderate to strong
Amenities: No drinking water; pit toilets
Entry fee: No
Topo: Bedford Point 7½'

Driving Instructions: Big Eddy is 35.0 miles southeast of Oregon
City. Follow the driving instructions of Swimming Hole #1 to the intersection of Highways 224 and 211 in Estacada. Stay straight on Highway 224
and continue to the turnoff marked for Big Eddy, 13.0 miles, between
mileposts 37 and 38, on the right. Be prepared for rough gravel when
leaving the highway to enter the parking area.

Comments: A varied shoreline provides pebbles, sand and formation
rock. There are rapids both upstream and downstream. Portland General
Electric Company warns of fluctuating water levels at all Clackamas River
locations.

3. Buck Lake •

Rating: 10
Location: Mount Hood National Forest
Water quality: Excellent; transparent to bottom
Vital statistics: 11 acres; 30' deep; 72° F (August); light algae; sand
and boulder bottom; light to moderate use
Setting: Forested foothills at 4000'; no litter
Swim skill: Moderate
Amenities: No-fee, primitive camping; no drinking water; pit toi-
lets
Entry fee: No
Topo: Timothy Lake 7½'

Driving Instructions: Buck Lake is 61.5 miles southeast of Oregon
City. Follow the driving instructions for Swimming Hole #1 to the

intersection of Highways 224 and 211 in Estacada. Stay straight on Highway 224 and continue to where it ends at its junction with Forest Roads 57 and 46, 25.7 miles. Bear left onto Forest Road 57 to its junction with Forest Road 58, 7.4 miles. Jog left onto Forest Road 58 to its junction with Forest Road 5810, 1.0 mile. Turn right onto Forest Road 5810 and go to the Buck Lake turnoff, 4.8 miles, between mileposts 4 and 5. Turn left onto a gravel road and drive to the trailhead, 0.6 mile. Parking is on the left, next to the trailhead. (See detail map.)

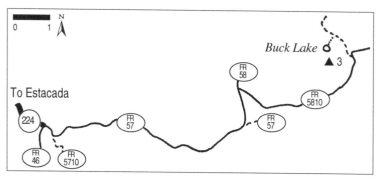

Hiking Instructions: Hike on a moderately ascending trail to the lake, 0.5 mile.

Comments: What a lake! Blue hues sparkle. Two rockfalls slide into the lake. One of them enters the lake 250 feet clockwise from where the trail meets the lake. That is a fine place to perch on and to swim from. There are salamanders and some log fall. Vine maple and rhododendrons abound. The maple turns a vibrant red in late summer. The lake is beauty in the midst of devastation. Much of the way on Forest Road 5810 is through an area shattered by logging. The trail to the lake goes from ratty new-growth to outstanding old-growth forest.

4. Collawash River confluence of East • • • • • • • • and Hot Springs Forks

Rating: 8

Location: Mount Hood National Forest

Water quality: Excellent; transparent to bottom

Vital statistics: 110' wide; at least 12' deep; light current; 63° F (August); light algae; rock and boulder bottom; light to moderate use

Setting: Forested valley at 1720'; light to moderate litter

Swim skill: Moderate

Amenities: No drinking water; pit toilets

Entry fee: No

Topo: Bull of the Woods 7½′

Driving Instructions: Collawash River confluence is 55.3 miles southeast of Oregon City. Follow the driving instructions for Swimming Hole #1 to the intersection of Highways 224 and 211 in Estacada. Stay straight on Highway 224 and continue to where it ends at its junction with Forest Roads 57 and 46, 25.7 miles. Bear right onto Forest Road 46 and drive to its junction with Forest Road 63, 3.7 miles. Turn right onto Forest Road 63 and drive to its junction with Forest Road 70, 3.7 miles. Continue straight on Forest Road 63 to the asphalt turnout on the left, 0.2 mile. (See detail map.)

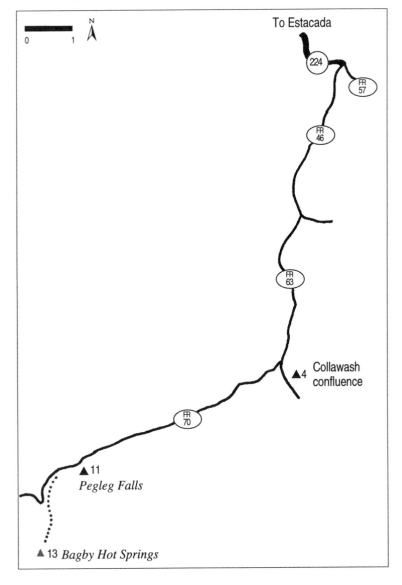

Comments: A picnic ground is at the entry down to the confluence site. There is a broad, 130-foot gravel beach with some sand. A nice cliff and some rock outcrops are on the opposite bank.

5. Dodge Park on Sandy River ••••••••••••••

Rating: 6
Location: Portland City Park
Water quality: Fair; 2′ transparency
Vital statistics: 90′ wide; at least 9′ deep; moderate current; 75° F (August); light algae; sand bottom; moderate to heavy use
Setting: Wooded valley at 270′; moderate litter
Swim skill: Moderate
Amenities: No drinking water; pit toilets
Entry fee: No
Topo: Sandy 7½′

Driving Instructions: Dodge Park is 26.2 miles east of Oregon City. From the intersection of I-205 (Exit 9) and Highway 99E in Oregon City, head northeast on I-205 to Exit 12, the exit for the town of Estacada and for Highways 224 and 212, 3.2 miles. Take the exit and follow it to a stoplight, 0.2 mile. Turn right onto Highways 224 and 212 and drive to the point where they split, 3.2 miles. Continue straight on Highway 212 to Highway 26, 8.4 miles (make a right turn in Boring to stay on Highway 212). Turn right and go to Ten Eyck Road (which becomes Lusted Road) in Sandy, 5.0 miles. Turn left and drive to the park entrance, 6.1 miles (stay straight at 3.5 miles). Turn right and into parking on gravel, 0.1 mile. (See detail map on next page.)
Comments: A rope swing and a 180-foot sandy beach await.

6. Feyrer Park on Molalla River •••••••••••••••

Rating: 7
Location: County Park
Water quality: Good; transparent to bottom
Vital statistics: 90′ wide; at least 12′ deep; light current; 73° F (August); light algae; rock and boulder bottom; moderate to heavy use
Setting: Forested valley at 360′; moderate litter
Swim skill: Moderate
Amenities: Drinking water; flush toilets
Entry fee: No
Topo: Molalla 7½′

Driving Instructions: Feyrer Park is 20.9 miles south of Oregon City. From the intersection of I-205 (Exit 9) and Highway 99E in Oregon City, head northeast on I-205 to Exit 10, the exit for Highway 213, 0.8 mile.

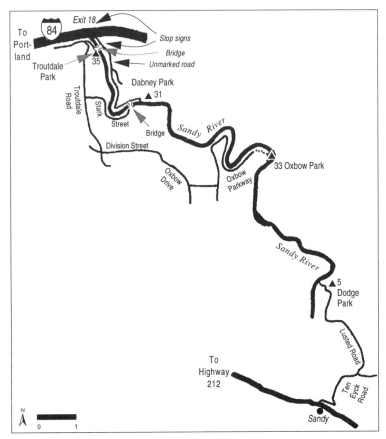

Head south on Highway 213 to Highway 211, approximately 16 miles. Turn left and drive through Molalla to Feyrer Park Road, 2.1 miles. Turn right and go to the park entrance, 1.9 miles. Turn left and into parking, 0.1 mile.

Comments: The hole is across from the bathrooms. A pebble bank and upstream rapids contribute to a pleasant hole. The adjacent park is lush.

7. High Rocks on Clackamas River • • • • • • • • • • •

Rating: 7
Location: Gladstone City Park
Water quality: Fair; 6′ transparency
Vital statistics: 150′ wide; at least 18′ deep; moderate current; 64° F (August); moderate algae; boulder on bedrock bottom; moderate to heavy use
Setting: Urban valley at 20′; heavy litter
Swim skill: Moderate to strong

Amenities: Drinking water; flush toilets
Entry fee: No
Topo: Gladstone 7½'

Driving Instructions: High Rocks is 2.5 miles northeast of Oregon City. From the intersection of I-205 (Exit 9) and Highway 99E in Oregon City, head northeast on I-205 to Exit 11 for Gladstone, 1.6 miles. Take the exit and go to a stop signal on 82nd Drive, 0.3 mile. Turn left and drive to a dead end at a bridge crossing the river at Cross Park, 0.6 mile. Cross Park is downstream and High Rocks Park is upstream of the bridge and accessed by a 380-foot asphalt path 0.1 mile back, on the left side of the road. However, the only nearby public parking is at Cross Park. To get to that parking, turn right onto Columbia Avenue just before reaching the dead end, and go to 1st Street, one block. Turn left and drive to Yale Avenue, 0.2 mile. Turn left and drive to parking, one block. (See detail map.)

Comments:
Beautiful, but trashed, basalt lines the spectacular, 0.2-mile river channel upstream of the bridge. Dropoffs to deep water are sheer. The water becomes shallow downstream of the bridge. There are up- and downstream rapids, and there is considerable slackwater. The river runs right next to I-205 at this spot. Graffiti are a travesty. Portland General Electric Company warns of fluctuating water levels at all Clackamas River locations.

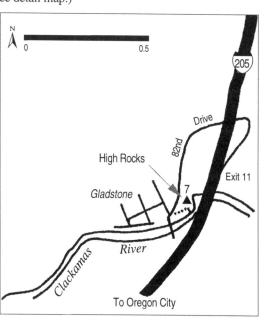

8. McIver Park on Clackamas River •••••••••

Rating: 7
Location: State Park
Water quality: Fair; 8' transparency
Vital statistics: 150' wide; at least 8' deep; swift current; 73° F (Au-

gust); moderate algae; gravel and rock bottom; heavy
use

Setting: Forested valley at 300'; moderate litter
Swim skill: Strong
Amenities: For-fee camping; drinking water; flush toilets
Entry fee: Yes, during summer
Topo: Estacada 7½'

Driving Instructions: McIver Park is 20.3 miles east of Oregon City. From the intersection of I-205 (Exit 9) and Highway 99E in Oregon City, head northeast on I-205 to Exit 12, the exit for the town of Estacada and for Highways 224 and 212, 3.2 miles. Take the exit and follow it to a stop sign, 0.2 mile. Turn right onto Highways 224 and 212 and drive to the point where they split, 3.2 miles. Take the right fork at this split, Highway 224, to another fork, 1.1 miles. Bear right at this fork and cross the Clackamas River to Springwater Road, 0.2 mile. Bear left and drive to the McIver Park turnoff, 9.1 miles. Turn left into the park and go to a fork, 0.5 mile. Bear right at this fork and proceed to the day-use area, past the campground, 2.6 miles. Turn left into the parking area and drive as far downstream as possible to park, 0.2 mile. (See detail maps.)

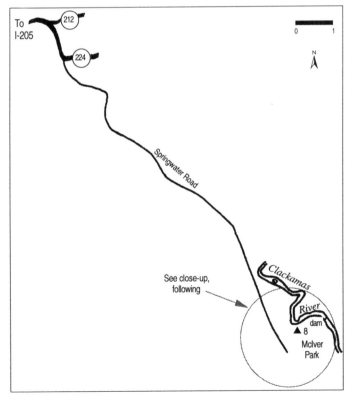

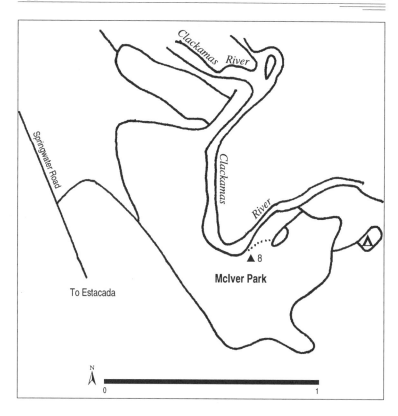

Hiking Instructions: Walk on the trail closest to the river, down-stream to a river cove, where a creek comes in on the left, 0.1 mile.

Comments: The cove along the river is created by a small tributary. Adults should be prepared to catch any kids tubing the stream. It is necessary to watch the current, which is swift and follows closely around the gravel-and-pebble beach. The current is difficult to swim against in spots, particularly close to the beach, so a plan for the return to the beach area is required. The current along the opposite shore is relatively weak, and a swim far enough upriver for a charge across the river is usually successful and certainly exciting. There are a few boulders along the left margin, downstream from the beach. The water is deep downriver for approximately 500 feet, where it becomes shallow and develops rapids. Birds of prey frequently soar overhead. The water often is full of driftboaters, but there is a nice ambiance. Portland General Electric Company warns of fluctuating water levels at all Clackamas River locations.

9. Molalla River Park ●

Rating: 5
Location: State Park

Water quality: Fair; 6' transparency
Vital statistics: 350' wide; at least 14' deep; light current; 70° F
(July); light to moderate algae; sandy bottom; moderate use
Setting: Wooded valley at 60'; moderate litter
Swim skill: Moderate
Amenities: Drinking water; pit and flush toilets
Entry fee: No
Topo: Canby 7½'

Driving Instructions: Molalla River Park is 10.5 miles southwest of Oregon City. From the intersection of I-205 (Exit 9) and Highway 99E in Oregon City, head southwest on Highway 99E to Territorial Road, 7.1 miles. Turn right and go to Holly Street, 1.6 miles. Turn right and proceed to the park turnoff, 1.4 miles. Turn left and drive to parking, 0.4 mile.

Hiking Instructions: Follow the river, on a pleasant gravel-road trail, upstream to the place set aside for swimming, 0.7 mile.

Comments: A couple of 30-foot, packed-sand beach spots front the river.

10. The Narrows on Clackamas River •••••••••

Rating: 7
Location: Mount Hood National Forest
Water quality: Good; 14' transparency
Vital statistics: 50' wide; at least 24' deep; moderate current; 61° F
(August); moderate algae; bedrock bottom; moderate use
Setting: Forested valley at 1040'; moderate litter
Swim skill: Moderate to strong
Amenities: None
Entry fee: No
Topo: Three Lynx 7½'

Driving Instructions: The Narrows is 41.6 miles southeast of Oregon City. Follow the driving instructions for Swimming Hole #1 to the intersection of Highways 224 and 211 in Estacada. Stay straight on Highway 224 and continue to an asphalt turnout above the river, 19.6 miles, between mileposts 43 and 44, on the right.

Hiking Instructions: Walk the moderate trail down to the river, 0.1 mile.

Comments: Generally low, blistered formation rock lines this gorgeous basalt channel where dropoffs to deep water are sheer. Upstream is a chute. There are some suds. Portland General Electric Company warns of fluctuating water levels at all Clackamas River locations.

11. Pegleg Falls on Hot Springs Fork •••••••••
Collawash River

Rating:	8
Location:	Mount Hood National Forest
Water quality:	Excellent, transparent to bottom
Vital statistics:	60′ wide; at least 22′ deep; moderate current; 61° F (August); light algae; boulder on bedrock bottom; moderate use
Setting:	Forested valley at 2040′; moderate to heavy litter
Swim skill:	Moderate
Amenities:	No-fee camping; no drinking water; pit toilets
Entry fee:	No
Topo:	Bagby Hot Springs 7½′

Driving Instructions: Pegleg Falls is 60.7 miles southeast of Oregon City. Follow the driving instructions for Swimming Hole #1 to the intersection of Highways 224 and 211 in Estacada. Stay straight on Highway 224 and continue to where it ends at its junction with Forest Roads 57 and 46, 25.7 miles. Bear right onto Forest Road 46 and drive to its junction with Forest Road 63, 3.7 miles. Turn right and drive to Forest Road 70, 3.7 miles. Turn right and go to the Pegleg Falls Campground turnoff (which may not have a sign), 5.5 miles, on the left side of the road. Turn in and drive to parking, less than 0.1 mile. (See detail map for Swimming Hole #4.)

Hiking Instructions: The hole is upstream from parking, partly along a metal fence, less than 0.1 mile.

Comments: The 17-foot falls is lovely, with a beautiful gem of a pool at its base and ropes for swinging. The pool is lined with bedrock. The overall effect is marred by a fish ladder.

12. Trillium Lake •••••••••••••••••••••••••

Rating:	5
Location:	Mount Hood National Forest
Water quality:	Good; 12′ transparency
Vital statistics:	57 acres; 16′ deep; 70° F (August); moderate shore-line weeds; sand and rock bottom; moderate to heavy use
Setting:	Forested foothills at 3600′; light to moderate litter
Swim skill:	Low to moderate
Amenities:	For-fee camping; drinking water; pit toilets
Entry fee:	No
Topo:	Mount Hood South 7½′

Driving Instructions: Trillium Lake is 49.9 miles east of Oregon City. Follow the driving instructions for Swimming Hole #1 to the point where Highways 224 and 212 split. Continue straight on Highway 212 to Highway 26, 8.4 miles (make a right turn in Boring to stay on Highway 212). Turn right and go to the turnoff for the lake at Forest Road 2656, about 33 miles. Turn right and drive to parking near the dam at the south end of the lake, 1.9 miles, on the left side of the road.

Comments: The swim area is adjacent to the dam on this natural lake. There are a beautiful view of Mount Hood and an adequate sandy beach.

Clackamas County Points of Interest

13. Bagby Hot Springs •
Mount Hood National Forest

> **Type:** Developed hot springs
> **Hours:** Daily
> **Fee:** No

Driving Instructions: Bagby Hot Springs is 61.2 miles southeast of Oregon City. Follow the driving instructions for Swimming Hole #1 to the intersection of Highways 224 and 211 in Estacada. Stay straight on Highway 224 and continue to where it ends at its junction with Forest Roads 57 and 46, 25.7 miles. Bear right onto Forest Road 46 and drive to its junction with Forest Road 63, 3.7 miles. Turn right and drive to Forest Road 70, 3.7 miles. Turn right and go to the Bagby Hot Springs turnoff, 6.0 miles. Turn left and drive to parking, less than 0.1 mile. (See detail map for Swimming Hole #4.)

Hiking Instructions: Hike to the springs on a well-maintained and pleasant trail, 1.4 miles. The trail follows the Hot Springs Fork of the Collawash River through old-growth forest dominated by Douglas fir. (There are swimmable spots along the way, particularly at the 0.4- and 1.2-mile points, but they are really too cold.)

Comments: At 2280 feet elevation, the hot springs is managed cooperatively by the Forest Service and a volunteer group, the Friends of Bagby. For the pleasure of a developed, but still rustic, hot springs, there is no better place in Oregon. There are three bathing areas. The New Bathhouse is composed of five private rooms, each equipped with a cedar-log tub, or "canoe." The adjacent Lower Bathhouse is furnished with three log tubs and a large circular tub, all set on a roofed deck. The smaller, Upper Bathhouse, 300 feet up the trail from the others, has a single large, circular tub. The cedar tubs are two to three feet wide and ten feet long. One-hundred-thirty-six-degree water from the springs, just above the main complex, is piped by wood flumes to the bathhouses, where wooden valves and stoppers are used to control the flow. Cold spring water is available for mixing to achieve the desired temperature. Nudity is to be expected. It is requested that no soap be used and that users clean out their tubs with brushes, which are provided after each use. Heavily used, the springs may be best enjoyed at odd hours and times of the year and in crummy weather. Bullies and vandals have sometimes been a problem at this otherwise extraordinary place.

14. Hart's Reptile World ••••••••••••••••••••
11264 South Macksburg Road, Canby; (503) 266-7236

> **Type:** Reptile zoo
> **Hours:** Daily, 11 A.M. to 7 P.M.
> **Fee:** Yes

Driving Instructions: Hart's Reptile World is 14.6 miles south of Oregon City. From the intersection of I-205 (Exit 9) and Highway 99E in Oregon City, head southwest on Highway 99E to a stoplight in Canby at Ivy Street (also called Canby Marquam Highway), 8.9 miles. Turn left and go to Macksburg Road, 3.4 miles. Turn left onto Macksburg Road, where there is a jog right off from, then left back onto, Macksburg Road, starting at 0.8 mile. Continue to the turnoff for Hart's Reptile World, 1.4 miles more. Turn right onto a gravel road and drive to parking near a long, metal-sheeted building, less than 0.1 mile.

Comments: An intimate and educational view of snakes and other reptiles is offered.

15. Little Crater Lake ••••••••••••••••••••••••
Mount Hood National Forest

> **Type:** Geologic site
> **Hours:** Daily
> **Fee:** No

Driving Instructions: Little Crater Lake is 75.4 miles east of Oregon City. Follow the driving instructions for Swimming Hole #1 to the intersection of Highways 224 and 211 in Estacada. Stay straight on Highway 224 and continue to where it ends at its junction with Forest Roads 57 and 46, 25.7 miles. Bear left onto Forest Road 57 and go to its junction with Forest Road 58, 7.4 miles. Jog left and go to Forest Road 5810, 1.0 mile. Turn right onto Forest Road 5810 and drive until it rejoins Forest Road 57, 8.1 miles. Follow Forest Road 57 past Timothy Lake to Forest Road 42, 3.8 miles. Turn left and drive to Forest Road 58, 4.2 miles. Turn left and go to the Little Crater Lake turnoff, 2.3 miles. Turn left and travel to parking at the trailhead for Little Crater Lake, 0.3 mile, on the right side of the road.

Hiking Instructions: The hike to the lake is on a handicapped-accessible trail, less than 0.2 mile long.

Comments: Forty-five feet deep, the lake was formed and is fed by an artesian spring along a fault line. It is a marvelous deep-blue color. This would be a great place for a swim except for the temperature! And swimming is not allowed.

16. McLoughlin House National Historic Site ● ● ● ● ● ●
713 Center Street, Oregon City; (503) 656-5146

> **Type:** Historic home
> **Hours:** Tuesday to Saturday, 10 A.M. to 4 P.M.; Sunday 1–4
> P.M.; closed Mondays, holidays and in January
> **Fee:** Yes

Driving Instructions: From the intersection of I-205 (Exit 9) and Highway 99E in Oregon City, head southwest on Highway 99E to 10th Street (which becomes 7th Street), 0.4 mile. Turn left and drive to Center Street, 0.3 mile (bear left at the top of the hill). Turn left. McLoughlin House is immediately on the left side of the road.

Comments: This is the retirement home, built in 1846, of the head of the Hudson's Bay Company in the Oregon Territory.

Clatsop County
(County Seat: Astoria)

Often too cool and breezy for swimming comfort, Clatsop County can be very nice for swimming on warm summer days. Driving instructions begin in Astoria at the junction of Highway 101 and Highway 30, along Marine Drive, at the entry to the bridge connecting Oregon and Washington.

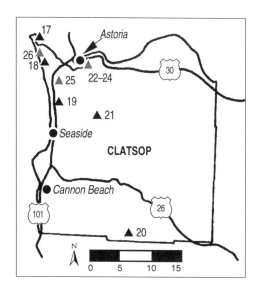

Clatsop County Swimming Holes

17. Clatsop Spit on Columbia River
18. Coffenbury Lake
19. Cullaby Lake
20. Spruce Run Park on Nehalem River
21. Youngs River Falls

Clatsop County Points of Interest

22. Astor Column on Coxcomb Hill
23. Columbia River Maritime Museum
24. Flavel House
25. Fort Clatsop National Memorial
26. Fort Stevens Historic Area and Military Museum

Clatsop County Swimming Holes

17. Clatsop Spit on Columbia River • • • • • • • • • •

Rating: 7
Location: State Park
Water quality: Fair; 4' transparency
Vital statistics: 4.0 miles wide; at least 14' deep; light current; 70° F
(August); moderate algae; sand bottom; moderate use
Setting: Grassy coast at sea level; light to moderate litter
Swim skill: Moderate
Amenities: For-fee camping; drinking water; pit toilets
Entry fee: Yes
Topo: Warrenton 7½'

Driving Instructions: Clatsop Spit is 13.4 miles northwest of Astoria.
From the junction of Highway 101 and Highway 30 in Astoria, head
southwest on Highway 101 to Business Highway 101, 3.8 miles. Turn right
and drive to Main Avenue, 0.9 mile. Turn left and go to 18th Street (which
joins Ridge Road), 0.2 mile. Turn right and drive to the day-use entrance of
Fort Stevens State Park, 3.6 miles. Turn left into the park and drive to Parking
Area D on the northeast extension of the spit, 4.9 miles. (See detail map.)

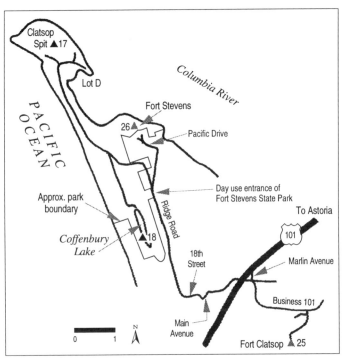

Hiking Instructions: Hike to the sheltered side of the spit, to the south.

Comments: Tall coastal grass covers the sand, except for a wide strip of glorious beach next to the water. There is some limited wave action in the brackish water. The place has a sheltered ocean feel. The ocean is just a few paces away, on the other side of the spit. It can be very windy here.

18. Coffenbury Lake ••••••••••••••••••••••

Rating: 6
Location: State Park
Water quality: Fair; 6' transparency
Vital statistics: 56 acres; 9' deep; 72° F (August); heavy bottom weeds outside roped area; sand and silt bottom; moderate to heavy use
Setting: Wooded coast at 19'; light to moderate litter
Swim skill: Low to moderate
Amenities: For-fee camping; drinking water; flush toilets
Entry fee: Yes, during summer
Topo: Warrenton 7½'

Driving Instructions: Coffenbury Lake is 11.3 miles west of Astoria. From the junction of Highway 101 and Highway 30 in Astoria, head southwest on Highway 101 to Business Highway 101, 3.8 miles. Turn right and drive to Main Avenue, 0.9 mile. Turn left and go to 18th Street (which joins Ridge Road), 0.2 mile. Turn right and drive to the day-use entrance of Fort Stevens State Park, 3.6 miles. Turn left into the park and go to a swimming turnoff, 1.2 miles. Turn left and drive to the turnoff for the lake, 1.5 miles. Turn right and go to parking, less than 0.1 mile. (See detail map for Swimming Hole #17.)

Comments: A roped-off swim area is at the north end of the lake in Fort Stevens Park. There is a 190-foot sandy beach alongside the tea-brown water.

19. Cullaby Lake ••••••••••••••••••••••••••

Rating: 5
Location: County Park
Water quality: Fair; 3' transparency
Vital statistics: 220 acres; 12' deep; 75° F (August); heavy bottom weeds; sand and silt bottom; moderate use
Setting: Wooded coast at 8'; light litter
Swim skill: Moderate
Amenities: Drinking water; flush toilets
Entry fee: No
Topo: Gearhart 7½'

Driving Instructions: Cullaby Lake is 9.0 miles southwest of Astoria. From the junction of Highway 101 and Highway 30 in Astoria, head southwest on Highway 101 to Cullaby Lake Road, 8.0 miles. Turn left and drive to Hawkins Road, 0.2 mile. Turn right and drive to parking near the lake, 0.8 mile.

Comments: A struggling grass bank fronts the tea-brown lake next to a playground and picnic area. There is tall aquatic weed-growth to the surface, beginning at about where swimmable depth is reached. It is necessary to stroke another 75 feet to be mostly free of weeds.

20. Spruce Run Park on Nehalem River ••••••••

Rating:	8
Location:	County Park
Water quality:	Good; 5' transparency
Vital statistics:	130' wide; at least 7' deep; light current; 66° F (August); light to moderate algae; bedrock bottom; heavy use
Setting:	Wooded valley at 320'; moderate litter
Swim skill:	Moderate
Amenities:	For-fee camping; drinking water; pit and flush toilets
Entry fee:	No
Topo:	Elsie 7½'

Driving Instructions: Spruce Run Park is 44.2 miles south of Astoria. From the junction of Highway 101 and Highway 30 in Astoria, head southwest on Highway 101 to where Highway 26 splits to the left, 19.1 miles, at milepost 25. Drive on Highway 26 to Nehalem River Road, 19.7 miles, between mileposts 19 and 20. Turn right and drive to the park, 5.4 miles, between mileposts 5 and 6. Turn in to parking on the right, alongside the river.

Comments: For the Nehalem River, this is a huge hole, complete with swinging rope, occupying a sizable area at the upstream end of the park. Low rock outcrops are along the shore, particularly at the downstream end of the pool. There is a rapids downstream.

21. Youngs River Falls •••••••••••••••••••••

Rating:	6
Location:	County Park
Water quality:	Good; 6' transparency
Vital statistics:	80' wide; at least 17' deep; moderate current; 62° F (August); light algae; boulder and gravel bottom; moderate use
Setting:	Forested valley at 50'; moderate to heavy litter

Swim skill: Moderate to strong
Amenities: None
Entry fee: No
Topo: Olney 7½'

Driving Instructions: Youngs River Falls is 13.8 miles south of Astoria. From the junction of Highway 101 and Highway 30 in Astoria, head southwest on Highway 101 to the turnoff for Highway 202, 0.4 mile. Bear left and drive to a stop, 0.1 mile. Continue straight, still on Highway 202, to Youngs River Loop, 9.4 miles (stay left when Business Highway 101 splits off at 1.3 miles), between mileposts 9 and 10. Turn right onto Youngs River Loop and drive to the falls turnoff, 3.8 miles (stay right where two roads enter from the left at 0.7 mile). Turn left and go to parking above the falls, 0.1 mile.

Comments: A spectacular, 60-foot falls creates a lot of action in the boulder-lined pool at its base. There is a 90-foot gravel beach downstream.

Clatsop County Points of Interest

22. Astor Column •••••••••••••••••••••••••••
Coxcomb Hill, Astoria

Type: Historic monument
Hours: Daily
Fee: No

Driving Instructions: From the junction of Highway 101 and Highway 30 in Astoria, head northeast on Highway 30 to the point on 8th Street at which there is a jog and the highway becomes one-way, 1.0 mile. Follow the jog onto Commercial Street and proceed to 12th Street, 0.2 mile. Turn right and drive to Franklin Avenue, 0.2 mile. Turn left and drive to 14th Street, 0.1 mile. Turn right and go to Jerome Avenue, 0.2 mile. Turn left and proceed to 15th Street, 0.1 mile. Turn right and go to Coxcomb Drive, 0.1 mile. Turn left and head to parking at the base of the column, 0.8 mile.

Comments: Offering a great view of the region, the column depicts the discovery and settlement of the Pacific Northwest. It is 166 steps to the top.

23. Columbia River Maritime Museum •••••••••
1792 Marine Drive, Astoria; (503) 325-2323

Type: Maritime museum
Hours: Daily, 9:30 A.M. to 5 P.M.
Fee: Yes

Driving Instructions: From the junction of Highway 101 and Highway 30 in Astoria, head northeast on Highway 30 to the point on 8th Street at which there is a jog and the highway becomes one-way, 1.0 mile. Follow the jog onto Commercial Street and proceed to the turnoff for the museum, 0.5 mile, on the left side of the road.

Comments: This museum, the largest of its kind in the Northwest, provides glimpses into various aspects of nautical life and history.

24. Flavel House ••••••••••••••••••••••••••
441 8th Street, Astoria; (503) 325-2563

> **Type:** Historic home
> **Hours:** Daily, 10 A.M. to 5 P.M. during summer; 11 A.M. to 4 P.M. during winter
> **Fee:** Yes

Driving Instructions: From the junction of Highway 101 and Highway 30 in Astoria, head northeast on Highway 30, curving onto 8th Street where the highway jogs to become one-way, 1.0 mile. Rather than continue on Highway 30 (Commercial Street), stay straight on 8th Street to the Flavel House, one block farther. It is on the right side of the road on the corner of 8th Street and Duane Avenue.

Comments: This ornate and stately 19th Century Victorian home was built in 1885.

25. Fort Clatsop National Memorial ••••••••••••
Fort Clatsop Road, Astoria; (503) 861-2471

> **Type:** National historic site
> **Hours:** Daily, 8 A.M. to 5 P.M.; open to 6 P.M. from June 16 to Labor Day
> **Fee:** Yes

Driving Instructions: Fort Clatsop National Memorial is 6.3 miles southwest of Astoria. From the junction of Highway 101 and Highway 30 in Astoria, along Marine Drive (at the entry to the bridge connecting Oregon to Washington), head southwest on Highway 101 to Marlin Avenue, 3.4 miles. Turn left and drive to Business Highway 101, 0.2 mile. Turn left and drive to Fort Clatsop Road, 1.9 miles. Turn right and go to the Fort Clatsop turnoff, 0.6 mile. Turn left and into parking, 0.2 mile. (See detail map for Swimming Hole #17.)

Comments: Lewis and Clark camped here during the winter of 1805-06. A replica of their quarters shows what it was like. A living history program operates seasonally.

26. Fort Stevens Historic Area and Military Museum
Fort Stevens State Park; (503) 861-2000

Type: Historic military base
Hours: Daily, 8 A.M. to 6 P.M. during summer; Monday
through Friday, 10 A.M. to 4 P.M. the rest of year
Fee: Yes

Driving Instructions: Fort Stevens Historic Area and Military Museum is 9.4 miles west of Astoria. Follow the driving instructions for Swimming Hole #17 to 18th Street. Turn right and drive to a stoplight on Pacific Drive, 4.3 miles. Turn left and go to the Fort Stevens entrance, 0.2 mile. Turn right at the entrance. (See detail map for Swimming Hole #17.)

Comments: A sobering place, the fort guarded the mouth of the Columbia River from Confederate attack during the Civil War. It was the only military installation in the continental United States to be fired on by foreign powers since the War of 1812, during World War II, June 1942. Self-guided and guided tours of the buildings and grounds are interesting.

Columbia County
(County Seat: St. Helens)

Columbia County provides nicely for swimmers along the Columbia River despite its relatively small amount of public land. Driving instructions begin in St. Helens at the intersection of Highway 30 and Columbia Boulevard.

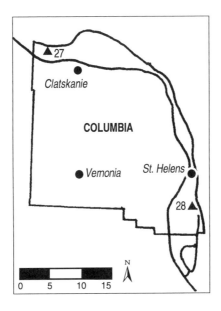

Columbia County Swimming Holes

27. Jones Beach on Columbia River
28. Sauvie Island Beaches on Columbia River

Columbia County Swimming Holes

27. Jones Beach on Columbia River • • • • • • • • • •

Rating:	8
Location:	Private
Water quality:	Fair; 3' transparency
Vital statistics:	1.0 mile wide; at least 14' deep; moderate current; 70° F (August); light algae; sand bottom; moderate to heavy use
Setting:	Wooded valley at 2'; light to moderate litter

Swim skill: Moderate to strong
Amenities: No-fee, primitive camping; no drinking water; pit toilets
Entry fee: No
Topo: Nassa Point 7½'

Driving Instructions: Jones Beach is 41.6 miles northwest of St. Helens. From the intersection of Highway 30 and Columbia Boulevard in St. Helens, head north on Highway 30 to Woodson Road, approximately 39 miles, between mileposts 67 and 68. Turn right and drive to River Front Road, 1.8 miles (turn right after crossing a bridge a short way off the highway). Turn right and drive to parking next to the beach, 0.8 mile. Parking and the beach are on the left side of the road. (See detail map.)

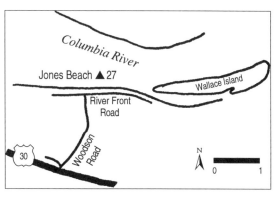

Comments: A favorite of windsurfers and anglers, the beach unfortunately is also a haunt for ATVs, though they seem to be confined. The wind can whip up some good wave action. The beach is 1.2 miles long.

28. Sauvie Island Beaches on Columbia River • • • •

Rating: 9
Location: State Department of Fish and Wildlife
Water quality: Good; 5' transparency
Vital statistics: 0.5 mile wide; at least 56' deep; light current; 67° F (July); light algae and bottom weeds; sand bottom; moderate to heavy use
Setting: Wooded valley at 10'; moderate to heavy litter
Swim skill: Moderate
Amenities: No drinking water; pit toilets
Entry fee: Yes
Topo: St. Helens 7½'

Driving Instructions: Sauvie Island Beaches are 29.6 miles southeast of St. Helens. From the intersection of Highway 30 and Columbia Boulevard St. Helens, head south on Highway 30 to Sauvie Island Road,

17.8 miles, between mileposts 10 and
11. Turn left, cross the bridge and
drive to Reeder Road, 2.1 miles. Turn
right and proceed to its junction with
Gillihan Road, 4.3 miles. Turn left,
continuing on Reeder Road to a long
turnout by pit toilets on the left side of
the road, 5.4 miles. Walton Beach is
accessed by stairways on the right
side of the road. It is 1.2 miles beyond
the start of Walton Beach to McNary
parking on the left side of the road.
The beach at McNary is accessed by
short trails on the right side of the
road. The road ends in parking at
North Unit beyond the start of McNary
parking, 2.0 miles farther. Cross over
a stile to the beach. The last 2.3 miles
of road are gravel. (See detail map.)

Comments: Part of the Sauvie
Island Wildlife Area, these long extensions of sandy beaches are glorious. The calm, steady current provides
the backdrop to a scene that is relatively peaceful, given its proximity to
Portland. Cattle are allowed to run in
the North Unit area, so watch for pies.

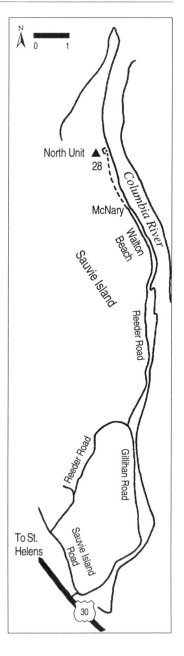

Multnomah County
(County Seat: Portland)

Multnomah County, despite the fact it boasts the largest urban concentration in the state, has a few decent places to swim along the Columbia and Sandy rivers. There are many city sights to choose from and even a couple of fountains to cool off in, if the need arises. While in downtown Portland—roughly bounded by the Willamette River to the north and east, and by I-405 to the south and west—it is probably best to find a place to park and use the ample public transportation furnished by Tri-Met. This part of Portland is designated "Fareless Square," so the rides are free. Driving instructions begin in Portland at the junction of I-5 and I-84.

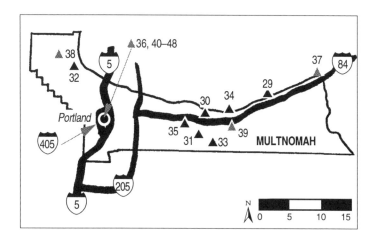

Multnomah County Swimming Holes

29. Benson Lake
30. Blue Lake
31. Dabney Park on Sandy River
32. Kelly Point Park on Columbia River
33. Oxbow Park on Sandy River
34. Rooster Rock Park on Columbia River
35. Troutdale Park on Sandy River

Multnomah County Points of Interest

36. American Advertising Museum
37. Bonneville Dam
38. Bybee House and Howell Territorial Park on Sauvie Island
39. Columbia River Scenic Highway

40. Keller Fountain
41. Lovejoy Fountain
42. Oregon History Center
43. Oregon Museum of Science and Industry (OMSI)
44. Pittock Mansion
45. Portland Art Museum
46. Portland Saturday Market
47. Salmon Street Springs
48. Washington Park Zoo

Multnomah County Swimming Holes

29. Benson Lake •

Rating:	6
Location:	State Park
Water quality:	Fair; 3′ transparency
Vital statistics:	25 acres; 8′ deep; 79° F (August); moderate algae; sand bottom; moderate use
Setting:	Wooded valley at 40′; light litter
Swim skill:	Low to moderate
Amenities:	Drinking water; flush toilets
Entry fee:	Yes, during summer
Topo:	Multnomah Falls 7½′

Driving Instructions: Benson Lake is 28.7 miles east of Portland. From the junction of I-5 and I-84 in Portland at Exit 301, head east on I-84 to Exit 30, 28.4 miles, between mileposts 30 and 31. Take the exit and drive to parking, 0.3 mile. Note that there is access only for traffic heading east.

Comments: This lake is pleasant, though there is noise from cars and trains. There is a hard-packed sand beach area. The park is grassy around the west end of the lake.

30. Blue Lake •

Rating:	6
Location:	County Park
Water quality:	Good; 7′ transparency
Vital statistics:	61 acres; 24′ deep; 72° F (July); moderate shoreline weeds; sand in swim area, otherwise silt and gravel bottom; heavy use
Setting:	Urban valley at 14′; light litter
Swim skill:	Low to moderate
Amenities:	Drinking water; flush toilets

Entry fee: Yes
Topo: Camas 7½'

Driving Instructions: Blue Lake is 16.2 miles east of Portland. From the junction of I-5 and I-84 in Portland at Exit 301, head east on I-84. Drive to Exit 13, the exit for Blue Lake Park and 181st Avenue, 10.5 miles. Take the exit and drive to 181st Avenue, 0.3 mile. Turn left and drive to Sandy Boulevard/Highway 30 Bypass, 0.4 mile. Turn right and go to 223rd Avenue, 2.1 miles. Turn left and drive to the park turnoff, 0.9 mile. Turn left and go to the park entrance, 0.5 mile. Enter the park and stay straight past the booth and to swim parking at the end of the park road, 1.5 miles.

Comments: There is a marked-off swimming area at this natural lake with a dam. Children ages four and under are not permitted in the water. In the swim area there is a 130-foot sand beach.

31. Dabney Park on Sandy River • • • • • • • • • • • •

Rating: 6
Location: State Park
Water quality: Fair; 2' transparency
Vital statistics: 90' wide; at least 8' deep; moderate current; 73° F (August); light algae; rock and sand bottom; moderate use
Setting: Wooded valley at 40'; light to moderate litter
Swim skill: Moderate
Amenities: Drinking water; flush toilets
Entry fee: Yes, during summer
Topo: Washougal 7½'

Driving Instructions: Dabney Park is 19.2 miles east of Portland. From the junction of I-5 and I-84 in Portland at Exit 301, head east on I-84 to Exit 18, 15.8 miles, at milepost 18. Exit and drive to a stop sign, 0.1 mile. Turn left onto an unmarked road and drive to another stop sign, 0.4 mile. Continue straight ahead to Stark Street, 2.4 miles. Still continuing straight ahead, drive to the Dabney turnoff, 0.4 mile. Turn right and find parking, 0.1 mile. (See detail map for Swimming Hole #5.)

Comments: The river is murky but pleasant, with a 100-foot sandy spot adjacent to the boat ramp. A neat island is an easy swimming objective. The bank is sand and rock, with a somewhat brushy shoreline. There is some slack water.

32. Kelly Point Park on Columbia River • • • • • • • •

Rating: 6
Location: City Park

Water quality:	Fair; 4′ transparency
Vital statistics:	0.6 mile wide; at least 36′ deep; light current; 69° F (July); light algae; sand bottom; moderate use
Setting:	Urban valley at 10′; light litter
Swim skill:	Moderate
Amenities:	Drinking water; flush toilets
Entry fee:	No
Topo:	Sauvie Island 7½′

Driving Instructions: Kelly Point Park is 12.1 miles northwest of Portland. From the junction of I-5 and I-84 in Portland at Exit 301, head north on I-5 to Marine Drive Exit 307, 5.5 miles. Exit and drive to a fork, 0.4 mile. Bear toward Marine Drive West and to a stop light, 0.5 mile. Turn right onto Marine Drive and drive to Portland Road, 1.1 miles. Jog left onto Portland Road, then right, back onto Marine Drive again, 0.5 mile. Drive to the turnoff for the park, 3.4 miles. Turn right and go to the farthest parking, 0.7 mile.

Hiking Instructions: A mostly asphalt trail leads from parking to the beach, less than 0.1 mile.

Comments: The park is a nice one despite the presence of a number of old pilings which jut from the water and considerable upstream shipping activity on both sides of the river. The large, coarse-sand beach is inviting. Watch for yellow alert signs which are put up when body contact with the water is not advised.

33. Oxbow Park on Sandy River • • • • • • • • • • • • •

Rating:	6
Location:	Regional Park
Water quality:	Fair; 2′ transparency
Vital statistics:	90′ wide; at least 9′ deep; moderate current; 74° F (August); light algae; rock and sand bottom; heavy use
Setting:	Forested valley at 90′; light litter
Swim skill:	Moderate
Amenities:	For-fee camping; drinking water; pit toilets
Entry fee:	Yes
Topo:	Sandy 7½′

Driving Instructions: Oxbow Park is 30.1 miles east of Portland. Follow the driving instructions for Swimming Hole #31 to Stark Street. Turn right and across the bridge and travel to Troutdale Road, 2.0 miles. Turn left and drive to a stop at Division Street, 1.7 miles. Bear left and go to Oxbow Drive, 1.4 miles. Turn right and head to Oxbow Parkway, 2.2

miles. Turn left and drive to the park entry booth, 1.6 miles. Continue on the park roadway to parking at the trail to Group Camp 3 and River Access, 2.5 miles. (See detail map for Swimming Hole #5.)

Hiking Instructions: Hike to the group camp, 0.2 mile. Continue through the camp and on the trail to where the river takes a sharp bend, 0.2 mile. From this point cross a rock beach to the river and the best swimming spot in the park, 250 feet farther.

Comments: Some sand and a lot of coarse-grained large rocks and gravel compose the bank. A nice rockface graces the opposite shore. A road follows along the other side of the river. Expect nudity.

34. Rooster Rock Park on Columbia River ••••••

Rating: 7
Location: State Park
Water quality: Fair; 2′ transparency
Vital statistics: 0.8 mile wide; at least 6′ deep; light current; 79° F (August); light algae; sand bottom; moderate to heavy use
Setting: Scrub valley at 40′; light litter
Swim skill: Low to moderate
Amenities: Drinking water; flush toilets
Entry fee: Yes, during summer
Topo: Bridal Veil 7½′

Driving Instructions: Rooster Rock Park is 22.9 miles east of Portland. From the junction of I-5 and I-84 in Portland at Exit 301, head east on I-84 to Exit 25, the exit for Rooster Rock, 22.4 miles, between mileposts 24 and 25. Take the exit and drive to parking along the river, about 0.5 mile.

Comments: Here is a 0.1-mile sandy beach marked for swimming between rows of mooring posts. It is a great place, marred by noise from boats, cars and trains.

35. Troutdale Park on Sandy River ••••••••••

Rating: 7
Location: Community Park
Water quality: Fair; 2′ transparency
Vital statistics: 100′ wide; at least 10′ deep; moderate current; 73° F (August); light to moderate algae; sand and boulder bottom; moderate to heavy use
Setting: Urban valley at 20′; moderate litter
Swim skill: Moderate to strong
Amenities: Drinking water; flush toilets

Entry fee: No
Topo: Camas 7½'

Driving Instructions: Troutdale Park is 16.4 miles east of Portland. From the junction of I-5 and I-84 in Portland at Exit 301, head east on I-84 to Exit 18, 15.8 miles, at milepost 18. Exit and drive to a stop sign, 0.1 mile. Turn left onto an unmarked road and drive to another stop sign, 0.4 mile. Turn right, cross a bridge and, just across the bridge, turn left into parking, less than 0.1 mile farther. (See detail map for Swimming Hole #5.)

Hiking Instructions: Head down the path that leads from parking to the river, 0.1 mile.

Comments: The park is an agreeable surprise. A broad sand beach stretches along the shoreline. A small upstream rapids empties into the hole. The water is milky. It channels through mid-sized boulders under the bridge with a fair current that can be swum against with effort. Close to the bank, the water moves slowly.

Multnomah Points of Interest

36. American Advertising Museum ● ● ● ● ● ● ● ● ● ● ● ●
9 NW 2nd Avenue, Portland; (503) 226-0000

Type: Advertising museum
Hours: Wednesday through Friday, 11 A.M. to 5 P.M.; Saturday and Sunday, noon to 5 P.M.
Fee: Yes

Driving Instructions: American Advertising Museum is in northwest Portland. From the junction of I-5 and I-84 in Portland at Exit 301, head south on I-5 to Exit 300B, the exit for the Oregon Museum of Science and Industry (OMSI), 0.3 mile. Exit to the right and drive to the exit for City Center and Morrison Street, 0.5 mile. Bear right at the exit, onto what becomes SW Washington Street, and drive to the Front Avenue turnoff, 0.3 mile. Bear right to SW Front Avenue, 0.1 mile. Turn left and drive to SW Ash Street, 0.1 mile. Turn left and go to SW 2nd Avenue, 0.1 mile. Turn right, cross Burnside Street and park, 0.1 mile. The museum is on the left side of 2nd Avenue. (See detail maps of Portland, following. These maps show only the streets necessary to get to points of interest. For greater detail, use a commercial map.)

Comments: The museum maintains exhibits of the best and worst of print, radio and television advertising. A video collection of classic television ads is full of chuckles and nostalgia.

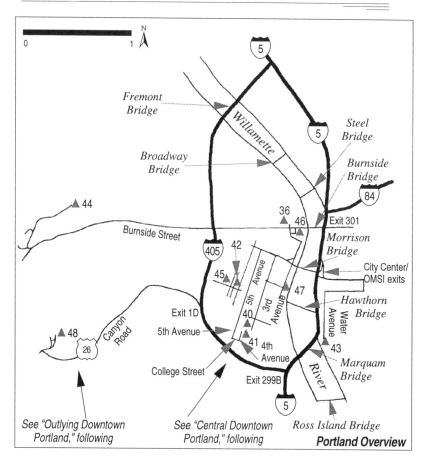

Portland Overview

See "Outlying Downtown Portland," following

See "Central Downtown Portland," following

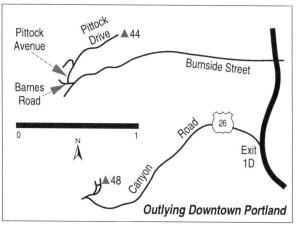

Outlying Downtown Portland

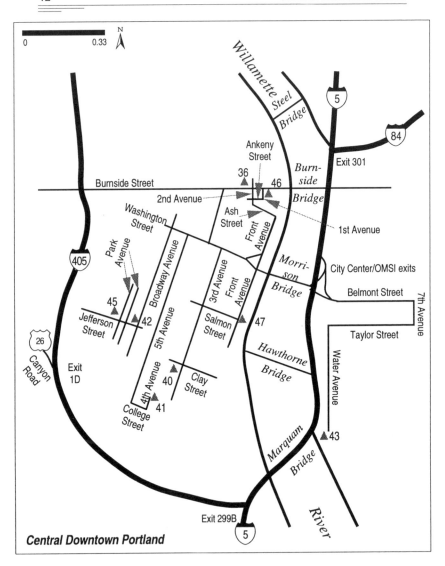

Central Downtown Portland

37. Bonneville Dam •
Army Corps of Engineers; (503) 374-8820

Type: River dam
Hours: Daily, 9 A.M. to 5 P.M.; extended hours during summer
Fee: No

Driving Instructions: Bonneville Dam is 39.3 miles east of Portland. From the junction of I-5 and I-84 in Portland at Exit 301, head east on I-

84 and drive to Exit 40, the exit for Bonneville Dam, 38.0 miles, between mileposts 40 and 41. Take the exit and drive to parking following the signs, 1.3 miles.

Comments: If you want to see a dam, this is it. There are extensive exhibits and glassed viewing areas where fish can be seen working their way past the dam. Visitor's centers are on both the Oregon and the Washington sides. Bradford Island Regional Visitor Center, on the Oregon side, is massive and interesting. The dam is a National Historic Landmark.

38. Bybee House and Howell Territorial Park • • • • •
Sauvie Island; (503) 621-3344

> **Type:** Historic home
> **Hours:** Wednesday through Sunday, noon to 5 P.M. from June through Labor Day
> **Fee:** No, donation requested

Driving Instructions: Bybee House and Howell Territorial Park is 17.5 miles northwest of Portland. From the junction of I-5 and I-84 in Portland at Exit 301, head north on I-5 to Exit 302B, the exit for Highway 30, St. Helens and I-405, 1.6 miles. Take Exit 302B onto I-405 southbound and drive to Exit 3, the exit for Highway 30 heading west, 1.3 miles. Take Exit 3 and go on Highway 30 (also designated Yeon Avenue and St. Helens Road) to Sauvie Island Road, 13.3 miles, between mileposts 10 and 11. Turn right, cross Sauvie Island Bridge and drive to Howell Park Road, 1.2 miles (across the bridge, bear left). Turn right and drive to parking, which is on the left, 0.1 mile.

Comments: The 19th Century farm and agricultural museum are maintained through the cooperative effort of Multnomah County and the Oregon Historical Society.

39. Columbia River Scenic Highway • • • • • • • • • •
Columbia River Gorge

> **Type:** Scenic drive
> **Hours:** Daily
> **Fee:** No

Driving Instructions: Columbia River Scenic Highway is east of Portland. From the junction of I-5 and I-84 in Portland at Exit 301, head east on I-84 to Exit 16B, 14.1 miles. Take Exit 16B and follow signs for the scenic route, an approximately 22-mile stretch of road, begun in 1913, that runs between Troutdale and Ainsworth State Park.

Comments: Also called Columbia River Historic Highway and Crown Point Highway, the route winds its way through the Columbia

River Gorge, offering views of the river and trails to various waterfalls along the way. In Crown Point State Park, on the rim of the gorge, is Vista House. Multnomah Falls, along the way, is the nation's second highest at 620 feet. (Multnomah Falls has its own exit from I-84, Exit 31, on the left side of the road, if there is not enough time for the scenic route.)

40. Keller Fountain •••••••••••••••••••••••
SW 3rd Avenue, Portland

Type: Water fountain
Hours: Daily
Fee: No

Driving Instructions: Keller Fountain is in southwest Portland. Follow the driving instructions of Point of Interest #36 onto SW Washington Street, and drive to SW 3rd Avenue, 0.4 mile. Turn left and go to SW Clay Street, 0.5 mile. The fountain is just past Clay Street, on the right side of the road. It will be necessary to look for a place to park. (See detail maps for Point of Interest #36.)

Comments: Here is an 18-foot urban waterfall, suitable as a fun place to watch people and to refresh oneself.

41. Lovejoy Fountain •••••••••••••••••••••••
SW 4th Avenue, Portland

Type: Water fountain
Hours: Daily
Fee: No

Driving Instructions: Lovejoy Fountain is in southwest Portland. From the junction of I-5 and I-84 in Portland at Exit 301, head south on I-5 to Exit 300B, the exit for OMSI, 0.3 mile. Exit to the right and drive to the exit for City Center and Morrison Street, 0.5 mile. Bear right at the exit, onto what becomes SW Washington Street, and drive to SW 5th Avenue, 0.6 mile. Turn left and go to SW College Street, 0.8 mile. Turn left and drive to SW 4th Avenue, less than 0.1 mile. Turn left and find a place to park. Lovejoy Park, where the fountain is located, is on the right. (See detail maps for Point of Interest #36.)

Hiking Instructions: Look for a brick walkway to the fountain.

Comments: Here is a cozy fountain nestled among tall buildings.

42. Oregon History Center •••••••••••••••••
1200 SW Park Avenue, Portland; (503) 222-1741

Type: History museum
Hours: Monday through Saturday, 10 A.M. to 5 P.M.; Sunday, noon to 5 P.M.

Fee: Yes

Driving Instructions: Oregon History Center is in southwest Portland. Follow the driving instructions of Point of Interest #36 onto what becomes SW Washington Street, and drive to SW Broadway Avenue, 0.7 mile. Turn left and go to SW Jefferson Street, 0.4 mile. Turn right and go to SW Park Avenue, one block. Turn right. The center is immediately on the right side of the road. (See detail maps for Point of Interest #36.)

Comments: The center is a well-interpreted regional museum which, in permanent and changing exhibits, explores different facets of Oregon history.

43. Oregon Museum of Science •••••••••••• and Industry (OMSI)
1945 SE Water Avenue, Portland; (503) 797-4000

Type: Science museum
Hours: Daily, 9:30 A.M. to 5:30 P.M.; open to 9 P.M. Thursday and Friday; closed Christmas
Fee: Yes

Driving Instructions: Oregon Museum of Science and Industry is in southeast Portland. From the junction of I-5 and I-84 in Portland at Exit 301, head south on I-5 to Exit 300B, the exit for OMSI, 0.3 mile. Exit to the right and drive to another exit for OMSI, 0.5 mile. Bear left at the exit, onto SE Belmont Street, and drive to SE 7th Avenue, 0.5 mile. Turn right and go to SE Taylor Street, 0.1 mile. Turn right and drive to SE Water Avenue, 0.3 mile. Turn left and go to the OMSI entrance and parking, on the right side of the road, 0.4 mile. The museum is on the east bank of the Willamette River. Coming from the south, take the OMSI and Water Avenue Exit from I-5 and follow the signs. (See detail maps for Point of Interest #36.)

Comments: Dedicated to hands-on science exploration and discovery, OMSI is a fascinating place.

44. Pittock Mansion ••••••••••••••••••••••••
3229 NW Pittock Drive, Portland; (503) 823-3623

Type: Historic home
Hours: Daily, noon to 4 P.M.
Fee: Yes

Driving Instructions: Pittock Mansion is in northwest Portland. Follow the driving instructions of Point of Interest #36 onto what becomes SW Washington Street, and drive to SW 4th Avenue, 0.5 mile. Turn right and go to W Burnside Street, 0.2 mile. Turn left and head to NW Barnes Road, 2.3

miles. Turn right and drive to NW Pittock Avenue, 0.1 mile. Turn right and proceed to NW Pittock Drive, 0.2 mile. Turn right and go to parking near the mansion, 0.4 mile. (See detail maps for Point of Interest #36.)

Comments: This 1914 mansion displays incredible opulence and has an incredible view of Portland, particularly at night.

45. Portland Art Museum • • • • • • • • • • • • • • • • • •
1219 SW Park Avenue, Portland; (503) 226-2811

> **Type:** Art museum
> **Hours:** Tuesday through Saturday, 11 A.M. to 5 p.m.; Sunday 1–5 P.M.
> **Fee:** Yes (the first Thursday of the month is free from 4–9 P.M.)

Driving Instructions: Portland Art Museum is in southwest Portland. Follow the driving instructions of Point of Interest #36 onto what becomes SW Washington Street, and drive to SW Broadway Avenue, 0.7 mile. Turn left and go to SW Jefferson Street, 0.4 mile. Turn right and drive to SW Park Avenue, one-way to the left, two blocks. The museum is on the on the right side of the road. (See detail maps for Point of Interest #36.)

Comments: Historic and contemporary art from around the world is displayed in an eclectic and not overwhelming collection.

46. Portland Saturday Market • • • • • • • • • • • • • • • •
108 W Burnside Street, Portland

> **Type:** Street market
> **Hours:** Weekends, March to December
> **Fee:** No

Driving Instructions: Portland Saturday Market is in southwest Portland. Follow the driving instructions of Point of Interest #36 onto what becomes SW Washington Street, and drive to the turnoff for Front Avenue, 0.3 mile. Bear right and drive to SW Front Avenue, 0.1 mile. Turn left and drive to SW Ash Street, 0.1 mile. Turn left and go to SW 2nd Avenue, 0.1 mile. Turn right and drive to SW Ankeny Street, one block. Turn right and go to SW 1st Avenue, one block. The market is underneath the Burnside Bridge, 180 feet to the left, down SW 1st Avenue. It will be necessary to drive around to find parking. (See detail maps for Point of Interest #36.)

Comments: Discover an open-air marketplace of handcrafts, art, entertainment and food.

47. Salmon Street Springs • • • • • • • • • • • • • • • • • •
SW Front Avenue, Portland

Type: Water fountain
Hours: Daily
Fee: No

Driving Instructions: Salmon Street Springs is in southwest Portland. Follow the driving instructions of Point of Interest #36 onto what becomes SW Washington Street, and drive to SW 3rd Avenue, 0.4 mile. Turn left and go to SW Salmon Street, 0.3 mile. Turn left and drive to SW Front Avenue and the fountain, 0.1 mile. (See detail maps for Point of Interest #36.)

Comments: Part of McCall Waterfront Park, the fountain is close to the center of downtown bustle and is within sight of the Willamette River.

48. Washington Park Zoo • • • • • • • • • • • • • • • • • •
4001 SW Canyon Road, Portland; (503) 226-1561

Type: Wildlife zoo
Hours: Daily, 9:30 A.M. to 5 P.M. (6 P.M. during summer); closed Christmas
Fee: Yes

Driving Instructions: Washington Park Zoo is in southwest Portland. From the junction of I-5 and I-84 in Portland at Exit 301, head south on I-5 to Exit 299B, the exit for I-405 and Beaverton, 1.6 miles. Exit and head on I-405 to Exit 1D, the exit for Highway 26, 0.9 mile. Exit and drive to the zoo exit, 2.0 miles. Exit, bear to the right and drive to parking, 0.4 mile. (See detail maps for Point of Interest #36.)

Comments: This is a very congenial zoo, which has humanely structured enclosures, approximating natural habitats, for its more than 650 animals. Also in Washington Park are the International Rose Test Gardens, the Japanese Garden, the Hoyt Arboretum, the World Forestry Center and the Oregon Vietnam Veterans Living Memorial.

Tillamook County
(County Seat: Tillamook)

Rivers that pool in profusion before emptying into the ocean make
Tillamook County a county of abundance for swimmers. The great-
sounding names beckon—the Nehalem, the Kilchis, the Nestucca. Driving
instructions begin in Tillamook at the intersection of Highway 101 (Main
Avenue, heading south) and Highway 6 (3rd Street, heading east).

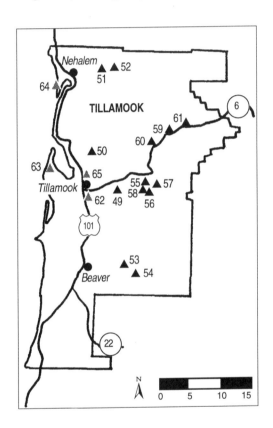

Tillamook County Swimming Holes

49. Dam Hole on Trask River
50. Kilchis Park on Kilchis River
51. Nehalem Falls on Nehalem River
52. Nehalem River, near milepost 9
53. Nestucca River, near milepost 7
54. Nestucca River, near milepost 9

55. North Fork Trask River
56. South Fork Trask River
57. South Fork Trask River tributary
58. Trask Park on North Fork Trask River
59. Wilson River at Jones Creek
60. Wilson River at Keenig Creek
61. Wilson River, near milepost 27

Tillamook County Points of Interest

62. Blimp Hangar Museum
63. Cape Meares Park
64. Nehalem Bay Spit
65. Tillamook Cheese Factory

Tillamook County Swimming Holes

49. Dam Hole on Trask River •••••••••••••

Rating:	8
Location:	Tillamook State Forest
Water quality:	Good; 14′ transparency
Vital statistics:	80′ wide; at least 20′ deep; light current; 68° F (August); light to moderate algae; sand bottom; moderate use
Setting:	Wooded valley at 160′; moderate litter
Swim skill:	Moderate
Amenities:	None
Entry fee:	No
Topo:	Siskeyville 7½′

Driving Instructions: Dam Hole is 9.8 miles east of Tillamook. From the intersection of Highway 101 and Highway 6 in Tillamook, head east on Highway 6 to the Trask River Road turnoff, 2.5 miles. Turn right onto Olson Road and go to Trask River Road, 1.9 miles. Turn left and go to a gravel turnout on the right, 5.4 miles, between mileposts 6 and 7. (See detail map on next page.)

Hiking Instructions: Hike down to the beach from the turnout, 190 feet.

Comments: A deep hole is at the end of a 250-foot rock-lined chute. Pockmarked and mossy climbing rocks abound, but take care. There are some nice holes above the main chute, and below the main pool as well. There are decent shallows, too. The 80-foot beach is coarse sand. The water is a bit sudsy. Look for big anadromous fish.

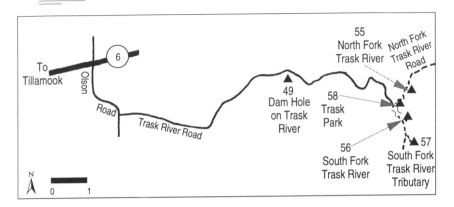

50. Kilchis Park on Kilchis River • • • • • • • • • • • • •

Rating: 7
Location: County Park
Water quality: Excellent; transparent to bottom
Vital statistics: 90' wide; at least 9' deep; light current; 63° F (August); light to moderate algae; rock bottom; moderate use
Setting: Forested valley at 80'; light litter
Swim skill: Moderate
Amenities: No-fee camping; drinking water; flush toilets
Entry fee: No
Topo: Kilchis River 7½'

Driving Instructions: Kilchis Park is 7.8 miles north of Tillamook. From the intersection of Highway 101 and Highway 6 in Tillamook, head east on Highway 6 to Highway 101 (Pacific Avenue, heading north), one block. Turn left onto Highway 101 and jog left, then right, 0.1 mile. Still on Highway 101, head to Alderbrook Road, 2.6 miles, between mileposts 62 and 63. Turn right and go to Kilchis River Road, 1.0 mile. Turn right and drive to a stop sign in the park, 4.1 miles, just past milepost 4. Turn onto the gravel road that angles farthest to the right and stop where it nears the river, less than 0.1 mile.

Hiking Instructions: There is a short trail from the road that leads to the river.

Comments: Gravel and stone carpet 200 feet of the bank at the downstream end of the park. There are plenty of shallows. A stretch of rock outcropping on the opposite bank, where the river narrows, is the place to find the deeper water.

51. Nehalem Falls on Nehalem River • • • • • • • • •

Rating: 8

Location: Tillamook State Forest
Water quality: Good; 7' transparency
Vital statistics: 60' wide; at least 9' deep; moderate current; 65° F (August); moderate to heavy algae; bedrock bottom; moderate use
Setting: Wooded valley at 120'; light to moderate litter
Swim skill: Moderate to strong
Amenities: No-fee camping; no drinking water; pit toilets
Entry fee: No
Topo: Foley Peak 7½'

Driving Instructions: Nehalem Falls is 28.8 miles north of Tillamook. From the intersection of Highway 101 (Main Avenue, heading south) and Highway 6 (3rd Street, heading east) in Tillamook, head east on Highway 6 to Highway 101 (Pacific Avenue, heading north), one block. Turn left onto Highway 101 and jog left, then right, 0.1 mile. Still on Highway 101, head to Highway 53, the turnoff for Mohler and Necanicum, 19.3 miles, between mileposts 46 and 47. Turn right and drive to unmarked Miami River Road, 1.3 miles. Turn right and go to Foss Road, just after crossing railroad tracks, 1.0 mile. Turn left and drive to the end of the pavement, 6.7 miles. Now on gravel, continue to the turnoff for the campground, 0.2 mile, between mileposts 6 and 7. Turn left and drive along the river to the campground next to the falls, 0.2 mile.

Comments: Not a falls in the sense of a sheer drop, the water here descends a steep chute and then enters a wonderland of rock forms through a 190-foot-long rock-lined channel. Above the chute there is a small swimmable pool, and beyond that a wide, placid stream. But the best swimming is between the chute and the bridge. In this 0.4-mile stretch, there are several distinct pools, each separated from the others by rapids. The best place is 400 feet downstream of the chute. There the pool is over 0.1 mile long, and it boasts small, sandy pockets along the bank. The current is not strong, except in the areas of rapids. There is a fish ladder beside the chute. Fish may be abundant.

52. Nehalem River, near milepost 9 • • • • • • • • • •

Rating: 6
Location: Tillamook State Forest
Water quality: Good; 6' transparency
Vital statistics: 25' wide; at least 9' deep; light current; 66° F (August); moderate algae; gravel and rock on bedrock bottom; light to moderate use
Setting: Wooded valley at 120'; moderate litter
Swim skill: Moderate
Amenities: No-fee, primitive camping; no drinking water

Entry fee: No
Topo: Cook Creek 7½'

Driving Instructions: Nehalem River, near milepost 9 is 31.0 miles north of Tillamook. Follow the driving instructions for Swimming Hole #51, but continue to the turnoff for a primitive camp overlooking the river, 2.5 miles, between mileposts 9 and 10. Turn left and drive to the camp on a dirt road, 0.1 mile.

Comments: Slack water flows through an easy rapids, then into a pleasantly whirling pool. Upstream there is a channel. There are some suds. There is some sand along the bank. One-fifth of a mile downstream is another good, basic hole.

53. Nestucca River, near milepost 7 ••••••••••

Rating: 5
Location: Siuslaw National Forest
Water quality: Good; 6' transparency
Vital statistics: 40' wide; at least 7' deep; moderate current; 61° F (September); moderate algae; rock on bedrock bottom; moderate use
Setting: Forested valley at 280'; light to moderate litter
Swim skill: Moderate
Amenities: None
Entry fee: No
Topo: Blaine 7½'

Driving Instructions: Nestucca River, near milepost 7, is 21.8 miles southeast of Tillamook. From the intersection of Highway 101 (Main Avenue, heading south) and Highway 6 (3rd Street, heading east) in Tillamook, head south on Highway 101 to Blaine Road in Beaver, 14.6 miles. Turn left, following signs to Upper Nestucca River Recreation Area and drive to a fork in the road in Blaine, 6.6 miles. Bear to the right on Forest Road 85, Upper Nestucca Road, and drive to a dirt turnout on the right, 0.6 mile, between mileposts 7 and 8.

Comments: Here is a good hole, with some suds, made cozy by formation rock ledges and boulders. There is an upstream rapids. Resist jumping off the huge bank outcrop—an underwater rock ledge awaits below.

54. Nestucca River, near milepost 9 ••••••••••

Rating: 6
Location: Siuslaw National Forest
Water quality: Good; 7' transparency
Vital statistics: 60' wide; at least 8' deep; moderate current; 61° F

(September); moderate algae; sand and bedrock bottom; light to moderate use

Setting: Forested valley at 360'; light to moderate litter
Swim skill: Moderate
Amenities: None
Entry fee: No
Topo: Blaine 7½'

Driving Instructions: Nestucca River, near milepost 9, is 24.4 miles southeast of Tillamook. Follow the driving instructions for Swimming Hole #53 but continue to a gravel turnout on the right, 3.2 miles, between mileposts 9 and 10.

Hiking Instructions: Follow the short, steep trail that leads from the turnout to the river.

Comments: Shallow rapids curve around both sides of a mossy boulder perched in the middle of the river. The small hole is at the downstream base of the boulder. The water swirls nicely. A rock wall buttresses the road side of the river. Rocky ledges compose the bank, with a 30-foot sandy spot downstream of the hole. Crawdads may share the secluded feel of the place.

55. North Fork Trask River • • • • • • • • • • • • • • • • •

Rating: 8
Location: Tillamook State Forest
Water quality: Excellent; transparent to bottom
Vital statistics: 80' wide; at least 13' deep; moderate current; 66° F (August); moderate to heavy algae; gravel and bedrock bottom; moderate use
Setting: Wooded valley at 320'; moderate to heavy litter
Swim skill: Moderate to strong
Amenities: No-fee, primitive camping; no drinking water
Entry fee: No
Topo: Trask 7½'

Driving Instructions: North Fork Trask River is 15.5 miles east of Tillamook. Follow the driving instructions for Swimming Hole #49 to Trask River Road. Turn left and go to North Fork Trask River Road, 10.6 miles, between mileposts 11 and 12. Turn left and go on gravel to a spur turnout on the right, 0.5 mile. (See detail map for Swimming Hole #49.)

Hiking Instructions: A trail leads from the turnout to the river, 100 feet.

Comments: Relatively clear water for these parts bubbles and churns through a maze in the bedrock and drops into a sizeable pool. Formation rock ledges abut the water. There are some shallows downstream. Huge salmon and sturgeon prowl the bottom. The grandeur of the place, including the shadows and noises of big fish, can make this a spooky swim.

56. South Fork Trask River • • • • • • • • • • • • • • • • • • •

Rating: 7
Location: Tillamook State Forest
Water quality: Excellent; transparent to bottom
Vital statistics: 40′ wide; at least 10′ deep; light current; 61° F (August); moderate algae; bedrock bottom; light use
Setting: Wooded valley at 320′; light litter
Swim skill: Moderate
Amenities: None
Entry fee: No
Topo: Trask 7½′

Driving Instructions: South Fork Trask River is 16.9 miles east of Tillamook. Follow the driving instructions for Swimming Hole #49 to Trask River Road. Turn left and drive to the end of the pavement, just after a bridge crossing, 12.3 miles. Bear left across the bridge, avoiding a spur to the right (not on map), and continue on gravel to a turnout on the left side of the road, 0.2 mile. (See detail map for Swimming Hole #49.)

Hiking Instructions: There is a short, brushy trail from the turnout to the river.

Comments: This is a nice spot where the river channels through formation rocks, with a 3-foot falls upstream and a rapid downstream. The hole is a hangout for huge fish. Watch for nettles.

57. South Fork Trask River tributary • • • • • • • • • • • •

Rating: 6
Location: Tillamook State Forest
Water quality: Excellent; transparent to bottom
Vital statistics: 40′ wide; at least 6′ deep; moderate current; 61° F (August); moderate algae; bedrock bottom; light to moderate use
Setting: Wooded valley at 400′; moderate litter
Swim skill: Moderate
Amenities: None
Entry fee: No
Topo: Trask 7½′

Driving Instructions: South Fork Trask River tributary is 17.6 miles east of Tillamook. Follow the driving instructions of Swimming Hole #49 to Trask River Road. Turn left and drive to the end of the pavement, just after a bridge crossing, 12.3 miles. Bear left across the bridge and continue on gravel to a divide in the road, 0.6 mile. Bear left at this divide and drive to a three-way split in the road, 0.2 mile (the three-way split is not on the detail map). Take the far left fork of the split and drive on rough dirt to a primitive campsite along the river, less than 0.1 mile. (See detail map for Swimming Hole #49.)

Comments: A cute hole is nestled among rocky outcrops at the base of a 1-foot waterfall. There are downstream rapids.

58. Trask Park on North Fork Trask River • • • • • • •

Rating: 6
Location: Tillamook State Forest
Water quality: Excellent; transparent to bottom
Vital statistics: 50′ wide; at least 11′ deep; moderate current; 66° F (August); moderate algae; bedrock bottom; moderate use
Setting: Wooded valley at 280′; moderate litter
Swim skill: Moderate
Amenities: For-fee camping; drinking water; pit toilets
Entry fee: No
Topo: Trask 7½′

Driving Instructions: Trask Park is 15.2 miles east of Tillamook. Follow the driving instructions of Swimming Hole #49 to Trask River Road. Turn left and drive to the turnoff for the park, 10.8 miles, between mileposts 11 and 12. The park is on both sides of the road. Park on either side. (See detail map for Swimming Hole #49.)

Hiking Instructions: From parking, it is a short hike to the river on either side of the bridge.

Comments: There are two good spots. One is just downriver of the bridge where there is some sand in the bedrock. The South Fork of the Trask joins below. The other decent spot, just above the bridge, is a low, rock-lined channel marked by a lone concrete bridge piling with a Douglas-fir sapling growing from it.

59. Wilson River at Jones Creek • • • • • • • • • • • • •

Rating: 6
Location: Tillamook State Forest
Water quality: Excellent; transparent to bottom
Vital statistics: 50′ wide; at least 11′ deep; light current; 64° F (August); light algae; boulders and bedrock bottom; moderate use
Setting: Wooded valley at 520′; light to moderate litter

Swim skill: Moderate
Amenities: None
Entry fee: No
Topo: Jordan 7½'

Driving Instructions: Wilson River at Jones Creek is 22.8 miles northeast of Tillamook. From the intersection of Highway 101 and Highway 6 in Tillamook, head east on Highway 6 to the turnoff for Jones Creek Forest Camp, North Fork Road, 22.7, between mileposts 22 and 23. Turn left and go to the bridge crossing that overlooks the hole, less than 0.1 mile. (Parking is not easy, so it may be necessary to drive down the road a bit to find a reasonable place to stop.)

Comments: The river funnels through a bedrock channel that extends above and below the bridge. There are rapids upstream and shallows downstream.

60. Wilson River at Keenig Creek • • • • • • • • • • • •

Rating: 8
Location: Tillamook State Forest
Water quality: Excellent; transparent to bottom
Vital statistics: 80' wide; at least 19' deep; light current; 64° F (August); light algae; gravel and bedrock bottom; moderate use
Setting: Wooded valley at 320'; moderate litter
Swim skill: Moderate
Amenities: No-fee camping; drinking water; pit toilets
Entry fee: No
Topo: Jordan Creek 7½'

Driving Instructions: Wilson River at Keenig Creek is 17.9 miles northeast of Tillamook. From the intersection of Highway 101 and Highway 6 in Tillamook, head east on Highway 6 to the turnoff for Keenig Creek Forest Park, 17.8 miles, between mileposts 17 and 18. Turn left and go to the bridge crossing above the hole, less than 0.1 mile.

Hiking Instructions: There is a short trail on the downstream side of the bridge on the far side of the road.

Comments: The trail leads downstream to a rock bar with some coarse sand. The place is rock-walled, with areas of rapids above and below the hole. The deep water is downstream of the bridge and extends to the bar.

61. Wilson River, near milepost 27 • • • • • • • • • • • •

Rating: 6
Location: Tillamook State Forest

Water quality: Excellent; transparent to bottom
Vital statistics: 40′ wide; at least 8′ deep; moderate current; 61° F (August); light algae; gravel, boulder and bedrock bottom; moderate use
Setting: Wooded valley at 800′; moderate to heavy litter
Swim skill: Moderate
Amenities: None
Entry fee: No
Topo: Woods Point 7½′

Driving Instructions: Wilson River, near milepost 27, is 27.7 miles northeast of Tillamook. From the intersection of Highway 101 and Highway 6 in Tillamook, head east on Highway 6 to a turnout, just past a bridge crossing, 27.7 miles, between mileposts 27 and 28, on the left side of the road. The hole is just below the turnout.

Comments: The hole is wedged between a 4-foot falls and a formation rock face. The bank is rocky and dropoffs are sheer.

Tillamook County Points of Interest

62. Blimp Hangar Museum ••••••••••••••••••
4000 Blimp Boulevard, Tillamook; (503) 842-2413

Type: Aviation museum
Hours: Daily, 10 A.M. to 6 P.M. from mid-May to October; weekends and holidays the rest of the year
Fee: Yes

Driving Instructions: The Blimp Hanger Museum is 4.1 miles southeast of Tillamook. From the intersection of Highway 101 and Highway 6 in Tillamook, head south on Highway 101 to Long Prairie Road, 2.4 miles, between mileposts 68 and 69. Turn left and drive to Blimp Boulevard, 1.1 miles. Turn right and go to Hangar B Road, 0.3 mile. Turn right and go to parking next to the long edge of the hangar, 0.3 mile.

Comments: The museum is housed in Hangar B, one of the two largest wooden clear-span structures ever built—192 feet high, 1072 feet long, 296 feet wide. Constructed during World War II by the US Navy, the buildings were the base for blimp anti-submarine patrols. Hangar A burned down in 1992.

63. Cape Meares Park •••••••••••••••••••••
State Park; (503) 842-3182

Type: Unusual tree; historic lighthouse
Hours: Daily, 11 A.M. to 5 P.M. from March to October
Fee: No

Driving Instructions: Cape Meares Park is 9.7 miles west of Tillamook. From the intersection of Highway 101 and Highway 6 in Tillamook, head west on 3rd Street to the Cape Meares turnoff at Bayocean Road, 1.8 miles. Turn right and go to the turnoff for Cape Meares Park and Lighthouse, 5.3 miles. Turn left and drive to the park entrance, 2.0 miles. Turn right into the park and go to parking, 0.6 mile.

Hiking Instructions: The Octopus Tree is reached on a trail away from the ocean, 0.1 mile. The lighthouse is reached by an asphalt trail toward the ocean, 0.2 mile.

Comments: Attractions include the Cape Meares Lighthouse and the Octopus Tree. The Octopus Tree is a six-armed, mammoth Sitka spruce. The lighthouse is the only one on the coast where the public is allowed into the light room, which is staffed by volunteers. While not currently in use, the light fixture is pretty amazing to view.

64. Nehalem Bay Spit •
Nehalem Bay State Park; (503) 368-5943

> **Type:** Scenic location
> **Hours:** Daily
> **Fee:** Yes, during summer

Driving Instructions: Nehalem Bay Spit is 24.8 miles north of Tillamook. Follow the driving instructions of Swimming Hole #51 past the left/right jogs. Still on Highway 101, head to the turnoff to Nehalem Bay Park, 21.9 miles. Turn left and drive to a split in the road at the day-use area, 2.8 miles (prior to the split, curve to the right at 0.2 mile and stay straight at 1.2 miles). The left fork goes to the bay side and the fork straight ahead leads to the ocean side of the spit.

Comments: While not particularly accommodating as swimming locations, the two sides of the 4-mile-long spit offer an incredible contrast of ocean and bay environments.

65. Tillamook Cheese Factory • • • • • • • • • • • • • • • •
4175 Highway 101 North, Tillamook; (503) 842-4481

> **Type:** Cheese factory
> **Hours:** Daily, 8 A.M. to 6 P.M.; open to 8 P.M. during the summer
> **Fee:** No

Driving Instructions: Tillamook Cheese Factory is in Tillamook. Follow the driving instructions for Swimming Hole #51 past the left/right jogs. Still on Highway 101, head to the cheese factory turnoff, 1.9 miles. Turn right into the parking lot.

Comments: One of the most popular attractions in Oregon, the factory has become very commercial and crowded. The distant, glass-walled views of the cheese-making process are a far cry from the great tours of old.

Washington County
(County Seat: Hillsboro)

This county is the swimming-hole dud of the state. But Tillamook and Multnomah counties are close at hand.

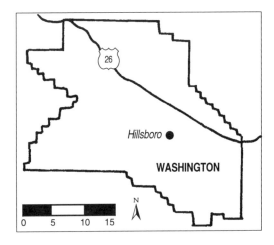

Yamhill County
(County Seat: McMinnville)

There is little for swimmers here, but the county has some interest. Driving instructions begin in McMinnville at the intersection of 3rd Street and Highway 99W.

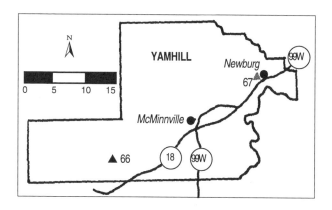

Yamhill County Swimming Hole

66. Blackwell Park on Willamina Creek

Yamhill County Point of Interest

67. Hoover-Minthorn House

Yamhill County Swimming Hole

66. Blackwell Park on Willamina Creek ••••••••
Rating:	5
Location:	County Park
Water quality:	Good; 8′ transparency
Vital statistics:	50′ wide; at least 8′ deep; light current; 63° F (August); light algae; sand and gravel bottom; moderate use
Setting:	Wooded valley at 320′; moderate litter
Swim skill:	Moderate
Amenities:	None
Entry fee:	No
Topo:	Stony Mountain 7½′

Driving Instructions: Blackwell Park is 22.6 miles west of McMinnville. From 3rd Street at Highway 99W in McMinnville, head southwest on Highway 99W (Adams Street in McMinnville) to Highway 18, 1.2 miles. Stay straight onto Highway 18 and drive to Business Highway 18, the turnoff for Willamina, 10.4 miles. Turn right and drive to Willamina Creek Road at a fork in Willamina, 6.3 miles. Bear right and go to the park turnoff, 4.6 miles. Turn left and drive to parking, less than 0.1 mile.

Comments: Below the bridge, this is a nice, basic country hole. There are upstream rapids, a rope swing and a 50-foot gravel beach.

Yamhill County Point of Interest

67. Hoover-Minthorn House • • • • • • • • • • • • • • • • • •
115 South River Street, Newberg; (503)538-6629

> **Type:** Historic home
> **Hours:** Wednesday through Sunday, 1–4 P.M. from March to November; weekends only, 1–4 P.M. during February and December; closed during January and holidays
> **Fee:** Yes

Driving Instructions: Hoover-Minthorn House is 14.7 miles northeast of McMinnville. From 3rd Street at Highway 99W in McMinnville, head northeast on Highway 99W (Baker Street in McMinnville) to River Street in Newberg, 14.7 miles. Turn right. The house is on the right side of the road, less than one block away.

Comments: This is the restored boyhood home of Herbert Hoover, 31st president of the United States. It was built in 1881.

Lower Northwest

The Lower Northwest spans the gamut from pure mountain stream to meandering, silt-loaded river. Stretching from the crest of the Cascades to the Pacific Ocean, split down the middle by the Willamette River, it is a region of diverse geography and immense enchantment. Dry, warm summers enhance the pleasure of water play. Pop in a Beach Boys tape for the trans-coast-range trip to the beach. Look for Douglas fir and hemlock forests and for cottonwood and oak trees in the low valleys.

Lower Northwest Region

Benton County
(County Seat: Corvallis)

The mature Willamette River presents itself in Benton County. Driving instructions begin in Corvallis at the junction of Highway 99W (4th Street, heading south) and Highways 34 and 20 (Harrison Avenue).

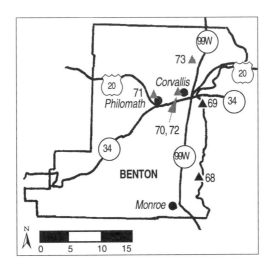

Benton County Swimming Holes

68. Irish Bend on Willamette River
69. Willamette Park on Willamette River

Benton County Points of Interest

70. Benton County Courthouse
71. Benton County Historical Museum
72. Monument to the Kalapuya
73. Peavy Arboretum

Benton County Swimming Holes

68. Irish Bend on Willamette River ● ● ● ● ● ● ● ● ● ● ●

> **Rating:** 6
> **Location:** County Park
> **Water quality:** Fair; 5′ transparency
> **Vital statistics:** 280′ wide; at least 16′ deep; swift current; 64° F (August); moderate algae; gravel and pebble bottom; moderate use

Setting: Wooded valley at 260'; light to moderate litter
Swim skill: Strong
Amenities: No-fee, primitive camping; no drinking water
Entry fee: No
Topo: Harrisburg 7½'

Driving Instructions: Irish Bend is 17.3 miles south of Corvallis. From the joining of Highway 99W and Highways 34 and 20 in Corvallis, head south on 99W to Old River Road, 12.9 miles, between mileposts 96 and 97. Turn left and head to Irish Bend Road, 2.1 miles. Turn left and drive to the end of the pavement, 1.1 miles. Continue on gravel to the bend, 1.2 miles.

Comments: The river moves powerfully beside a 0.2-mile gravel-and-pebble bar. There is a road along the opposite bank. Watch for poison oak.

69. Willamette Park on Willamette River •••••••

Rating: 8
Location: Corvallis City Park
Water quality: Fair; 5' transparency
Vital statistics: 300' wide; at least 20' deep; swift current; 70° F (August); moderate algae; rock and pebble bottom; moderate use
Setting: Wooded valley at 210'; light to moderate litter
Swim skill: Strong
Amenities: For-fee camping; drinking water; flush and pit toilets
Entry fee: No
Topo: Riverside 7½'

Driving Instructions: Willamette Park is 3.4 miles southeast of Corvallis. From the joining of Highway 99W and Highways 34 and 20 in Corvallis, head south on 99W to Goodnight Avenue, 2.2 miles. Turn left and drive to the end of the pavement, 0.7 mile. Continue straight on gravel into the park, and bear left at the fork to trailhead parking, 0.5 mile. (See detail map on next page.)

Hiking Instructions: Hike downriver on the wide, blackberry-lined trail to a three-way split in the trail, 0.3 mile. Take the right-hand fork to the river, less than 0.1 mile. Now continue downstream along the river to a large bar of gravel and pebbles, 0.2 mile. Watch for poison oak.

Comments: The gravel bar is over 0.2 mile long, ending along a backwater slough. There are some sandy spots along the shoreline, among pebbles and dirt. Just downriver from the bar is a pebble island. Beyond that is a boat ramp. The water is 3–4 feet deep to about halfway across the channel, then there is a precipitous dropoff. Because the current is stiff, an exit plan is needed. An upstream pulp plant contributes heavily to the dark coloration. Expect some nudity.

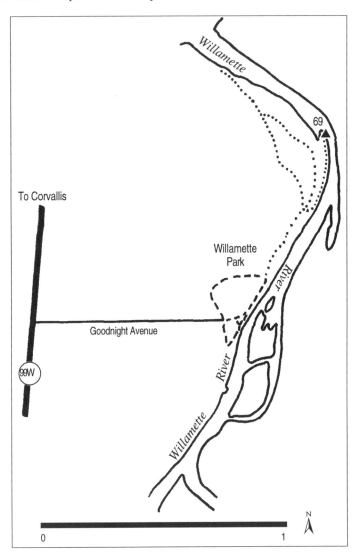

Benton County Points of Interest

70. Benton County Courthouse • • • • • • • • • • • • • •
120 Northwest 4th Street, Corvallis; (503) 757-6831

      Type: Operating courthouse

Hours: Monday through Friday, 8 A.M. to 5 P.M.; closed on holidays

Fee: No

Driving Instructions: From the joining of Highway 99W and Highways 34 and 20 in Corvallis, head south on 99W to the courthouse, 0.1 mile. The courthouse is on the right.

Comments: The building is the oldest operating courthouse in Oregon. A graceful and well-maintained structure, built in 1888, it is furnished with displays in the basement. Tours are given by appointment.

71. Benton County Historical Museum • • • • • • • • • •
1101 Main Street, Philomath; (503) 929-6230

Type: Historic museum

Hours: Tuesday through Saturday, 10 A.M. to 4:30 P.M.

Fee: No, donation requested

Driving Instructions: Benton County Historical Museum is 6.2 miles west of Corvallis. From the joining of Highway 99W and Highways 34 and 20 in Corvallis, head south on 99W to the point where Highway 20 splits to the right, 0.6 mile. Bear to the right and follow Highway 20 into Philomath to the museum entrance between 11th Street and 12th Street, 5.5 miles. Turn right and drive to parking, 0.1 mile.

Comments: Located in a unique building that once housed Philomath College, the museum presents a nice set of exhibits.

72. Monument to the Kalapuya • • • • • • • • • • • • • •

Type: History monument

Hours: Daily

Fee: No

Driving Instructions: From the joining of Highway 99W and Highways 34 and 20 in Corvallis, head south on 99W to where Highway 20 splits to the right, 0.6 mile. Bear to the right at the split, onto Highway 20, and at once be ready for a quick turn at the entrance into Pioneer Park, 0.4 mile. Turn left into the park and to the monument, where the road bends to the left, less than 0.1 mile.

Comments: A sobering monument has been placed along the Marys River, dedicated to the memory of the first inhabitants of the Willamette Valley, the Kalapuya Indians.

73. Peavy Arboretum •

Type: Arboretum

Hours: Daily

Fee: No

Driving Instructions: Peavy Arboretum is 6.3 miles north of Corvallis. From the joining of Highway 99W and Highways 34 and 20 in Corvallis, head south on 4th Street to Van Buren Avenue, one block. Turn left onto Van Buren Avenue and go to 3rd Street, one block. Turn left onto 3rd Street. This is Highway 99W, heading north. Drive on Highway 99W to Arboretum Road, 5.5 miles, between mileposts 77 and 78. Turn left and drive to Peavy Arboretum Road, the entrance to the arboretum, 0.8 mile. Turn left onto gravel in the arboretum, where there is an immediate fork. Bear left to parking for McDonald Forest access, 0.4 mile, or bear right to parking for Woodlands Trail, an interpreted nature trail, 0.1 mile.

Comments: A bevy of tree varieties from the Northwest and around the world are located here, including many along a marked nature trail.

Lane County
(County Seat: Eugene)

Stretching from the Cascades in the east to the Pacific Ocean in the west, Lane County is arguably the most varied and beautiful county of the state. Together with Douglas County to the south, it is part of the most luxuriant swimming-hole domain anywhere. The North Fork of the Middle Fork of the Willamette River, with its bulky name, is a felicitous gift of nature. Driving instructions begin in Eugene at the intersection of I-5 and I-105/Highway 126.

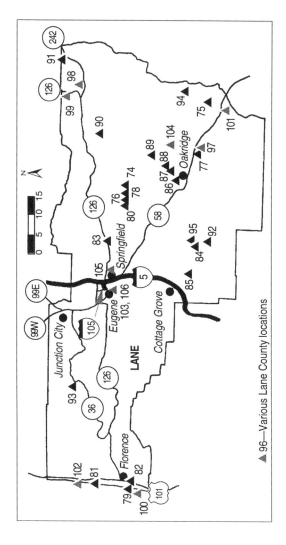

Lane County Swimming Holes

74. Bedrock on Fall Creek
75. Betty Lake
76. Big Pool on Fall Creek
77. Blue Pool on Salt Creek
78. Clark Creek on Fall Creek
79. Cleawox Lake in Honeyman Park
80. Dolly Varden on Fall Creek
81. Dune Lake
82. East Woahink Lake in Honeyman Park
83. Hendricks Bridge Wayside on McKenzie River
84. LaSells Stewart Park on Row River
85. Mosby Creek
86. North Fork of Middle Fork Willamette River, near milepost 1
87. North Fork of Middle Fork Willamette River, near milepost 3
88. North Fork of Middle Fork Willamette River, near milepost 5
89. North Fork of Middle Fork Willamette River, near milepost 11
90. Rider Creek Arm of Cougar Reservoir and Terwilliger Hot Springs
91. Scott Lake
92. Sharps Creek
93. Slide Rock on Lake Creek
94. Waldo Lake
95. Wildwood Falls Park on Row River

Lane County Points of Interest

96. Covered Bridges
97. McCredie Springs
98. McKenzie Highway
99. McKenzie River Hot Springs
100. Oregon Dunes National Recreation Area
101. Salt Creek Falls
102. Sea Lion Caves
103. University of Oregon Museum of Natural History and Oregon State Museum of Anthropology
104. Wall Creek Hot Springs
105. Wave Pool
106. Willamette Science and Technology Center (WISTEC)

Lane County Swimming Holes

74. Bedrock on Fall Creek • • • • • • • • • • • • • • • • •

Rating: 6
Location: Willamette National Forest

Water quality: Good; 6' transparency
Vital statistics: 50' wide; at least 6' deep; light current; 64° F (July); light algae; pebble and bedrock bottom; moderate to heavy use
Setting: Forested valley at 1040'; light litter
Swim skill: Moderate
Amenities: For-fee camping; drinking water; pit toilets
Entry fee: Yes
Topo: Saddleblanket Mountain 7½'

Driving Instructions: Bedrock is 36.0 miles southeast of Eugene. From the intersection of I-5 and I-105/Highway 126 in Eugene, head south on I-5 to Exit 188A, the exit for Willamette Highway, Oakridge and Highway 58, 5.2 miles, between mileposts 188 and 189. Exit and drive to a fork, 0.3 mile. Bear left at the fork onto Highway 58 and go to Jasper-Lowell Road, 13.2 miles, between mileposts 13 and 14. Turn left and drive to Big Fall Creek Road (which becomes Forest Road 18), 2.7 miles (jog to the left and right through Lowell). Turn right and drive to the Bedrock turnoff, 14.6 miles. Turn left and to parking across the bridge, less than 0.1 mile.

Hiking Instructions: The steep trail down to the hole is just upstream of the bridge. Watch for poison oak.

Comments: A nice backwater pool is downstream of a cascade and rapids. Further downstream is a narrow channel under the bridge. Formation rock and large pebbles compose the banks.

75. Betty Lake ••••••••••••••••••••••••••

Rating: 7
Location: Willamette National Forest
Water quality: Excellent; transparent to bottom
Vital statistics: 40 acres; at least 10' deep; 64° F (July); moderate shoreline weeds; gravel and silt bottom; light use
Setting: Forested mountains at 5570'; light litter
Swim skill: Low to moderate
Amenities: None
Entry fee: No
Topo: Waldo Lake 7½'

Driving Instructions: Betty Lake is 69.9 miles southeast of Eugene. Follow the driving instructions of Swimming Hole #74 onto Highway 58 and go to the Waldo Lake turnoff, 58.9 miles, between mileposts 58 and 59. Turn left onto Forest Road 5897 and follow it to the Betty Lake turnout on the left, 5.5 miles, between mileposts 5 and 6. (See detail map on next page.)

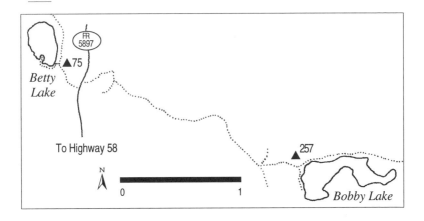

Hiking Instructions: Hike the Betty Lake Trail to a fork in the trail, 0.3 mile. Take the left-hand fork and go to the lake shore, less than 0.1 mile. Look across the lake, and to the left. There is a peninsula (sometimes island at high water) jutting out into the lake. Work around the lake in a clockwise direction to get to that peninsula, 0.1 mile.

Comments: Both shallows and depths can be accessed from this lovely spot. There is a narrow gravel shoreline. The bank back of it is a bit boggy. There is log fall along the shore.

76. Big Pool on Fall Creek • • • • • • • • • • • • • • • • • •

Rating:	6
Location:	Willamette National Forest
Water quality:	Good; transparent to bottom
Vital statistics:	40′ wide; at least 10′ deep; moderate current; 64° F (July); light algae; bedrock bottom; moderate use
Setting:	Forested valley at 960′; moderate litter
Swim skill:	Moderate
Amenities:	No-fee camping; no drinking water
Entry fee:	No
Topo:	Saddleblanket Mountain 7½′

Driving Instructions: Big Pool is 32.7 miles southeast of Eugene. Follow the driving instructions for Swimming Hole #74 to Big Fall Creek Road. Turn right and drive to a small gravel turnout, 11.3 miles, between mileposts 11 and 12, on the right. (An information turnout on the left is less than 0.1 mile farther.)

Comments: Low formation rock ledges line this channel between upstream and downstream rapids. There is a pebble bar upstream on the opposite shore.

77. Blue Pool on Salt Creek ••••••••••••••••••

Rating: 5
Location: Willamette National Forest
Water quality: Good; transparent to bottom
Vital statistics: 50′ wide; at least 7′ deep; light current; 60° F (June); moderate shoreline weeds; sand bottom; heavy use
Setting: Forested valley at 1920′; moderate litter
Swim skill: Low to moderate
Amenities: For-fee camping; drinking water; flush toilets
Entry fee: No
Topo: McCredie Springs 7½′

Driving Instructions: Blue Pool is 50.3 miles southeast of Eugene. Follow the driving instructions for Swimming Hole #74 onto Highway 58 and go to the Blue Pool Campground turnoff, 44.7 miles, between mileposts 44 and 45, on the right. Turn into the campground and go to parking, 0.1 mile.

Comments: The pool is adjacent to, and fed by, the creek. It is generally 2–3 feet deep, except near a monolith. There is considerable grass along the bank, and some coarse sand.

78. Clark Creek on Fall Creek ••••••••••••••

Rating: 7
Location: Willamette National Forest
Water quality: Excellent; transparent to bottom
Vital statistics: 50′ wide; at least 12′ deep; light current; 64° F (July); light algae; sand and gravel bottom; moderate to heavy use
Setting: Forested valley at 1000′; light litter
Swim skill: Moderate
Amenities: For-fee group camping; drinking water; pit toilets
Entry fee: No
Topo: Saddleblanket Mountain 7½′

Driving Instructions: Clark Creek is 34.2 miles southeast of Eugene. Follow the driving instructions for Swimming Hole #74 to Big Fall Creek Road. Turn right and drive to the turnoff for Clark Creek Group Camp parking, 12.8 miles, between mileposts 12 and 13, on the left.

Hiking Instructions: The hole is reached by a short trail across the road from the parking area.

Comments: There are upstream and downstream rapids and a pretty cascade opposite a bank of formation rocks. A beach area is wheelchair-accessible. Fall Creek is chock-full of swimmable locations.

79. Cleawox Lake in Honeyman Park •••••••••

Rating: 10
Location: State Park
Water quality: Good; 17' transparency
Vital statistics: 87 acres; 48' deep; 72° F (August); moderate bottom weeds; sand bottom; heavy use
Setting: Wooded coast at 67'; light litter
Swim skill: Low to moderate
Amenities: For-fee, camping; drinking water; flush toilets
Entry fee: Yes, during summer
Topo: Florence 7½'

Driving Instructions: Cleawox Lake is 70.2 miles west of Eugene. From the intersection of I-5 and I-105/Highway 126 in Eugene, head west on I-105 to Exit 4, the exit for Florence, 3.3 miles. Take the exit onto 6th Avenue and drive to Garfield Street, 4.0 miles. Turn left and go to 11th Avenue, 0.4 mile. Turn right and proceed west on Highway 126 to Florence and Highway 101, 58.8 miles. Turn left and go to the Honeyman State Park turnoff, 3.3 miles, between mileposts 193 and 194. Turn right and follow signs to Sand Dunes Picnic Area, 0.4 miles (bear left, then right, to day-use parking).

Hiking Instructions: Follow the short path at the end of the parking lot to the dunes beside the lake.

Comments: This is a wondrous place in the Oregon Sand Dunes. High dunes offer the opportunity for a breathtaking run down, followed by a splash into, the tea-brown lake. Often it is windy. The sand in the dunes is marvelous for digging, but be careful not to go overboard. Collapsed sand tunnels have been a source of tragedy.

80. Dolly Varden on Fall Creek ••••••••••••••

Rating: 6
Location: Willamette National Forest
Water quality: Excellent; transparent to bottom
Vital statistics: 60' wide; at least 11' deep; moderate current; 64° F (July); light algae; sand and rock bottom; moderate use
Setting: Forested valley at 920'; light litter
Swim skill: Moderate
Amenities: No-fee camping; no drinking water; pit toilet
Entry fee: No
Topo: Saddleblanket Mountain 7½'

Driving Instructions: Dolly Varden is 31.7 miles southeast of Eugene. Follow the driving instructions for Swimming Hole #74 to Big Fall Creek Road. Turn right and drive to the turnoff for Dolly Varden, 10.3 miles. Turn left and park.

Comments: There is a 60-foot sandy beach along a backwater stretch under a bridge. Downstream is a rapids that goes around a small island.

81. Dune Lake ••••••••••••••••••••••••••••

Rating: 7
Location: Siuslaw National Forest
Water quality: Good; 11′ transparency
Vital statistics: 0.1 mile wide; at least 11′ deep; 75° F (August); moderate to heavy bottom weeds; sand and silt bottom; moderate use
Setting: Wooded coast at 120′; light litter
Swim skill: Low to moderate
Amenities: For-fee camping; drinking water; flush toilets
Entry fee: No
Topo: Mercer Lake 7½′

Driving Instructions: Dune Lake is 73.4 miles west of Eugene. Follow the driving instructions for Swimming Hole #79 to Florence and Highway 101. Turn right and go to the Alder Dune Campground turnoff, 6.7 miles, between mileposts 183 and 184. Turn left and go to a left turn to day use, 0.2 mile. Take the turn and the road will curl to parking by the lake, 0.1 mile. (See detail map.)

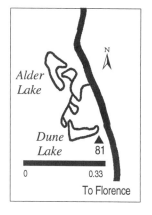

Comments: The tea-brown lake is small, with sandy shoreline openings. The aquatic growth is not a problem. Short but steep trails into the dunes are a treat.

82. East Woahink Lake in Honeyman Park •••••

Rating: 5
Location: State Park
Water quality: Excellent; 19′ transparency
Vital statistics: 820 acres; 68′ deep; 70° F (August); light bottom weeds; sand bottom; moderate to heavy use
Setting: Wooded coast at 39′; light litter
Swim skill: Low to moderate
Amenities: For-fee camping; drinking water; flush toilets

Entry fee: No
Topo: Florence 7½'

Driving Instructions: East Woahink Lake is 70.5 miles west of Eugene. Follow the driving instructions for Swimming Hole #79 to the Honeyman State Park turnoff. Turn left and drive to the East Woahink turnoff, 0.5 mile. Turn right and proceed to parking, 0.2 mile.

Comments: Actually on the northwest arm of the lake, the marked-off swim area can be seen on the left on the way to parking. It is a nice area for little children, insulated a little by space from the heavy, noisy boat use of the lake. The bank next to the sand beach is in well-groomed grass. The water is only three to four feet deep at the buoys, but does drop off to depth after that. It is less windy here than at Cleawox Lake, Swimming Hole #79, across the highway, but also less of an experience.

83. Hendricks Bridge Wayside on McKenzie River

Rating: 7
Location: State Park
Water quality: Good; transparent to bottom
Vital statistics: 300' wide; at least 12' deep; moderate current; 64° F (June); light algae; rock and sand on bedrock bottom; moderate use
Setting: Wooded valley at 560'; light litter
Swim skill: Low to moderate
Amenities: Drinking water; flush toilets
Entry fee: Yes, during summer
Topo: Walterville 7½'

Driving Instructions: Hendricks Bridge Wayside is 11.9 miles east of Eugene. From the intersection of I-5 and I-105/Highway 126 in Eugene, head east on Highway 126 to the end of the divided highway, 6.6 miles. Turn left onto Main Street, continuing on Highway 126, and drive to the park turnoff, 5.3 miles, between mileposts 11 and 12, on the right.

Comments: There is a roped-off area for kids which gets to three or four feet deep. The bank is grass and dirt. A decent spot for a good swimmer is across the river, a bit upstream from the roped area. Overlooked by a house on the opposite bank, and defined by large boulders, there is a nice deep hole.

84. LaSells Stewart Park on Row River • • • • • • • • •

Rating: 8
Location: County Park
Water quality: Good; 14' transparency

Vital statistics: 90' wide; at least 21' deep; moderate current; 62° F (August); light algae; rocks, boulder and bedrock bottom; moderate use

Setting: Forested valley at 1000'; moderate to heavy litter

Swim skill: Moderate

Amenities: No-fee, primitive camping; no drinking water

Entry fee: No

Topo: Culp Creek 7½'

Driving Instructions: LaSells Stewart Park is 35.7 miles southeast of Eugene. From the intersection of I-5 and I-105/Highway 126 in Eugene, head south on I-5 to Exity 174, the exit for Cottage Grove and Dorena, 19.1 miles. Take the exit and drive to Row River Road, 0.3 mile. Turn left and travel to the point where Row River Road splits to the left and Government Road goes straight ahead, 4.4 miels. Drive on Government Road to the point where it rejoins Row River Road., 6.6 miles. Continue on Row River Road to the turnoff for the park, 5.1 miles, between mileposts 17 and 18. Turn left and drive on a rough dirt and gravel road to parking, less than 0.2 mile. Cross an asphalt road on the way. (See detail map.)

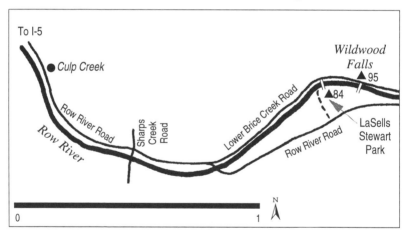

Comments: A terrific hole lies at the base of a lava curtain which curves halfway around the upstream end of the pool. The rest of the pool is surrounded by small boulders. A narrow, 13-foot falls feeds the pool, and above that is a smaller cascade. The falls create a circular current pattern. The rocks are great for climbing, and downstream there are other nice holes and a bit of sand. Watch for poison oak.

85. Mosby Creek ●

Rating: 5

Location: Private
Water quality: Good; transparent to bottom
Vital statistics: 40' wide; at least 6'
deep; light current;
66° F (July); light al-
gae; sand and debris
bottom; moderate use
Setting: Wooded valley at
800'; moderate litter
Swim skill: Moderate
Amenities: None
Entry fee: No
Topo: Blue Mountain 7½'

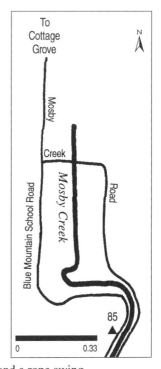

Driving Instructions: Mosby Creek
is 25.9 miles southeast of Eugene. Follow
the driving instructions for Swimming Hole
#84 to Row River Road. Turn left onto
Row River Road and go to Thornton Lane,
0.7 mile. Turn right and drive to Mosby
Creek Road, 0.1 mile. Turn left and travel
to Blue Mountain School Road, 4.7 miles.
Bear right and drive to a turnout, 1.0 mile,
on the left. (See detail map.)
Comments: The creek is a slow-mov-
ing waterway with dirt and grassy banks, and a rope swing.

86. North Fork of Middle Fork Willamette River, • • •
near milepost 1

Rating: 7
Location: Willamette National Forest
Water quality: Excellent; transparent to bottom
Vital statistics: 50' wide; at least 6' deep; moderate current; 66° F
(June); light algae; gravel and rock bottom; moderate
use
Setting: Forested valley at 1080'; light litter
Swim skill: Moderate
Amenities: None
Entry fee: No
Topo: Westfir East 7½'

Driving Instructions: North Fork of Middle Fork Willamette River,
near milepost 1, is 43.4 miles southeast of Eugene. Follow the driving

instructions for Swimming Hole #74 onto Highway 58. Go to the second Westfir turnoff, Westfir-Oakridge Road, 33.4 miles, between mileposts 33 and 34. Turn left and drive to Westfir Covered Bridge, on the left, 3.1 miles. Continue straight ahead on North Fork Road/Forest Road 19 to a gravel turnout on the left, 1.4 miles, between mileposts 1/57 and 2/56.

Hiking Instructions: From the turnout, take the trail to the river, 230 feet. Watch for poison oak.

Comments: This is one of many great spots on this branch of the Willamette. The bank is composed of formation rock and sand. There is an upstream rapid.

87. North Fork of Middle Fork Willamette River, • • • near milepost 3

Rating: 10
Location: Willamette National Forest
Water quality: Excellent; transparent to bottom
Vital statistics: 60' wide; at least 14' deep; moderate current; 66° F (June); light algae; boulder and gravel bottom; moderate to heavy use
Setting: Forested valley at 1160'; light to moderate litter
Swim skill: Moderate
Amenities: None
Entry fee: No
Topo: Westfir East 7½'

Driving Instructions: North Fork of Middle Fork Willamette River, near milepost 3 is 45.5 miles southeast of Eugene. Follow the driving instructions for Swimming Hole #74 onto Highway 58. As for Swimming Hole #86, drive to the Westfir Covered Bridge, then continue straight ahead on North Fork Road/Forest Road 19 to gravel and asphalt turnouts, 3.5 miles, between mileposts 3/55 and 4/54, on the left.

Hiking Instructions: The trails down to the river from the turnouts are steep but short.

Comments: This is a super place. It is a spot which handles use well. There are two pools—a smaller upper pool and a larger lower one—separated by a dangerous chute. A high cliff abuts the lower pool. Boulders and formation rock layer the bank.

88. North Fork of Middle Fork Willamette River, • • • near milepost 5

Rating: 8
Location: Willamette National Forest

Water quality: Excellent; transparent to bottom
Vital statistics: 50' wide; at least 18' deep; moderate current; 66° F (June); light algae; boulders and gravel bottom; light use
Setting: Forested valley at 1200'; light litter
Swim skill: Moderate
Amenities: None
Entry fee: No
Topo: Westfir East 7½'

Driving Instructions: North Fork of Middle Fork Willamette River, near milepost 5 is 47.3 miles southeast of Eugene. Follow the driving instructions for Swimming Hole #74 onto Highway 58. As for Swimming Hole #86, drive to the Westfir Covered Bridge, then continue straight ahead on North Fork Road/Forest Road 19 to a small asphalt turnout, 5.3 miles, between mileposts 5/53 and 6/52, on the left.

Hiking Instructions: There is a short, steep trail to the river from the turnout.

Comments: It does not look like much till you get there, but this place is what swimming holes are all about. There is a nice chute upstream and an easy rapids downstream. Boulders compose much of the bank. Abutted by a lava cliff, the pool is magnificent.

89. North Fork of Middle Fork Willamette River, • • • near milepost 11

Rating: 8
Location: Willamette National Forest
Water quality: Excellent; transparent to bottom
Vital statistics: 60' wide; at least 14' deep; moderate current; 66° F (August); light algae; bedrock bottom; light use
Setting: Forested valley at 1480'; light to moderate litter
Swim skill: Moderate
Amenities: None
Entry fee: No
Topo: Westfir East 7½'

Driving Instructions: North Fork of Middle Fork Willamette River, near milepost 11, is 53.0 miles east of Eugene. Follow the driving instructions for Swimming Hole #74 onto Highway 58. As for Swimming Hole #86, drive to the Westfir Covered Bridge, then continue straight ahead on North Fork Road/Forest Road 19 to a turnout, 11.0 miles, just before milepost 11/47, on the left.

Comments: A 90-foot-wide lava monolith abuts the stream, and the river curves around it. There is a small gravel beach off a backwater area, downstream of the monolith.

Elegantly sculpted Mt. Hood, Oregon's highest peak at 11,239 feet, towers over Swimming Hole #12, Trillium Lake.

At Swimming Hole #8, McIver Park on Clackamas River, a happy youngster "tubes" toward a safe landing in his parents' arms.

Intriguing "formation rock" lines Swimming Hole #10, The Narrows on Clackamas River.

**Two views of Swimming
Hole #218, South Umpqua
Falls on South Umpqua
River, a great spot for
moderate-to-strong swim-
mers.**

Good swimming and outstanding scenery are your rewards for making the 1.4-mile hike to Swimming Hole #308, Strawberry Lake, in Strawberry Mountain Wilderness.

Cliffs form a handsome backdrop for this angler/swimmer at Swimming Hole #323, Clarno Park on John Day River.

Swimming Hole #83, Hendricks Bridge Wayside on McKenzie River, is a fine choice for the whole family.

Swimming Hole #93, Slide Rock on Lake Creek, rates a big smile from this young swimmer.

Swimming Hole #207, Little Falls on Steamboat Creek: Little Falls plus a little kid add up to big-time fun.

At Swimming Hole #147, Three Pools on Little North Fork Santiam River, a joyous leap leads to a glorious splashdown.

Swimming Hole #235, Crowfoot Falls on Big Butte Creek, with its
luscious pool.

90. Rider Creek Arm of Cougar Reservoir •••••• and Terwilliger Hot Springs

Rating: 8
Location: Willamette National Forest
Water quality: Excellent; 25′ transparency
Vital statistics: 1280 acres; at least 100′ deep in this arm; 70° (July); light algae; mud bottom; heavy use
Setting: Forested valley at 1720′; light to moderate litter
Swim skill: Moderate
Amenities: For-fee camping around the lake; no drinking water; pit toilets
Entry fee: No
Topo: Cougar Reservoir 7½′

Driving Instructions: Rider Creek Arm of Cougar Reservoir and Terwilliger Hot Springs are 53.3 miles east of Eugene. From the intersec-

tion of I-5 and I-105/ Highway 126 in Eugene, head east on Highway 126 to the end of the divided highway, 6.6 miles. Turn left onto Main Street, continuing on Highway 126, and drive to the Cougar Reservoir turnoff, Forest Road 19, 39.0 miles, between mileposts 45 and 46. Turn right and drive to a dam, 3.4 miles. Turn right at the dam to go around the west side of the reservoir to the parking lot near the hot springs trailhead, 4.3 miles. (See detail map.)

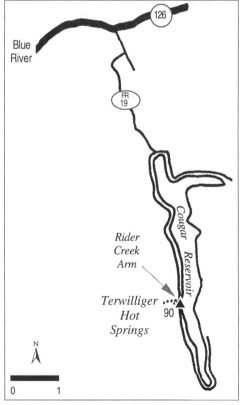

Hiking Instructions: From the parking lot, backtrack on foot to the Terwilliger Hot Springs Trailhead sign on the other side of the road. Take the path along the outside of the railing, less than 0.1 mile. From the trailhead sign it is an easy hike to the springs, 0.3 mile. From a second trailhead sign, 0.1 mile along the way to the springs, a spur trail goes to the left down to the swim spot.

Comments: There is a nice countercultural atmosphere here. Expect nudity at both the springs and the swimming hole. The hot springs consist of eight dammed pools from 3–10 feet across and 2–3 feet deep. They range in temperature from 109 to 112° F. They are gravel-bottomed and provide a totally lovely place for a soak. But if a swim is needed, that is available, too. The trail to the hot springs overlooks a very pleasant pool created by the reservoir and Rider Creek, with a waterfall in the background. The bank is dirt, but it is a very acceptable swim to the base of the falls and back. The area is day-use only.

91. Scott Lake ••••••••••••••••••••••••••••••

Rating: 8
Location: Willamette National Forest
Water quality: Excellent; transparent to bottom
Vital statistics: 26 acres; 19' deep; 68° (July); moderate shoreline weeds; silt bottom; moderate use
Setting: Forested mountains at 4806'; light litter
Swim skill: Low to moderate
Amenities: No-fee camping; no drinking water; pit toilets
Entry fee: No
Topo: Linton Lake 7½'

Driving Instructions: Scott Lake is 70.0 miles east of Eugene. From the intersection of I-5 and I-105/Highway 126 in Eugene, head east on Highway 126 to the end of the divided highway, 6.6 miles. Turn left onto Main Street, continuing on Highway 126, and drive to Highway 242, the McKenzie Pass scenic route, 46.4 miles, at milepost 55. Turn right and drive to the Scott Lake turnoff on a windy and bumpy passage, 16.1 miles, between mileposts 71 and 72. Turn left

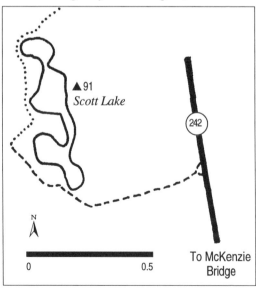

and drive on gravel to the trailhead, which gives access to the various parts of the lake, 0.9 mile. (See detail map on preceding page.)

Comments: This is such a lovely place. On the skyline to the east are North and Middle Sisters. The lake itself is really a series of three generally interconnected pools. The shoreline is mostly dirt and gravel. There is a particularly nice spot on the channel connecting the middle and south pools. The water here is shallow, no more than 5 feet, with easy access to deeper water to the north. There are tons of tadpoles in the late spring and early summer. The smell of the place is divine.

92. Sharps Creek ••••••••••••••••••••••••••

Rating:	6
Location:	Bureau of Land Management
Water quality:	Good; 11′ transparency
Vital statistics:	40′ wide; at least 14′ deep; light current; 65° F (July); moderate algae; bedrock and gravel bottom; moderate to heavy use
Setting:	Forested valley at 1120′; light litter
Swim skill:	Low to moderate
Amenities:	For-fee camping; drinking water; pit toilets
Entry fee:	No
Topo:	Culp Creek 7½′

Driving Instructions: Sharps Creek is 38.0 miles southeast of Eugene. Follow the driving instructions of Swimming Hole #84 to the rejoining with Row River Road. Continue on Row River Road to Sharps Creek Road, 4.2. Turn right and drive to Sharps Creek Recreation Site, 3.3 miles, between mileposts 3 and 4. Park on the left 0.1 mile past the recreation site sign.

Hiking Instructions: From parking, follow the pathway along a cyclone fence down to the pool. Watch for poison oak.

Comments: Bedrock and formation rock define this hole. There are cliffs and underwater rock ledges, a small gravel beach, and a small rapids upstream.

93. Slide Rock on Lake Creek ••••••••••••••••

Rating:	9
Location:	Bureau of Land Management
Water quality:	Good; transparent to bottom
Vital statistics:	60′ wide; at least 10′ deep; moderate current; 76° F (August); moderate to heavy algae; bedrock bottom; heavy use
Setting:	Forested valley at 480′; heavy litter
Swim skill:	Moderate

Amenities: None
Entry fee: No
Topo: Triangle Lake 7½′

Driving Instructions: Slide Rock is 44.5 miles west of Eugene. Follow the driving instructions for Swimming Hole #79 to Exit 4 onto 6th Avenue, which is Highway 99, and drive to Highway 36, 14.9 miles, between mileposts 111 and 112. Turn left, drive past Triangle Lake, and travel to a roughly developed parking lot, 26.3 miles, between mileposts 25 and 26, on the right.

Hiking Instructions: From the parking lot, hike west, downstream, beside the road to the long staircase that leads down to the creek, 0.2 mile. Be careful of cars. The staircase is on the left. Watch for poison oak.

Comments: Nature has constructed this gorge with large blocks on bedrock. There are some suds. There are three great pools on Lake Creek, a tributary of the Siuslaw River. The bottom of the staircase is adjacent to the middle pool. That pool is surrounded by formation rocks, off of which some people jump. Water flows from this pool 2–6 inches deep over a smooth bedrock layer for a distance of about 100 feet at about a 20–30 degree angle. At the bottom of this slide is a lower pool which sliders dump into. The best sliding is with tubes—they offer smooth riding and protection from getting banged up—but many people just slide on their posteriors. Be sure to wear only sturdy cutoffs or swim suits that are expendable. Take particular care of being pulled by rapids and jammed into the wall on the right side.

The upper pool is at the base of 18-foot Lake Creek Falls. It makes a fine place for dipping or sunning. The gorge is laid out east to west so that it gets maximum sun. But there is also plenty of shade. The place can absorb a lot of people, but even so it is overused. There are often far too many dogs. A fish ladder detracts. The slippery rocks make for excellent sliding, but also danger. (A terrible, though naturally occurring, tragedy occurred in this area in 1993. A shifting of the sandstone at the base of the slide created an uplifted, jagged lip which quickly led to two broken legs and the closure of the Slide Rock area to water play uses. The BLM intends to repair the problem by smoothing the damaged area, so that this great place can again be open to the public by Summer 1994.)

94. Waldo Lake ••••••••••••••••••••••••

Rating: 6
Location: Willamette National Forest
Water quality: Excellent; 52′ transparency
Vital statistics: 6298 acres; at least 420′ deep; 66° F (August); light algae; sand and silt bottom; moderate use

Setting: Forested mountains at 5414'; light litter
Swim skill: Moderate to strong
Amenities: For-fee camping; drinking water; flush toilets
Entry fee: No
Topo: Waldo Lake 7½'

Driving Instructions: Waldo Lake is 77.7 miles east of Eugene. Follow the driving instructions for Swimming Hole #74 onto Highway 58 and go to the Waldo Lake turnoff, 58.9 miles, between mileposts 58 and 59. Turn left onto Forest Road 5897, which becomes Forest Rd 5898, and drive to the turnoff for North Waldo Campground, 12.6 miles. Turn right and go to the parking lot and boat ramp, 0.7 mile.

Hiking Instructions: The easiest place to swim is adjacent to the parking lot and boat ramp. A more secluded place is at a rocky point 2.3 miles from the parking lot. Take the Waldo Lake Trail, accessed at the north edge of the parking area. It leads counterclockwise around the lake. Hike to a fork along the trail, 1.7 miles. Follow the left branch and till a swampy lake appears on the right, 0.5 mile. Just past this point the trail divides. Bear left and hike to the lake and a lovely formation rock outcrop, 0.1 mile.

Comments: Waldo is the second deepest lake in Oregon and one of the purest lakes in the world. Near the boat ramp (it is hard to understand why motors are allowed on this lake) there is a marked area with a swimming platform out from the shore and a small, sandy beach. There is also a rocky island to explore. From the formation rocks at the hike-in spot, there is easy, clambering access to the water. Of course, there are many places to swim, all around the lake.

95. Wildwood Falls Park on Row River • • • • • • • •

Rating: 10
Location: County Park
Water quality: Excellent; 16' transparency
Vital statistics: 90' wide; at least 19' deep; moderate current; 65° F (July); light algae; pebble bottom; moderate to heavy use
Setting: Forested valley at 1000'; light to moderate litter
Swim skill: Moderate
Amenities: None
Entry fee: No
Topo: Culp Creek 7½'

Driving Instructions: Wildwood Falls Park is 35.7 miles southeast of Eugene. Follow the driving instructions for Swimming Hole #84 to the rejoining with Row River Road. Continue on Row River Road to the turnoff for the park, 4.5 miles, between mileposts 16 and 17. Turn left and drive on Lower Brice Creek Road to a turnout on the right, 0.8 mile. (See detail map for Swimming Hole #84.)

Comments: Awesome! A 13-foot falls drops off a cliff which halfway circles the pool below. Access to the pool is a bit difficult and requires care, either by crossing the stream above the falls and clambering down on the other side or by jumping from the cliff. There is an easy circular current pattern created by the falls.

Lane County Points of Interest

96. Covered Bridges •
Throughout Lane County

> **Type:** Historic bridges
> **Hours:** Daily
> **Fee:** No

Comments: These bridges were built with covers that sheltered their wooden beams from Western Oregon's heavy rainfall and allowed the bridges to last longer. Lane County claims to have the most covered bridges of any county west of the Mississippi. Maps are at area visitor centers.

97. McCredie Springs •
Willamette National Forest

> **Type:** Natural hot springs
> **Hours:** Daily
> **Fee:** No

Driving Instructions: McCredie Springs is 50.7 miles southeast of Eugene. Follow the driving instructions for Swimming Hole #74 onto Highway 58 and go to the springs parking lot, 45.2 miles, between mileposts 45 and 46. There is a sign pointing to McCredie Station Road. The parking lot is next to the sign, on the right.

Hiking Instructions: The short trail is on the upstream side of the parking lot.

Comments: At 2,000 feet elevation, there are several hot pools on both sides of Salt Creek. Be cautious, and particularly alert with children. The creek is cold and swift, and the springs may be scalding. Temperatures generally range from 98 to 114° F, but there are several hot spots where the temperature greatly exceeds that. The biggest of the pools is 30 by 35 feet, the smallest 3 feet across, and they may be up to 2 feet deep. Silt and organic debris are the primary bottom materials. Expect nudity at this heavily used place.

98. McKenzie Highway ••••••••••••••••••••
Willamette and Deschutes National Forests

Type: Scenic drive
Hours: Daily
Fee: No

Driving Instructions: McKenzie Highway is 53.0 miles east of Eugene. From the intersection of I-5 and I-105/Highway 126 in Eugene, head east on Highway 126 to the end of the divided highway, 6.6 miles. Turn left onto Main Street, continuing on Highway 126, and drive to the junction with Highway 242, the McKenzie Pass scenic route, 46.4 miles, at milepost 55. Turn right and proceed on this bumpy and windy road to the summit at McKenzie Pass, 17.9 miles, between mileposts 77 and 78. Enter Linn, then Deschutes counties at the top.

Comments: The highway to McKenzie Pass (5325 feet in elevation) provides an impressive scenic drive through the Cascades. It is closed by snow in the winter. Check out Wright Observatory at the summit. See Point of Interest #266 for the eastern approach to McKenzie Pass, which passes through landscape scenically quite different from the west side.

99. McKenzie River Hot Springs ••••••••••••••
Willamette National Forest

Type: Natural hot springs
Hours: Daily
Fee: No

Driving Instructions: McKenzie River Hot Springs is 58.2 miles east of Eugene. From the intersection of I-5 and I-105/Highway 126 in Eugene, head east on Highway 126 to the end of the divided highway, 6.6 miles. Turn left onto Main Street, continuing on Highway 126, and drive to the junction with Highway 242, the McKenzie Pass scenic route, 46.4 miles. Continue straight on Highway 126 to Forest Road 2654, 5.2 miles. Turn left and cross a bridge to parking on the right, less than 0.1 mile.

Hiking Instructions: Walk the nearest trail along the river, downstream to the hot springs, 340 feet.

Comments: This luscious spot is tucked in the bank right alongside the roaring McKenzie at 1800 feet elevation. The pool measures 8 by 13 feet, is 1 to 2 feet deep, is 104° F, and is floored with coarse sand. Expect nudity.

100. Oregon Dunes National Recreation Area •••••
Siuslaw National Forest

>   **Type:** Scenic location
>   **Hours:** Daily
>   **Fee:** No

Driving Instructions: Oregon Dunes National Recreation Area is west of Eugene. The Dunes extend along the Lane County coastline from Florence south and into Douglas and Coos counties (see Points of Interest #171 and #227).

Comments: A hike through the dunes to an oasis or isolated wind-blown beach is a lifetime experience. Be sure to carry water and stay together. Be cautious, particularly at night, of the disorienting effect of the dunes and of the dense belt of trees and shrubs that must be traversed between the dunes and the ocean. Shoes are a must. See Point of Interest #227 for information about the dunes visitor center operated by the Siuslaw National Forest.

101. Salt Creek Falls •••••••••••••••••••••••••
Willamette National Forest

>   **Type:** Scenic location
>   **Hours:** Daily
>   **Fee:** No

Driving Instructions: Salt Creek Falls is 63.3 miles southeast of Eugene. Follow the driving instructions for Swimming Hole #74 onto Highway 58 and go to the falls turnoff, 57.1 miles, between mileposts 57 and 58. Turn right and drive to parking, 0.7 mile.

Comments: This pretty waterfall is Oregon's second highest, after Multnomah Falls.

102. Sea Lion Caves •••••••••••••••••••••••••••
91560 Highway 101, Florence; (503) 547-3111

>   **Type:** Wildlife habitat
>   **Hours:** Daily, 9 A.M. (8 A.M. during summer) to about an hour
>   before dark, depending on cave visibility; closed
>   Christmas
>   **Fee:** Yes

Driving Instructions: Sea Lion Caves is 77.8 miles west of Eugene. Follow the driving instructions for Swimming Hole #79 to Florence and

Highway 101, 58.8 miles. Turn right and go to Sea Lion Caves, 11.3 miles, between mileposts 179 and 180, on the left, with parking on either side.

Comments: Sea-lion observation points are on an outside ledge overlook and inside a cave. This is billed as the world's only mainland home of the Steller sea lion. Most of the animals gather outside during spring and summer, and inside during fall and winter.

103. University of Oregon Museum of Natural History and Oregon State Museum of Anthropology
1680 East 15th Avenue, Eugene; (503) 346-3024

> **Type:** Museum
> **Hours:** Wednesday through Sunday, noon to 5 P.M.; closed on university holidays
> **Fee:** No, donation requested

Driving Instructions: From the intersection of I-5 and I-105/Highway 126 in Eugene, head west on I-105 to Exit 1, the exit for University of Oregon, 1.1 miles. Take the exit and bear left at a fork, 0.2 mile. Now on Coburg Road, follow signs to the University of Oregon and drive to Broadway Avenue (which runs into Franklin Boulevard), 1.2 miles. Keep following the University of Oregon signs to Agate Street, 0.9 mile. Turn right and drive to 15th Street, 0.2 mile. Turn left and go to parking for the museum, less than 0.1 mile, on the right.

Comments: Combining natural history and anthropology, this is a small but attractive museum with frequently changing exhibits.

104. Wall Creek Hot Springs • • • • • • • • • • • • • • • • •
Willamette National Forest

> **Type:** Natural hot springs
> **Hours:** Daily
> **Fee:** No

Driving Instructions: Wall Creek Hot Springs is 50.6 miles southeast of Eugene. Follow the driving instructions for Swimming Hole #74 onto Highway 58 and go to Crestview Street in Oakridge, about 35 miles (Crestview Street is at a traffic signal and is signed to CITY CENTER). Turn left and drive to 1st Street, 0.2 mile. Turn right onto what becomes Salmon Creek Road/Forest Road 24, and follow it to Forest Road 1934, 9.4 miles. Turn left and go to the trailhead turnout on the left, 0.5 mile.

Hiking Instructions: From the trailhead, hike to the hot springs, 0.3 mile.

Comments: This is a very acceptable place for a soak at an elevation of 2160 feet. The pool is 18 feet in diameter, two feet deep and 96° F, with a sand and gravel bottom. Expect nudity.

105. Wave Pool •
6100 Thurston Road, Springfield; (503) 747-9283 or 726-2752

      Type: Swimming pool
    Hours: Monday through Saturday, 6:30–9 P.M.; Saturday and Sunday, noon to 5 p.m; additional summer hours are Monday through Friday, 10 A.M. to 5 P.M.
       Fee: Yes

Driving Instructions: Wave Pool is 7.5 miles east of Eugene. From the intersection of I-5 and I-105/Highway 126 in Eugene, head east on Highway 126 to the end of the divided highway, 6.6 miles. Turn left onto Main Street and go to 58th Street, 0.1 mile (there is a sign to Municipal Pool). Turn left and travel to Thurston Road, 0.5 mile. Turn right, following the sign to Lively Park Swim Center, and proceed to the pool turnoff at signs for Willamalane Park and Recreation District, 0.3 mile, on the left.

Comments: If one hankers for waves without the salt, sand and sun, this is the place. The waves are artificially generated.

106. Willamette Science and Technology Center • • (WISTEC)
2300 Centennial Boulevard, Eugene; (503) 484-9027

      Type: Science museum
    Hours: Wednesday through Sunday, noon to 6 P.M.
       Fee: Yes

Driving Instructions: From the intersection of I-5 and I-105/Highway 126 in Eugene, head west on I-105 to Exit 1, the exit for University of Oregon, 1.1 miles. Take the exit, following signs to Autsen Stadium, and bear left at a fork, 0.2 mile. Now on Coburg Road, drive to Country Club Road, 0.4 mile. Turn right and go to Centennial Boulevard, 0.5 mile. Bear right and proceed to Harris Parkway, 0.3 mile. Turn right and go to the WISTEC turnoff, 0.1 mile. Turn right and drive to parking, 0.1 mile.

Comments: This is a hands-on science museum. Though not on the scale of OMSI, WISTEC allows for close and personal science discovery.

Lincoln County
(County Seat: Newport)

There are a lot of sights in Lincoln County and few respectable places to swim. Driving instructions begin in Newport at the intersection of Highway 20 (Olive Street) and Highway 101 (North Coast Highway).

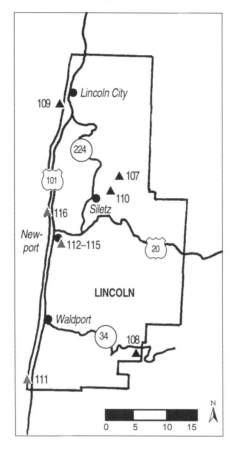

Lincoln County Swimming Holes

107. Moonshine Park on Siletz River
108. River Edge on Alsea River
109. Siletz Bay
110. Twin Bridges Park on Siletz River

Lincoln County Points of Interest

111. Cape Perpetua

112. Hatfield Marine Science Center
113. Oregon Coast Aquarium
114. Undersea Gardens
115. Yaquina Bay Park and Lighthouse
116. Yaquina Head Natural Area

Lincoln County Swimming Holes

107. Moonshine Park on Siletz River • • • • • • • • • •

Rating: 8
Location: County Park
Water quality: Excellent; transparent to bottom
Vital statistics: 90' wide; at least 13' deep; moderate current; 64° F (August); light algae; boulder, rock and gravel bottom; moderate use
Setting: Forested valley at 240'; light to moderate litter
Swim skill: Moderate
Amenities: For-fee camping; drinking water; flush toilets
Entry fee: No
Topo: Euchre Mountain 7½'

Driving Instructions: Moonshine Park is 24.9 miles northeast of Newport. From the intersection of Highway 20 and Highway 101 in Newport, head east on Highway 20 to Highway 229, 5.7 miles, between mileposts 5 and 6. Turn left and drive to Logsden Road in Siletz, 7.4 miles, between mileposts 23 and 24. Turn right and go to Moonshine Park Road, 7.8 miles, between mileposts 7 and 8. Turn left and drive to the park entrance, 3.9 miles (stay left on pavement when the road bends left and a gravel road branches off). Turn into parking on the right, less than 0.1 mile. (See detail map on next page.)

Hiking Instructions: From parking, the short trail to an upper hole is across the grass and down the bank. A lower hole is downstream, less than 0.1 mile.

Comments: The two holes are equally wonderful. The upper hole is at the base of a confluence and rapids. There is a 130-foot gravel beach. The downstream hole has a somewhat smaller gravel beach across from a wispy falls on the opposite bank. Floating between them is fun. Farther downstream are lots of shallows over bedrock.

108. River Edge on Alsea River • • • • • • • • • • • • •

Rating: 5
Location: Siuslaw National Forest

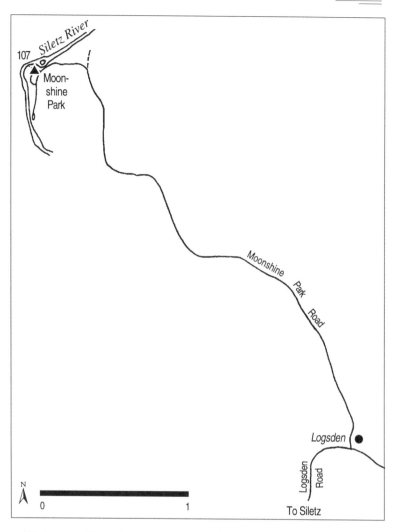

Water quality: Good; transparent to bottom
Vital statistics: 60' wide; at least 6' deep; moderate current; 68° F (August); moderate algae; bedrock bottom; moderate use
Setting: Forested valley at 160'; light litter
Swim skill: Moderate
Amenities: For-fee, group camping by permit, call 487-5811; drinking water; pit toilets
Entry fee: No
Topo: Hellion Rapids 7½'

Driving Instructions: River Edge is 38.7 miles southeast of Newport. From the intersection of Highway 20 and Highway 101 in Newport, head south on Highway 101 to Highway 34 in Waldport, 15.6 miles, between mileposts 155 and 156. Turn left and drive to the turnoff for River Edge, 23.1 miles, between mileposts 23 and 24. Turn right into parking.

Comments: Flat formation rock abuts this hole which is at the bottom of a slide for boat launching. There are a few suds.

109. Siletz Bay ••••••••••••••••••••••••••••

Rating:	8
Location:	State Park
Water quality:	Good; 8' transparency
Vital statistics:	1.8 miles wide; at least 23' deep; light current; 61° F (August); tidal zone aquatic vegetation; sand bottom; moderate to heavy use
Setting:	Wooded coast at sea level; light litter
Swim skill:	Moderate to strong
Amenities:	Drinking water; flush toilets
Entry fee:	No
Topo:	Lincoln City 7½'

Driving Instructions: Siletz Bay is 22.7 miles north of Newport. From the intersection of Highway 20 and Highway 101 in Newport, head north on Highway 101 to 51st Street, just after crossing Schooner Creek at the south end of Lincoln City, 22.4 miles. Turn left and drive to parking, 0.3 mile.

Comments: At the mouth of the bay, this is a sandy and sheltered, yet stimulating, ocean site. The amount of wave action encountered can be varied by moving toward or away from the ocean.

110. Twin Bridges Park on Siletz River •••••••••

Rating:	6
Location:	County Park
Water quality:	Good; transparent to bottom
Vital statistics:	100' wide; at least 12' deep; light current; 66° F (August); light algae; bedrock bottom; light to moderate use
Setting:	Forested valley at 140'; light litter
Swim skill:	Moderate
Amenities:	No drinking water; pit toilets
Entry fee:	No
Topo:	Eddyville 7½'

Driving Instructions: Twin Bridges Park is 17.9 miles northeast of Newport. Follow the driving instructions of Swimming Hole #107 to Logsden Road. Turn right and go to the park turnoff, 4.7 miles, between mileposts 4 and 5. Turn right, cross the bridge, and turn into the main park entrance, on the left, or turn right and onto a gravel turnout immediately on the right, 0.1 mile.

Hiking Instructions: From the park entrance there is a boat ramp to the water; from the turnout, there is a short trail.

Comments: The hole starts above the bridge, but widens below it next to a 50-foot sandy beach spot. There are swinging ropes on both sides of the river.

Lincoln County Points of Interest

111. Cape Perpetua ••••••••••••••••••••••
Siuslaw National Forest; (503) 547-3289

> **Type:** Scenic location
> **Hours:** Daily, 9 A.M. to 5 P.M. from Memorial Day to Labor Day; Saturday and Sunday, 10 A.M. to 4 P.M. the rest of the year
> **Fee:** No

Driving Instructions: Cape Perpetua is 27.2 miles south of Newport. From the intersection of Highway 20 and Highway 101 in Newport, head south on Highway 101 to the Siuslaw Forest Visitor Center turnoff, 27.0 miles, between mileposts 167 and 168. Turn left and go to parking, 0.2 mile.

Comments: The cape is a turbulent and beautiful headland, where a massive volcanic basalt protrusion meets the sea. Spectacular views of the ocean, churning water, trails, beaches and tidepooling are all here. The visitor center is a pleasant starting point.

112. Hatfield Marine Science Center ••••••••••
2030 South Marine Science Drive, Newport; (503) 867-0226

> **Type:** Science center
> **Hours:** Daily, 10 A.M. to 6 P.M. from mid-June to Labor Day; 10 A.M. to 4 P.M. the rest of the year
> **Fee:** No

Driving Instructions: From the intersection of Highway 20 and Highway 101 in Newport, head south on Highway 101 to the Aquarium and Science Center turnoff, just after crossing the bridge, 1.8 miles. Turn right onto OSU Drive and go to the center turnoff, 0.7 mile (check out the driftwood house on the left 0.2 mile along the way). Turn right and into parking, less than 0.1.

Comments: Here are an aquarium and other displays of the marine environment of the Pacific Northwest.

113. Oregon Coast Aquarium • • • • • • • • • • • • • • • •
2820 Southeast Ferry Slip Road, Newport; (503) 867-3474

> **Type:** Aquarium
> **Hours:** Daily, 9 A.M. to 6 P.M.; closed Christmas day
> **Fee:** Yes

Driving Instructions: From the intersection of Highway 20 and Highway 101 in Newport, head south on Highway 101 to the Aquarium and Science Center turnoff, just after crossing the bridge, 1.8 miles. Turn right onto OSU Drive and go to Ferry Slip Road, 0.4 mile (check out the driftwood house on the left 0.2 mile along the way). Turn right and go to the aquarium entrance, 0.1 mile. Turn left at the entrance and drive to parking, 0.1 mile.

Comments: The aquarium focuses exclusively on marine life found along the Oregon Coast. Both inside and outside exhibits present animals and plants in their natural habitats. It is a very nice place.

114. Undersea Gardens •
267 Southwest Bay Boulevard, Newport; (503) 265-7541

> **Type:** Commercial aquarium
> **Hours:** Daily, 10 A.M. to 5 P.M.; 9 A.M. to 8 P.M. during the
> summer; closed Christmas
> **Fee:** Yes

Driving Instructions: From the intersection of Highway 20 and Highway 101 in Newport, head south on Highway 101 to the bay-front turnoff at Hurbert Street (which becomes Fall Street), 0.3 mile. Turn left and ease downhill to Bay Boulevard, 0.3 mile. Turn left and drive to Undersea Gardens, a little over 0.1 mile, on the right. Across the street from it is parking. (Also across the street are Ripley's Believe It or Not and Wax Work Museum, for those who want to be amused. Ask about family rates and rates to see all three attractions.)

Comments: Windows onto the bay floor give views of marine life.

115. Yaquina Bay Lighthouse • • • • • • • • • • • • • • • • •
Yaquina Bay State Park, Newport; (503) 867-7451

> **Type:** Historic lighthouse

Hours: Daily, 11 A.M. to 5 P.M. from Memorial Day to September 30; Saturday and Sunday, noon to 4 P.M. the rest of the year
Fee: No, donation requested

Driving Instructions: From the intersection of Highway 20 and Highway 101 in Newport, head south on Highway 101 to the state park turnoff, 1.0 mile, on the right just before crossing the bridge. Take the turnoff and go to parking below the lighthouse, 0.2 mile.

Comments: Built in 1871, this authentically refurbished 19th Century lighthouse and keeper's dwelling is staffed by volunteers. The beach below is very pleasant.

116. Yaquina Head Natural Area ● ● ● ● ● ● ● ● ● ● ● ● ●
Bureau of Land Management; (503) 265-2863

Type: Scenic location
Hours: Daily, 6 A.M. to dusk
Fee: No

Driving Instructions: Yaquina Head Natural Area is 3.7 miles north of Newport. From the intersection of Highway 20 and Highway 101 in Newport, head north on 101 to the natural-area turnoff, 2.7 miles. Turn left onto Lighthouse Road and to parking, 1.0 mile.

Comments: There is superlative, if overused, tidepooling to the south of the lighthouse. Take the long staircase down to see the wonders. BLM is hoping to open the working lighthouse for tightly controlled tours by the spring of 1994, but as with so many things, it depends on funding.

Linn County
(County Seat: Albany)

Linn County is well-endowed with both cozy farmland creeks and clear, high-mountain streams. Driving instructions begin in Albany at I-5 Exit 233, at the freeway intersection with Highway 20.

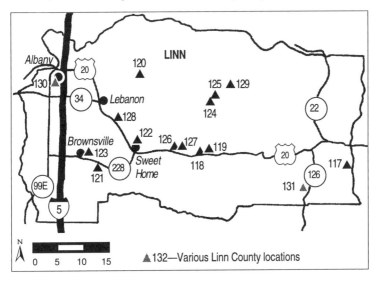

Linn County Swimming Holes

117. Big Lake
118. Cascadia Park on South Santiam River
119. High Rocks on South Santiam River in Cascadia Park
120. Larwood Park on Crabtree Creek
121. McKercher Park on Calapooia River
122. Northside Park on South Santiam River
123. Pioneer Park on Calapooia River
124. Quartzville Creek, boulder beach
125. Quartzville Creek, gravel beach
126. South Santiam River at bridge crossing
127. South Santiam Tree Farm Park on South Santiam River
128. Waterloo Park on South Santiam River
129. Yellowbottom on Quartzville Creek

Linn County Points of Interest

130. Albany Historic Districts
131. Blue Hole on McKenzie River
132. Covered Bridges

Linn County Swimming Holes

117. Big Lake •

Rating:	5
Location:	Willamette National Forest
Water quality:	Excellent; 43′ transparency
Vital statistics:	190 acres; 77′ deep; 67° F (August); light algae; gravel and rock bottom; heavy use
Setting:	Forested mountains at 4644′; light litter
Swim skill:	Moderate
Amenities:	For-fee camping; drinking water; pit toilets
Entry fee:	No
Topo:	Mount Washington 7½′

Driving Instructions: Big Lake is 82.3 miles east of Albany. From I-5 Exit 233 in Albany, at the freeway intersection with Highway 20/Santiam Highway, head east on Highway 20 to Santiam Pass and the turnoff for Big Lake, 78.9 miles, at milepost 80. Turn right and drive to Big Lake Road/Forest Road 2690, 0.9 mile. Turn left and drive to Big Lake Campground, 2.5 miles, or to East Big Lake Campground, 0.8 mile more.

Comments: The lake could be a fine one for swimming and quiet use, under the tranquil gaze of Mount Washington. Unfortunately, it has been turned over to motorboaters. They are omnipresent and oppressive. It is a sad fate for such a pure and beautiful lake in its otherwise serene surroundings.

118. Cascadia Park on South Santiam River • • • • •

Rating:	7
Location:	State Park
Water quality:	Excellent; transparent to bottom
Vital statistics:	50′ wide; at least 7′ deep; moderate current; 66° F (August); light algae; rock and gravel bottom; heavy use
Setting:	Forested valley at 800′; light to moderate litter
Swim skill:	Moderate
Amenities:	For-fee camping; drinking water; flush toilets
Entry fee:	No
Topo:	Cascadia 7½′

Driving Instructions: Cascadia Park is 40.3 miles southeast of Albany. From I-5 Exit 233 in Albany, at the freeway intersection with Highway 20/Santiam Highway, head east on Highway 20 to the park turnoff, 40.2 miles, between mileposts 41 and 42. Turn left and then bear right into the park after crossing the bridge, 0.1 mile. There are several day-use areas.

Hiking Instructions: Take an asphalt trail from one of the parking lots to the steps down to the river. From the first parking lot there is a wooden railing that leads to the steps, less than 0.2 mile.

Comments: This is a beautiful place of low formation rock where the water chutes through a narrow, 50-foot channel. It is a fun place for tubing, with a 40-foot gravel beach.

119. High Rocks on South Santiam River in • • • • • Cascadia Park

         Rating: 10
      Location: State Park
  Water quality: Excellent; transparent to bottom
  Vital statistics: 50' wide; at least 21' deep; light current; 68° F (August); light algae; sand, pebble and bedrock bottom; moderate to heavy use
        Setting: Forested valley at 840'; light to moderate litter
    Swim skill: Moderate
    Amenities: None
    Entry fee: No
          Topo: Cascadia 7½'

Driving Instructions: High Rocks is 41.1 miles southeast of Albany. From I-5 Exit 233 in Albany, at the freeway intersection with Highway 20/Santiam Highway, head east on Highway 20 to the long gravel turnouts on either side of Wolf Creek, 41.1 miles, between mileposts 42 and 43, on the left.

Hiking Instructions: From the turnouts, look for access points down steep trails a bit west of Wolf Creek. A cable allows scaling past a sheer wall at the base of the path which starts alongside the creek, but clambering down it is hazardous. Whatever path is chosen to descend into this gorge, great care should be exercised.

Comments: What a place! The 300-foot gorge is bounded by cliffs and boulders on both side of its incredible length. Dropoffs to deep water are sheer. There are shallows and rapids upstream. It presents an alluring vision, far removed from the traffic sounds which filter down from the highway above.

120. Larwood Park on Crabtree Creek • • • • • • • •

         Rating: 6
      Location: County Park

Water quality: Good; transparency to bottom
Vital statistics: 90′ wide; at least 7′ deep; light current; 71° F (August); light algae; bedrock bottom; heavy use
Setting: Wooded valley at 440′; heavy litter
Swim skill: Low to moderate
Amenities: No drinking water; pit toilets
Entry fee: No
Topo: Jordan 7½′

Driving Instructions: Larwood Park is 16.7 miles east of Albany. From I-5 Exit 233 in Albany, at the freeway intersection with Highway 20/Santiam Highway, head east on Highway 20 to Highway 226, 5.6 miles. Turn left and drive to Fish Hatchery Drive, 4.3 miles. Turn right and drive to a stop sign, 6.4 miles. Bear left at the stop sign, continuing on Fish Hatchery Drive to Larwood Drive, 0.3 mile. Turn left and go to parking on the left, less than 0.1 mile.

Comments: At the confluence of Crabtree Creek and Roaring River, this spot is an admirable setting, with the creek running under a covered bridge built in 1939. Though the water is not terribly deep, people jump off the bridge. It seems dangerous. There are great rock banks and shallows. But watch for glass.

121. McKercher Park on Calapooia River ● ● ● ● ● ●

Rating: 7
Location: County Park
Water quality: Good; transparency to bottom
Vital statistics: 80′ wide; at least 7′ deep; light current; 73° F (August); light algae; sand and gravel bottom; moderate to heavy use
Setting: Wooded valley at 440′; light litter
Swim skill: Moderate
Amenities: No drinking water; pit toilets
Entry fee: No
Topo: Union Point 7½′

Driving Instructions: McKercher Park is 26.7 miles southeast of Albany. From I-5 Exit 233 in Albany, at the freeway intersection with Highway 20/Santiam Highway, head south on I-5 to Exit 216, the exit for Brownsville, 16.5 miles, between mileposts 216 and 217. Take the exit and go to a stop, 0.3 mile. Turn left onto Highway 228 and drive to a gravel turnout 9.7 miles (this is 0.2 mile before the main entrance to the park), at milepost 12, on the right.

Comments: A myriad of channels and pools are above the hole. There is a 3-foot falls and there is a small downstream rapid. An 80-foot gravel beach, with some sand, is alongside. Watch for poison oak.

122. Northside Park on South Santiam River • • • • •

Rating: 7
Location: Sweet Home City Park
Water quality: Excellent; transparent to bottom
Vital statistics: 190′ wide; at least 10′ deep; moderate current; 66° F
(August); moderate algae; sand and rock bottom;
moderate use
Setting: Forested valley at 480′; light litter
Swim skill: Moderate to strong
Amenities: Drinking water; flush toilets
Entry fee: No
Topo: Sweet Home 7½′

Driving Instructions: Northside Park is 26.6 miles southeast of
Albany. From I-5 Exit 233 in Albany, at the freeway intersection with
Highway 20/Santiam Highway, head east on Highway 20 to Sweet Home
at 12th Avenue, 26.2 miles. Turn left and go to Redwood Street, 0.3 mile.
Turn left and drive to parking, less than 0.1 mile.

Hiking Instructions: From parking, walk across the grass, upstream,
to the river, 250 feet.

Comments: A 200-foot sandy beach lies along the water. The river
here is suited to an array of swimming abilities. The dropoff in the
downstream backwater area is steep, and the current varies widely in
different parts of the river.

123. Pioneer Park on Calapooia River • • • • • • • •

Rating: 6
Location: Brownsville City Park
Water quality: Good; transparent to bottom
Vital statistics: 40′ wide; at least 10′ deep; light current; 73° F (Au-
gust); light algae; sand and gravel bottom; light to
moderate use
Setting: Wooded valley at 320′; light to moderate litter
Swim skill: Low to moderate
Amenities: For-fee camping; drinking water; flush and pit toilets
Entry fee: No
Topo: Brownsville 7½′

Driving Instructions: Pioneer Park is 22.3 miles south of Albany.
From I-5 Exit 233 in Albany, at the freeway intersection with Highway 20/
Santiam Highway, head south on I-5 to Exit 216, the exit for Brownsville,

16.5 miles, between mileposts 216 and
217. Take the exit and go to a stop, 0.3
mile. Turn left onto Highway 228 and
drive to Main Street in Brownsville, 3.9
miles. Turn left and drive to Park Avenue, 0.5 mile. Turn left and go to the
park entrance, 0.2 mile. Stay left on a
gravel road, toward the ball field, and
park on the other side of the ball field, 0.3
mile. (See detail map.)

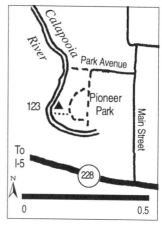

Hiking Instructions: Walk to the
hole across the grass, away from the ball
field, and through the trees, less than 0.1
mile.

Comments: Here is a very acceptable spot with a 130-foot sand-and-
gravel bank. There are shallows as well as depths. The adjacent park is nice
and has a playground next to the ball field.

124. Quartzville Creek, boulder beach ••••••••

Rating: 8
Location: Bureau of Land Management
Water quality: Excellent; transparent to bottom
Vital statistics: 50' wide; at least 18' deep; light current; 68° F (Au-
gust); light algae; pebble and boulder bottom; light to
moderate use
Setting: Forested valley at 1200'; light litter
Swim skill: Moderate
Amenities: No-fee, primitive camping by road; no drinking water
Entry fee: No
Topo: Yellowstone Mountain 7½'

Driving Instructions: Quartzville Creek, boulder beach, is 50.3 miles
east of Albany. From I-5 Exit 233 in Albany, at the freeway intersection with
Highway 20/Santiam Highway, head east on Highway 20 to the Green Peter
and Quartzville turnoff, 31.9 miles (for a fun exercise along the way, look for
the magic faucet just east of milepost 22, on the right), at milepost 33. Turn
left, skirt the Foster and Green Peter reservoirs and drive along Quartzville
Creek to a wide gravel turnout, 18.4 miles (0.3 mile past the Dogwood Picnic
Area turnout), on the right. Watch for logging trucks.

Hiking Instructions: It is a short, steep clamber down to the creek
from the turnout.

Comments: The 90-foot beach is composed of small boulders and
large pebbles, which are what make this place unique. The water is

marvelously clear. There is a rapids area upstream and shallows down-stream from the deep water. A rock wall lines the opposite bank.

125. Quartzville Creek, gravel beach

Rating: 7
Location: Bureau of Land Management
Water quality: Excellent; transparent to bottom
Vital statistics: 80' wide; at least 11' deep; light current; 66° F (August); light algae; gravel and pebble bottom; moderate use
Setting: Forested valley at 1280'; light litter
Swim skill: Moderate
Amenities: No-fee, primitive camping by road; no drinking water
Entry fee: No
Topo: Yellowstone Mountain 7½'

Driving Instructions: Quartzville Creek, gravel beach, is 51.8 miles east of Albany. Follow the driving instructions for Swimming Hole #124 past the reservoirs and continue along Quartzville Creek to a wide gravel turnout, 19.9 miles (1.8 miles past the Dogwood Picnic Area turnout), on the right. Watch for logging trucks.

Hiking Instructions: It is a short hike down to the creek on a good trail which begins on the downriver end of the turnout.

Comments: An 80-foot, coarse-sand and gravel beach is on the road side, and along the opposite bank is a rock wall. There are rapids upstream and downstream and some shallows. A small creek enters upstream.

126. South Santiam River at bridge crossing

Rating: 7
Location: Private
Water quality: Excellent; transparent to bottom
Vital statistics: 40' wide; at least 10' deep; moderate current; 70° F (August); light algae; gravel and bedrock bottom; moderate use
Setting: Forested valley at 760'; light litter
Swim skill: Moderate
Amenities: None
Entry fee: No
Topo: Green Peter 7½'

Driving Instructions: South Santiam River at bridge crossing is 37.1 miles southeast of Albany. From I-5 Exit 233 in Albany, at the freeway intersection with Highway 20/Santiam Highway, head east on Highway

20 to a turnout adjacent to a bridge crossing, 37.1 miles, between mileposts 38 and 39. The turnout and bridge crossing are on the left.

Comments: The river channels through low formation walls. There is a rapids upstream. Dropoffs to deep water are sheer.

127. South Santiam Tree Farm Park on • • • • • • • • South Santiam River

Rating: 7
Location: Private
Water quality: Good; transparent to bottom
Vital statistics: 40' wide; at least 14' deep; moderate current; 70° F (August); light algae; bedrock bottom; moderate use
Setting: Forested valley at 760'; light to moderate litter
Swim skill: Moderate to strong
Amenities: No drinking water; pit toilets
Entry fee: No
Topo: Green Peter 7½'

Driving Instructions: South Santiam Tree Farm Park is 37.4 miles southeast of Albany. From I-5 Exit 233 in Albany, at the freeway intersection with Highway 20/Santiam Highway, head east on Highway 20 to the turnoff for the park, 37.4 miles, between mileposts 38 and 39, on the left.

Hiking Instructions: A short trail through the park leads to the river. Work upstream along the rocks to get down to the water.

Comments: The river channels 150 feet between basaltic walls after passing through a myriad of chutes and cascades upstream. There are some suds. Dropoffs to deep water are sheer.

128. Waterloo Park on South Santiam River • • • • •

Rating: 6
Location: County Park
Water quality: Good; transparent to bottom
Vital statistics: 200' wide; at least 9' deep; light current; 66° F (August); moderate algae; rock bottom; moderate use
Setting: Wooded valley at 380'; moderate to heavy litter
Swim skill: Moderate
Amenities: No drinking water; pit toilets
Entry fee: No
Topo: Waterloo 7½'

Driving Instructions: Waterloo Park is 18.7 miles southeast of Albany. From I-5 Exit 233 in Albany, at the freeway intersection with

Highway 20/Santiam Highway, head east on Highway 20 to the Waterloo turnoff, 17.6 miles, between mileposts 18 and 19. Turn left and drive to just past the small community of Waterloo, to where the road curves to the left and to a stop sign, 1.1 miles. Either park in the lot on the right or go across the intersecting road and park on the other side. Do not cross the bridge. **Comments:** There is a large backwater stretch both above and below the bridge, and a chute above the bridge. The bank is gravel and rocks with some sand.

129. Yellowbottom on Quartzville Creek • • • • • • •

Rating: 8
Location: Bureau of Land Management
Water quality: Excellent; transparent to bottom
Vital statistics: 110' wide; at least 20' deep; light current; 70° F (August); light algae; sand and gravel bottom; moderate to heavy use
Setting: Forested valley at 1440'; light to moderate litter
Swim skill: Moderate
Amenities: For-fee camping; drinking water; pit toilets
Entry fee: No
Topo: Quartzville 7½'

Driving Instructions: Yellowbottom is 55.6 miles east of Albany. Follow the driving instructions for Swimming Hole #124 past the reservoirs and continue along Quartzville Creek to the Yellowbottom Campground, 23.7 miles. Day-use parking is on the right. Watch for logging trucks.

Comments: A nifty spine of lava, 13 feet tall and 100 feet long, juts out into the creek, creating a great pool alongside its downstream edge. Upstream of the spine, there are shallows and a 2-foot falls. Shallows are also downstream. The beach is sand and gravel.

Linn County Points of Interest

130. Albany Historic Districts • • • • • • • • • • • • • • •
8th and Ellsworth Streets, Albany; (503) 928-5008

Type: Historic buildings
Hours: Daily; on summer Sundays, noon to 4 P.M. from July to August, exploration can by done from horse-drawn carriages, with guides in Victorian-era costumes.
Fee: No, except for the carriages

Driving Instructions: From I-5 Exit 233 in Albany, at the freeway intersection with Highway 20/Santiam Highway, head west on Highway 20 to Pacific Boulevard, 1.1 mile. Turn left onto Pacific Boulevard and go to the turnoff for Albany City Center, Highway 20 and Corvallis, 0.8 mile. Exit to the right onto Lyon Street and then almost immediately turn in to parking at the Historic Districts Information Center on 8th Street, on the left, less than 0.1 mile. If unable to safely cross the lane of traffic at the merging point, continue to 7th Street, 0.1 mile. Turn left and go to the other side of the block. Turn left onto Ellsworth Street and immediately left again into parking by the information center gazebo.

Comments: A guide, including maps and tour routes of the historic districts, is available at the gazebo. There are 350 historic homes which, it is claimed, include every major architectural style popular in the United States since 1850.

131. Blue Hole on McKenzie River ••••••••••••
Willamette National Forest

Type: Scenic location
Hours: Daily
Fee: No

Driving Instructions: Blue Hole is 77.3 miles southeast of Albany. From I-5 Exit 233 in Albany, at the freeway intersection with Highway 20/Santiam Highway, head east on Highway 20 to its junction with Highway 126, about 66 miles. Turn right and drive to the trailhead turn-off at the north end of Trail Bridge Reservoir, 10.8 miles, between mileposts 10 and 11. Turn right, bear right after crossing the bridge and drive to the trailhead, 0.5 mile (the last 0.3 mile is on gravel). Parking is on the left and the trail is on the right. (See detail map.)

Hiking Instructions: Take the trail, walking upstream, to the hole, 1.9 miles.

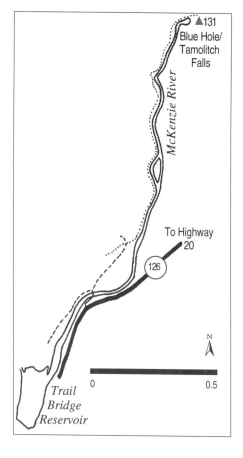

Comments: The trail goes through a moss-carpeted forest. Blue Hole, alternately known as Tamolitch Falls, is a great upwelling of water that begins the McKenzie River. It is not a place to swim at 45° F in August, but is a dazzling place to view.

132. Covered Bridges •••••••••••••••••••••
Throughout Linn County

> **Type:** Historic bridges
> **Hours:** Daily
> **Fee:** No

Comments: These bridges were built with covers that sheltered their wooden beams from Western Oregon's heavy rainfall and allowed the bridges to last longer. They also have served the cause of romance by furnishing protected meeting places. Maps are available at area visitor centers.

Marion County
(County Seat: Salem)

One of the best, but most abused, swimming streams in the state is in Marion County. The Little North Fork of the Santiam River abounds with tremendous places to swim. It's just too darn bad it has to be trashed. Driving instructions begin in Salem at the junction of Highway 22 with I-5 at Exit 253.

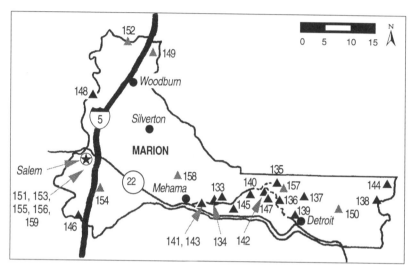

Marion County Swimming Holes

133. Bear Creek Park on Little North Fork Santiam River
134. Canyon Creek on Little North Fork Santiam River
135. La Cascada de los Ninos on Little North Fork Santiam River
136. Cedar Creek
137. Elk Lake
138. First Lake
139. French Creek on Detroit Lake
140. Little North Fork Santiam River, cliff pool
141. Little North Fork Santiam River, near milepost 26
142. Little North Fork Santiam River, Spur 211
143. North Fork Park on Little North Fork Santiam River
144. Russ Lake
145. Salmon Falls Park on Little North Fork Santiam River
146. Santiam River Rest Area
147. Three Pools on Little North Fork Santiam River
148. Wheatland Ferry on Willamette River

Marion County Points of Interest

149. Aurora National Historic District
150. Breitenbush Hot Springs
151. Bush House
152. Champoeg Park
153. Deepwood Estate
154. Enchanted Forest
155. Gilbert House Children's Museum
156. Mission Mill Village
157. Opal Pool on Opal Creek
158. Silver Falls Park
159. State Capitol

Marion County Swimming Holes

133. Bear Creek Park on Little North Fork •••••••
Santiam River

Rating:	7
Location:	County Park
Water quality:	Excellent; transparent to bottom
Vital statistics:	60′ wide; at least 7′ deep; moderate current; 71° F (July); light algae; rock, pebble and bedrock bottom; moderate to heavy use
Setting:	Forested valley at 920′; moderate to heavy litter
Swim skill:	Moderate
Amenities:	No drinking water; pit toilets
Entry fee:	No
Topo:	Mill City North 7½′

Driving Instructions: Bear Creek Park is 29.6 miles east of Salem. From the junction of Highway 22 and I-5 in Salem, head southeast on Highway 22 to the turnoff for Little North Santiam Recreation Area and Little North Fork Road, 21.9 miles, between mileposts 23 and 24. Turn left and drive to the park, 7.6 miles, between mileposts 30 and 31, on the left (0.4 mile past the Canyon Creek turnoff). Drive to parking, 0.1 mile. (See detail map on next page.)

Hiking Instructions: The trail to the river begins next to the pit toilets. Hike to the stream, 220 feet. Walk to holes 200 feet upstream or 130 feet downstream.

Comments: This is a tremendous spot when it is not crowded and littered. Otherwise, because the pool areas are small, it may seem closed in. The bank is mostly large rocks and small boulders, but beside the upstream pool is a 60-foot-long coarse-sand beach that can be very comfortable. The downstream hole is at the base of a rock outcrop.

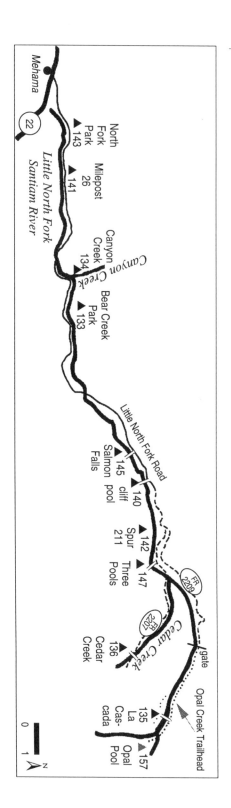

134. Canyon Creek on Little North Fork • • • • • • • • Santiam River

Rating: 8
Location: Bureau of Land Management
Water quality: Excellent; transparent to bottom
Vital statistics: 60′ wide; at least 10′ deep; moderate current; 71° F (July); light algae; pebble and gravel bottom; moderate to heavy use
Setting: Forested valley at 880′; moderate litter
Swim skill: Moderate
Amenities: Drinking water; pit toilets
Entry fee: No
Topo: Mill City North 7½′

Driving Instructions: Canyon Creek is 29.1 miles east of Salem. Follow the driving instructions for Swimming Hole #133 to the recreation-area turnoff. Turn left and drive to the Canyon Creek entrance, 7.2 miles, between mileposts 30 and 31. Turn left into the park. (See detail map for Swimming Hole #133.)

Hiking Instructions: The short trail to the river is down a stairway near the pit toilets.

Comments: Though this is a relatively small hole at a crook in the river, it is a wonderful spot. There are both shallows and depths. During high water there is a nice rapids upstream of the hole. Coarse sand and pebbles make a fine beach. Sunning rocks across the river are an easy swim from the beach, and beautiful high cliffs tower above. A house a short way downstream adds the only jarring note.

135. La Cascada de los Ninos on • • • • • • • • • • • • Little North Fork Santiam River

Rating: 7
Location: Willamette National Forest
Water quality: Excellent; transparent to bottom
Vital statistics: 60′ wide; at least 8′ deep; moderate current; 61° F (July); light algae; rock, boulder and bedrock bottom; light use
Setting: Forested valley at 2040′; light litter
Swim skill: Moderate to strong
Amenities: None
Entry fee: No
Topo: Battle Ax 7½′

Driving Instructions: La Cascada de los Ninos is 42.8 miles east of Salem. Follow the driving instructions for Swimming Hole #133 to the recreation-area turnoff. Turn left and drive to the end of the pavement, at the entry into Willamette National Forest, 15.3 miles. Continue on gravel to where the road forks, 1.4 miles. Forest Road 2209 goes to the left; Forest Road 2207 goes to the right. Go left to a closed gate, the entry to the Opal Creek area, 4.2 miles. (See detail map for Swimming Hole #133.)

Hiking Instructions: From the gate, hike 2.1 miles on a dirt road (which the detail map shows as a trail) to the Opal Creek Trailhead. Do not take the Opal Creek Trail (right), but continue on the road (left) to La Cascada, on the right, 0.4 mile.

Comments: The Opal Creek area contains the largest contiguous ancient forest in the western Cascades. Trees are up to 500 years old. La Cascada's 7-foot falls splashes into a lovely pool. Boulders and large rocks compose the banks.

136. Cedar Creek ••••••••••••••••••••••••

Rating: 7
Location: Private
Water quality: Excellent; transparent to bottom
Vital statistics: 50' wide; at least 17' deep; moderate current; 60° F (July); light algae; pebble and boulder bottom; light to moderate use
Setting: Forested valley at 2000'; light to moderate litter
Swim skill: Strong
Amenities: None
Entry fee: No
Topo: Elkhorn 7½'

Driving Instructions: Cedar Creek is 43.2 miles east of Salem. Follow the driving instructions for Swimming Hole #133 to the recreation-area turnoff. Turn left and continue as for Swimming Hole #135 to the fork of Forest Roads 2209 and 2207. Go right to a gravel turnout, 4.6 miles, on the left. (See detail map for Swimming Hole #133.)

Hiking Instructions: Hike to the creek down a well-defined path, 120 feet.

Comments: Here is a classic swimming hole, surrounded by breath-taking cliffs and secluded by a profusion of shrubs and trees. If the water were warmer and if the trees were not cedar and fir, it would be easy to imagine this was a tropical locale. The water here is 10–15° colder than holes further downstream. But coolness, together with a 13-foot waterfall and darting fish, makes for an invigorating swim.

137. Elk Lake •

Rating: 7
Location: Willamette National Forest
Water quality: Excellent; transparent to bottom
Vital statistics: 64 acres; 30' deep; 70° F (August); light shoreline
weeds; gravel, sand and silt bottom; moderate use
Setting: Forested foothills at 3702'; light litter
Swim skill: Moderate
Amenities: No-fee campground; no drinking water; pit toilets
Entry fee: No
Topo: Mother Lode Mountain 7½'

Driving Instructions: Elk Lake is 58.5 miles east of Salem. From the
junction of Highway 22 and I-5 in Salem, head southeast on Highway 22
to the Breitenbush turnoff, Forest Road 46, 48.6 miles, just past milepost
50. Turn left and drive along the Breitenbush River to the turnoff for Elk

Lake, 4.4 miles,
between mile-
posts 4 and 5.
Turn left onto
Forest Road
4696 and go to
Forest Road
4697/Elk Lake
Road, 0.8 mile.
Turn left onto
this rough
gravel road and
proceed to a
fork, 4.7 miles.
Elk Lake is up
the left fork,
which is very
rough. It is prob-
ably best to park
and hike this last
stretch unless the
car is expendable
or tough. (See
detail map, on

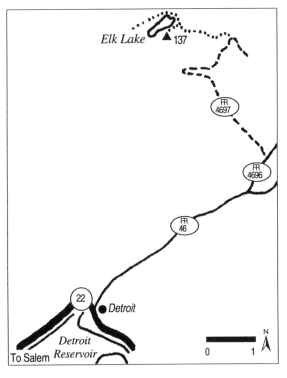

which "this last stretch" is shown as a trail.)

Hiking Instructions: The hike is pleasant. Hike to the point on the
road where there are primitive campsites on both sides, just before the road

crosses a small stream, 1.4 miles. Bear left and pick up the trail to the lake, 0.1 mile. Or continue on to the campground on the far side of the lake.

Comments: The shoreline is uniform and boggy, but there is a nice openness to the lake. Salamanders share it. The view of Battle Ax Mountain to the west is great.

138. First Lake ••••••••••••••••••••••••••••

Rating: 7
Location: Mount Hood National Forest
Water quality: Excellent; transparent to bottom
Vital statistics: 250′ wide; at least 14′ deep; 63° F (July); light shoreline weeds; silt and rock bottom; light use
Setting: Forested mountains at 4960′; light litter
Swim skill: Moderate
Amenities: No-fee, primitive camping; no drinking water
Entry fee: No
Topo: Olallie Butte 7½′

Driving Instructions: First Lake is 84.9 miles east of Salem. Follow the driving instructions for Swimming Hole #137 to the Breitenbush turnoff. Turn left and drive to the turnoff for Forest Road 4690 and Olallie Lake, 23.4 miles, between mileposts 21 and 22. Turn right and head generally eastward to Forest Road 4220, 8.1 miles (the last 1.9 miles are on gravel; stay straight where the pavement ends). Turn right, on rough gravel, to the turnout beside First Lake, 4.8 miles, on the right. (See detail map on next page.)

Hiking Instructions: Access the lake from the trail at the turnout, 220 feet.

Comments: Do not be put off by the marshy appearance of the finger of the lake next to the road. The lake is pretty, and not as exposed and windy as others nearby. There is a nice rock outcrop abutting the lake that makes getting in without stirring up the silty bottom a bit easier. A beam has been placed for diving, but it is right over boulders which are too close to the surface for comfort.

139. French Creek on Detroit Lake •••••••••••

Rating: 6
Location: Willamette National Forest
Water quality: Excellent; 20′ transparency
Vital statistics: 80′ wide; at least 36′ deep; 76° F (July); light algae; gravel and sand bottom; moderate to heavy use
Setting: Forested valley at 1520′; heavy litter
Swim skill: Moderate

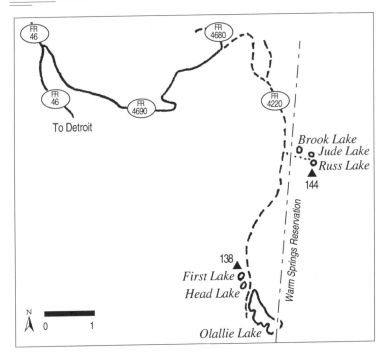

Amenities: No-fee, primitive camping; no drinking water
Entry fee: No
Topo: Detroit 7½'

Driving Instructions: French Creek is 48.5 miles east of Salem. From the junction of Highway 22 and I-5 in Salem, head southeast on Highway 22 to the turnoff up French Creek, Forest Road 2223, about 48.4 miles, between mileposts 49 and 50. Turn left and drive to turnouts on the right, 0.1 mile.

Hiking Instructions: It is a short, steep walk down to the water from the turnouts.

Comments: This is a pleasant enough stop along a backwater arm of the reservoir. (Skip the main lake as far as swimming is concerned. The number and noise level of motors are oppressive.) The shore is lined with low rock walls, which may be covered at high water, and is easily accessible. The bank behind the walls is gravel and dirt. There are some stumps. Dropoffs to deep water are sheer.

140. Little North Fork Santiam River, cliff pool • • • •

Rating: 10
Location: Willamette National Forest

Water quality: Excellent; transparent to bottom
Vital statistics: 100' wide; at least 13' deep; moderate current; 66° F (July); light algae; boulder and pebble bottom; light to moderate use
Setting: Forested valley at 1200'; light to moderate litter
Swim skill: Moderate
Amenities: No-fee, primitive camping; no drinking water
Entry fee: No
Topo: Elkhorn 7½'

Driving Instructions: Little North Fork Santiam River, cliff pool, is 37.5 miles east of Salem. Follow the driving instructions for Swimming Hole #133 to the recreation-area turnoff. Turn left and drive to the end of the pavement, at the entry into Willamette National Forest, 15.3 miles. There is a rough dirt spur road to the right, where the pavement ends. Follow that spur road to the point where it forks, 0.2 mile (the spur may be impassable if it has been raining). Take the right fork to a primitive parking and camping area, 0.1 mile. (See detail maps for Swimming Hole #133 and on this page.)

Hiking Instructions: The best trail to the hole begins at the first turnout to the right as the parking area is entered. The hike is very steep at the end, a little over 0.1 mile. The more used trail, past a huge bastion of rock, is positively unsafe.

Comments: This is a spectacular place of precipitous cliffs and bedrock that shelter a pool of great beauty. The pool lies at the base of a 6-foot waterfall. There is a pebble bar downstream of the pool.

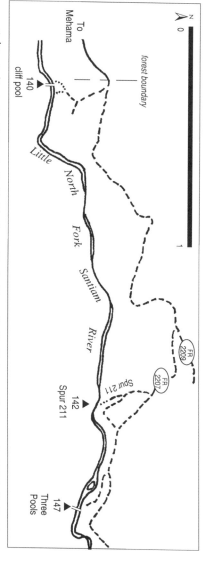

141. Little North Fork Santiam River, near milepost 26

Rating: 7
Location: Bureau of Land Management
Water quality: Excellent; transparent to bottom
Vital statistics: 50' wide; at least 17' deep; moderate current; 75° F (July); light algae; gravel and bedrock bottom; moderate use
Setting: Forested valley at 760'; moderate to heavy litter
Swim skill: Moderate
Amenities: None
Entry fee: No
Topo: Lyons 7½'

Driving Instructions: Little North Fork Santiam River, near milepost 26, is 25.1 miles east of Salem. Follow the driving instructions for Swimming Hole #133 to the recreation-area turnoff. Turn left and drive to a gravel turnout, 3.2 miles (this is 1.2 miles past North Fork County Park), between mileposts 26 and 27, on the right at the upstream end of a spur road (this spur road is not shown on the detail map). (See detail map for Swimming Hole #133.)

Hiking Instructions: It is a short hike down to the river. Watch for poison oak.

Comments: Though the area is littered, there is beauty in the ledges and boulders around a clear pool. Rapids are above and below the pool.

142. Little North Fork Santiam River, Spur 211 ••••

Rating: 8
Location: Willamette National Forest
Water quality: Excellent; transparent to bottom
Vital statistics: 60' wide; at least 11' deep; light current; 66° F (July); light algae; rock and pebble bottom; light to moderate use
Setting: Forested valley at 1360'; light to moderate litter
Swim skill: Moderate
Amenities: No-fee, primitive camping; no drinking water
Entry fee: No
Topo: Elkhorn 7½'

Driving Instructions: Little North Fork Santiam River, Spur 211, is 39.2 miles east of Salem. Follow the driving instructions for Swimming Hole #133 to the recreation-area turnoff. Turn left and continue as for Swimming Hole #135 to the fork of Forest Roads 2209 and 2207. Go right to Spur 211, 0.4 mile, on the right. Turn onto Spur 211, which is a rough dirt road, and drive to a primitive campsite, 0.2 mile (bear right at the fork). (See detail maps for Swimming Holes #133 and #140.)

Hiking Instructions: The best trail starts to the left of a snag toward the river, a little over 0.1 mile.

Comments: The bank is lined with formation rocks and gravel bars. There is a small rapids upstream, while downstream the bedrock is punched with myriad holes.

143. North Fork Park on Little North Fork • • • • • • • • Santiam River

Rating: 9
Location: County Park
Water quality: Excellent; transparent to bottom
Vital statistics: 90' wide; at least 11' deep; moderate current; 75° F (July); light algae; rock and bedrock bottom; heavy use
Setting: Forested valley at 720'; heavy litter
Swim skill: Moderate
Amenities: No drinking water; pit toilets
Entry fee: No
Topo: Lyons 7½'

Driving Instructions: North Fork Park is 23.9 miles east of Salem. Follow the driving instructions for Swimming Hole #133 to the recreation-area turnoff. Turn left and drive to the park turnoff, 1.9 miles, between mileposts 25 and 26, on the right. The grade down to the parking lot is steep, less than 0.1 mile. (See detail map for Swimming Hole #133.)

Hiking Instructions: The short trail entry to the swimming area is to the right in the parking lot.

Comments: Here is a broad pebble beach that partially arches around a luscious curve in the river alongside a lovely pool. The water is a bit cloudier than at other Little North Fork locations, but still fairly clear. Extensive rock ledges also partially line the pool, and there is a nice rapids upstream which feeds the pool.

144. Russ Lake •

Rating: 6
Location: Confederated Tribes of Warm Springs
Water quality: Excellent; transparent to bottom
Vital statistics: 10 acres; 16' deep; 61° F (September); light algae; silt bottom; light use
Setting: Forested mountains at 4640'; light litter

Swim skill: Moderate
Amenities: No-fee camping at trailhead; no drinking water; pit toilets at trailhead
Entry fee: No
Topo: Olallie Butte 7½'

Driving Instructions: Russ Lake is 81.7 miles east of Salem. Follow the driving instructions for Swimming Hole #137 to the Breitenbush turnoff, then those for Swimming Hole #138 to Forest Road 4220. Turn right, on rough gravel, and drive to Olallie Meadows Campground, 1.4 miles. Turn left into the campground and go to the Russ Lake trailhead, 0.2 mile. (See detail map for Swimming Hole #138.)

Hiking Instructions: Hike to the lake following signs, 0.9 mile. On the way there are two other lakes, Brook and Jude. The trail is easy but rocky.

Comments: The lake is in an attractive bowl. There are some good-sized rocks on the shoreline, giving decent access to deep water.

145. Salmon Falls Park on Little North Fork ●●●●●● Santiam River

Rating: 8
Location: County Park
Water quality: Excellent; transparent to bottom
Vital statistics: 200' wide; at least 18' deep; moderate current; 71° (July); light algae; pebble bottom; moderate to heavy use
Setting: Forested valley at 1120'; moderate to heavy litter
Swim skill: Moderate to strong
Amenities: No drinking water; pit toilets
Entry fee: No
Topo: Elkhorn 7½'

Driving Instructions: Salmon Falls Park is 35.8 miles east of Salem. Follow the driving instructions for Swimming Hole #133 to the recreation-area turnoff. Turn left and drive to the park, 13.9 miles, on the right. (See detail map for Swimming Hole #133.)

Hiking Instructions: From the parking area hike an easy trail down to the water, 380 feet.

Comments: The dramatic feature of this spot is the 250-foot-long cliff wall that bisects the river bed. The water is deep all along the base of the wall. There are a small falls and a fish ladder near the far end of the wall. The bank consists of large pebbles and small boulders.

146. Santiam River Rest Area • • • • • • • • • • • • • • • •

Rating: 6
Location: State Rest Area
Water quality: Good; 11' transparency
Vital statistics: 100' wide; at least 14' deep; moderate current; 70° F (August); moderate algae; pebble bottom; light to moderate use
Setting: Wooded valley at 190'; moderate litter
Swim skill: Moderate to strong
Amenities: Drinking water; flush toilets
Entry fee: No
Topo: Albany 7½'

Driving Instructions: Santiam River Rest Area is 13.1 miles south of Salem. From the junction of Highway 22 and I-5 in Salem, head south on I-5 to the rest-area exit, 12.6 miles, between mileposts 241 and 242. Drive to parking, 0.5 mile.

Hiking Instructions: From parking, walk toward the river, following signs to the equestrian area, 0.2 mile. At the gravelled equestrian parking lot, walk across a line of jumbled concrete blocks to pick up the primitive road/trail just on the other side. Hike toward the river and then alongside it downstream to a large pebble-and-gravel bar, 0.5 mile. The trail forks twice; bear right both times. Stay out of the willow thickets.

Comments: There is slack water on the side near the bar, but the current picks up toward the opposite shore. The river divides into rapids just downriver.

147. Three Pools on Little North Fork Santiam River

Rating: 10
Location: Willamette National Forest
Water quality: Excellent; transparent to bottom
Vital statistics: 60' wide; at least 11' deep; moderate current; 64° F (July); light algae; sand and gravel on bedrock bottom; heavy use
Setting: Forested valley at 1360'; heavy litter
Swim skill: Moderate
Amenities: No drinking water; pit toilets
Entry fee: No
Topo: Elkhorn 7½'

Driving Instructions: Three Pools is 39.7 miles east of Salem. Follow the driving instructions for Swimming Hole #133 to the recreation-area turnoff. Turn left and continue as for Swimming Hole #135 to the fork of Forest Roads 2209 and 2207. Go right to the Three Pools turnoff, 0.9 mile, on the right. Take the turnoff and drive to parking, 0.2 mile. (See detail maps for Swimming Holes #133 and #140.)

Hiking Instructions: The trail from parking down to the pool is short but steep and slippery, 250 feet.

Comments: Wow! An eye-popper of a place, Three Pools is really a legion of green-hued pools and streams that shift and chute through volcanic walls and sedimentary layers. This is the grandest swimming hole complex on a superlative swimming stream. Unfortunately, the place is oftentimes hopelessly trashed by mindless users. The Forest Service has tried to spruce up the area, only to see improvements vandalized. It is a pity that such a truly wonderful place is so badly treated. Watch out for slippery rocks, and take care if jumping from the rocks. There have been many accidents here.

148. Wheatland Ferry on Willamette River ••••••

Rating: 5
Location: State Park
Water quality: Fair; 7' transparency
Vital statistics: 0.1 mile wide; at least 13' deep; moderate current; 68° F (July); moderate bottom weeds and algae; pebble bottom; moderate use
Setting: Wooded valley at 100'; light to moderate litter
Swim skill: Moderate to strong
Amenities: None, though drinking water and flush toilets are available in main park area
Entry fee: No, though required in main park area during summer
Topo: Mission Bottom 7½'

Driving Instructions: Wheatland Ferry is 15.3 miles north of Salem. From the junction of Highway 22 and I-5 in Salem, head north on I-5 to Exit 263, for Brooks, 9.5 miles. Exit to a stop at Brooklake Road, 0.2 mile. Turn left and go to Wheatland Road, 1.9 miles. Turn right and travel to Matheny Road, 3.2 miles. Turn left and drive to the ferry landing, 0.5 mile.

Comments: Part of Willamette Mission State Park, the pebble shoreline downstream of the landing is a popular recreation spot, as is the pebble shoreline on the opposite bank. Watch for poison oak. The not-always-reliable ferry hours are daily, 6 A.M. to 9:45 P.M.

Marion County Points of Interest

149. Aurora National Historic District ••••••••••
15008 Second Street, Aurora; (503) 678-5754

Type: Historic community
Hours: Wednesday through Saturday, 10 A.M. to 4:30 P.M. and Sunday, 1–4:30 P.M. from March to December; also open Tuesdays from June to August; Thursday through Sunday, 1–4:30 P.M. during January and February
Fee: Yes

Driving Instructions: Aurora National Historic District is 27.5 miles northeast of Salem. From the junction of Highway 22 and I-5 in Salem, head north on I-5 to Exit 278, the exit for Champoeg and Aurora, 24.5 miles, between mileposts 278 and 279. Take the exit to a stop at Ehlen Road, 0.2 miles. Turn right and drive to Martins Street (which becomes 2nd Street) in Aurora, 2.7 miles (0.1 mile after crossing railroad tracks as the town is entered). Turn left onto Martins Street, cross Highway 99E and go to Liberty Street, 0.1 mile. Be careful crossing the highway. The Old Aurora Colony and Museum are on the right.

Comments: A five-building complex, including the Ox Barn Museum, exhibits a 19th century experiment in communal living.

150. Breitenbush Hot Springs •••••••••••••••••
Breitenbush; (503) 854-3314

Type: Commercial hot springs
Hours: Daily, 9 A.M. to 6 P.M. generally, but call ahead
Fee: Yes, a facility use rate for half or full day.

Driving Instructions: Breitenbush Hot Springs is 59.1 miles east of Salem. Follow the driving instructions for Swimming Hole #137 to the Breitenbush turnoff. Turn left and drive to the Breitenbush Community turnoff, 9.1 miles. Turn right and cross a bridge in less than 0.1 mile. Now on gravel, bear left onto Forest Road 2231 and drive to Forest Road 890, 0.6 mile. Turn left and go to the resort's entry gate, 0.6 mile. Continue past the gate to parking, 0.1 mile.

Comments: At 2200 feet elevation there are three natural pools. The largest is 12 by 20 feet and 2 to 3 feet deep. The pools vary in temperature up to 105° F. Two of them are bottomed on silt, the other is rock-lined. Four hot tubs range up to 112° F. Expect nudity.

151. Bush House •••••••••••••••••••••••••••
600 Mission Street SE, Salem; (503) 363-4714

Type: Historic home
Hours: Tuesday through Sunday, 2–5 P.M.; opens at noon June to August

Fee: Yes

Driving Instructions: From the junction of Highways 22 and I-5 in Salem, head northwest on Highway 22 to where Mission Street splits off to the left, 2.2 miles. Proceed on Mission Street to the end of the parking area along Bush Park, 0.5 mile. Turn left into parking below the house.

Comments: This is a fine 19th Century Victorian home set in Bush Park. Outside there are pleasant rose gardens and a greenhouse.

152. Champoeg Park ••••••••••••••••••••••
8239 Champoeg Road, St. Paul; (503) 678-1251

Type: Historic and scenic site
Hours: Monday through Friday, 8 A.M. to 4 P.M.; Saturday and Sunday, noon to 4 P.M.; weekend hours from 9:30 A.M. to 5:30 P.M. during the summer
Fee: Yes, during summer

Driving Instructions: Champoeg Park is 30.6 miles north of Salem. Follow the driving instructions for Point of Interest #149 to the Ehlen Road stop. Turn left and go to Case Road, 3.6 miles. Turn right and drive to the park turnoff, 2.2 miles. Turn right into the park, then immediately right again into visitor center parking, 0.1 mile.

Comments: The state park visitor center, for which hours are given above, nicely explores the Native American and pioneer history of Champoeg and the site's importance to Oregon statehood. The park is set along the Willamette River.

153. Deepwood Estate ••••••••••••••••••••••
1116 Mission Street SE, Salem; (503) 363-1825

Type: Historic home
Hours: Sunday through Friday, noon to 4:30 P.M. from May to September; Sunday, Monday, Wednesday and Friday, 1–4 P.M. during the rest of the year; closed January
Fee: Yes

Driving Instructions: From the junction of Highway 22 and I-5 in Salem, head northwest on Highway 22 to the fork where Mission Street splits off to the left, 2.2 miles. Proceed on Mission Street to 12th Street, 0.1 mile. Turn left and then make a quick right turn into estate parking.

Comments: Built in 1894, this elegant home and grounds are owned by the City of Salem and operated by the Friends of Deepwood as a living museum.

154. Enchanted Forest •••••••••••••••••••••

8462 Enchanted Way, Turner; (503) 363-3060

> **Type:** Amusement park
> **Hours:** Daily, 9:30 A.M. to 6 P.M., mid-March to September
> **Fee:** Yes

Driving Instructions: Enchanted Forest is 6.4 miles south of Salem. From the junction of Highway 22 and I-5 in Salem, head south on I-5 to Exit 248, the exit for Sunnyside and Turner, 5.3 miles, between mileposts 248 and 249. Exit and drive to Delaney Road, 0.2 mile. Turn left and drive to Enchanted Way, 0.1 mile. Turn right and drive to the Enchanted Forest turnoff, 0.8 mile, on the left.

Comments: This amusement park features a storybook land, a haunted house, a western town and a bobsled ride. Fractured fairy tales are performed on the park stage.

155. Gilbert House Children's Museum ••••••••••

116 Marion Street, Salem; (503) 371-3631

> **Type:** Children's museum
> **Hours:** Tuesday through Saturday, 10 A.M. to 5 P.M.; Sunday,
> Monday and holidays, noon to 4 P.M.
> **Fee:** Yes

Driving Instructions: From the junction of Highway 22 and I-5 in Salem, head northwest on Highway 22 to the fork where Mission Street splits off to the left, 2.2 miles. Proceed on Mission Street to Liberty Street, 0.8 mile. Turn right and go to Ferry Street, 0.4 mile. Turn left and drive to the house turnoff at Court Street, 0.3 mile. Turn left and follow the road upriver to parking, 0.3 mile, on the right.

Comments: A place for creative play and learning, this hands-on museum is dedicated to the inventor of the Erector Set and the American Flyer railroad set, A. C. Gilbert.

156. Mission Mill Village •••••••••••••••••••••

1313 Mill Street SE, Salem; (503) 585-7012

> **Type:** Historic site
> **Hours:** Tuesday through Saturday, 10 A.M. to 4:30 P.M.; Sun-
> day, 1–4:30 P.M. during the summer
> **Fee:** Yes

Driving Instructions: From the junction of Highway 22 and I-5 in Salem, head northwest on Highway 22 to the fork where Mission Street splits off to the left, 2.2 miles. Bear right at this fork onto 12th Street and go to Mill Street, 0.1 mile. Turn right, then immediately left into parking.

Comments: The complex features the oldest buildings in Oregon including a cavernous woolen mill, established in 1889, which demonstrates the turn-of-the-century process of making fabric from wool. (The Marion Museum of History is located next door at 260 12th Street SE, (503) 364-2128.)

157. Opal Pool on Opal Creek •••••••••••••••
Willamette National Forest

> **Type:** Scenic location
> **Hours:** Daily
> **Fee:** No

Driving Instructions: Opal Pool is 42.8 miles east of Salem. Follow the driving instructions for Swimming Hole #133 to the recreation-area turnoff. Turn left and continue as for Swimming Hole #135 to the fork of Forest Roads 2209 and 2207. Go left to a closed gate, the entry to the Opal Creek area, 4.2 miles. (See detail map for Swimming Hole #133.)

Hiking Instructions: Follow the hiking instructions for Swimming Hole #135 past La Cascada and continue on the road to an information board at Jawbone Flats mining camp, 0.9 mile. Walk through the camp and across the bridge that crosses over the confluence of Opal and Battle Ax creeks (the beginning of the Little North Fork River), 0.1 mile. These turns/forks are not on the detail map (the scale is too coarse): just past the bridge, turn right and follow Opal Creek upstream to a sign for Opal Pool on the right side of the trail, 0.2 mile. Turn right onto the pool trail and hike to a high cliff overlook of the pool, 185 feet (bear right where the trail forks, 50 feet from the sign).

Comments: At 2280 feet in elevation, this is a magnificent place, but is too cold for swimming and dangerous to reach. Enclosed by sheer rock walls, the pool is overlooked by a 30-foot cliff.

158. Silver Falls Park ••••••••••••••••••••••••
State Park

> **Type:** Scenic location
> **Hours:** Daily
> **Fee:** Yes, during summer

Driving Instructions: Silver Falls Park is 21.8 miles east of Salem. From the junction of Highway 22 and I-5 in Salem, head southeast on Highway 22 to the exit for Silver Falls and Highway 214, 5.1 miles, between mileposts 6 and 7. Take the exit to a stop, 0.2 mile. Turn left onto Highway 214 and drive to the day-use entrance at the park, 16.2 miles (stay left on Highway 214 at 2.1 and 4.3 miles). Turn left into the park and go to parking, about 0.3 mile. (See detail map.)

Comments: One of Oregon's most enthralling scenic wonders is accessed by a trail that follows the North and South forks of Silver Creek at elevations ranging from 1000 to 1600 feet. The opportunity to see 10 waterfalls along a 7.7-mile hike is nearly compensation enough for the lack of good swimming.

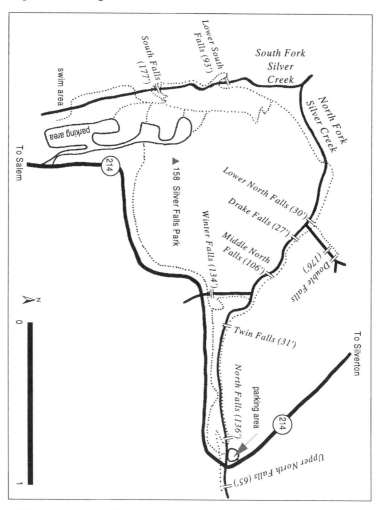

159. State Capitol •
Court Street, Salem; (503) 378-4423

Type: Government building
Hours: Monday through Friday, 7 A.M. to 6 P.M. (7 P.M. when in session); Saturday, 9 A.M. to 4 P.M.; Sunday, noon to

4 P.M.
Fee: No

Driving Instructions: From the junction of Highway 22 and I-5 in Salem, head northwest on Highway 22 to the fork where Mission Street splits off to the left, 2.2 miles. Bear right at this fork onto 12th Street and drive to Court Street, 0.4 mile. Turn left and proceed to the front of the Capitol, 0.2 mile, on the left. Street parking is generally findable at meters all around the complex, or there is parking under the mall to the north.

Comments: The gold-leaf-covered statue of an Oregon pioneer atop the Capitol Dome is unique. Guided tours of the building and films about Oregon are offered year-round. The Legislature is in session biennially (odd years) and is always interesting to observe.

Polk County
(County Seat: Dallas)

Despite its mostly farmland character, Polk County boasts a very acceptable creek for outdoor swimming enthusiasts. Driving instructions begin in Dallas at the intersection of Highway 223 and Ellendale Road.

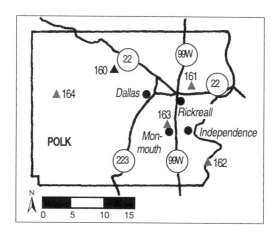

Polk County Swimming Holes

160. Mill Creek

Polk County Points of Interest

161. Brunk House
162. Buena Vista Ferry
163. Jensen Arctic Museum
164. Valley of the Giants Natural Area

Polk County Swimming Hole

160. Mill Creek •

Rating:	8
Location:	County Park and Bureau of Land Management
Water quality:	Excellent; transparent to bottom
Vital statistics:	40' wide; at least 11' deep; moderate current; 67° F (August); light algae; sand, rock and bedrock bottom; moderate use
Setting:	Forested valley at 560'; moderate litter
Swim skill:	Moderate
Amenities:	No-fee, BLM camping; no drinking water; pit toilets

Entry fee: No
Topo: Socialist Valley 7½'

Driving Instructions: Mill Creek is 12.4 miles northwest of Dallas. From the intersection of Highway 223 and Ellendale Road in Dallas, head north on Highway 223 to its junction with Highway 22, 2.6 miles. Turn left and drive to the turnoff for Mill Creek Road, 8.1 miles, between mileposts 4 and 5. Turn left and drive to several turnouts. There are turnouts on the left at 1.7 miles and 2.2 miles, and on the right at 2.8 miles (the last 0.4 mile to this turnout is on gravel; bear right at the end of the pavement). (See detail map on next page.)

Comments: The hole at the first stop, relatively large, has a rock-lined channel. At Mill Creek County Park, the second stop, there are a several nice pools with occasional sand-and-gravel spots nestled in the bank of a narrow, rock-lined gorge. The third stop is bounded by bedrock, gravel and dirt. There is a swinging rope. Watch for poison oak.

Polk County Points of Interest

161. Brunk House •
5705 Highway 22, Rickreall; (503) 623-2669

Type: Historic home
Hours: Monday, Tuesday, Thursday and Friday, 1–4 P.M.; Wednesday, 9 A.M. to noon.
Fee: No; donation requested

Driving Instructions: Brunk House is 10.1 miles east of Dallas. From the intersection of Highway 223 and Ellendale Road in Dallas, head north on Highway 223 to its intersection with Highway 22, 2.6 miles. Turn right and drive to the Brunk House turnoff, 7.5 miles, between mileposts 20 and 21, on the left.

Comments: The restored 1861 pioneer farmhouse and grounds are loaded with memorabilia from the turn of the century. The place exudes a nice, homey feel.

162. Buena Vista Ferry •
Buena Vista

Type: River ferry
Hours: The theoretical hours of operation are Wednesday through Friday, 7 A.M. to 5 P.M.; Saturday and Sunday, 9 A.M. to 7 P.M.
Fee: Yes

Driving Instructions: Buena Vista Ferry is 19.4 miles southeast of

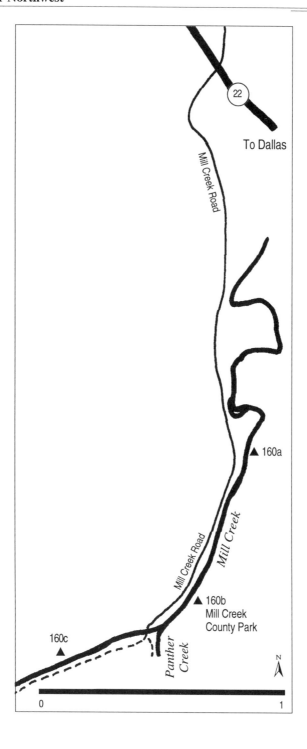

Dallas. From the intersection of Highway 223 and Ellendale Road in Dallas, head east on Ellendale Road to a fork, 3.3 miles. Bear right and drive to Highway 99W, 0.9 mile. Turn right and drive to the stop light in Monmouth at Highway 51, 5.5 miles. Turn left and drive to Main Street in Independence, 2.4 miles. Turn right onto Main Street, which becomes Corvallis Road, and drive to Buena Vista Road, 1.5 miles, between mileposts 1 and 2. Turn left and drive to Sequoia Street, 5.5 miles (take care to stay on Buena Vista Road 2.5 miles after the turn and not get sidetracked by another road). Turn left onto Sequoia Street, which becomes Riverview Street, and go to Willamette Ferry Street, 0.2 mile. Turn left and drive to the ferry landing, 0.1 mile.

Comments: This rustic operation carries folks and vehicles across the Willamette River for a nominal charge. However, it does not always operate at the times of its posted schedule.

163. Jensen Arctic Museum •••••••••••••••••
590 Church Street, Monmouth; (503) 838-8468

> **Type:** Museum
> **Hours:** Wednesday through Saturday, 10 A.M. to 4 P.M.
> **Fee:** No, donation requested

Driving Instructions: Jensen Arctic Museum is 10.2 miles southeast of Dallas. Follow the driving instructions of Point of Interest #162 to Highway 99W. Turn right and drive to a flashing orange light at Hoffman Road, 4.4 miles, between mileposts 62 and 63. Turn right and go to Riddell Road, 0.5 mile. Turn left and drive to Stadium Drive, 0.7 mile. Turn right and go to Church Street, 0.4 mile. Turn left and immediately left again into museum parking.

Comments: The museum houses cultural items of Native Americans from the far north. It is on the campus of Western Oregon State College.

164. Valley of the Giants Natural Area •••••••••
Bureau of Land Management; (503) 375-5646

> **Type:** Scenic location
> **Hours:** Daily
> **Fee:** No

Driving Instructions: Valley of the Giants Natural Area is 39.8 miles west of Dallas. From the intersection of Highway 223 and Ellendale Road in Dallas, head southwest on Highway 223 to the turnoff to Falls City, at Fern Corner, about 6 miles, between mileposts 8 and 9. Turn right and drive to Bridge Street in Falls City, 4.3 miles. Turn left across the bridge to the end of the pavement, 0.7 mile. Continue on gravel to a gate posted

KEEP OUT (it blocks the road to the now-defunct town of Valsetz), 13.7 miles. Bear left to a bridge crossing, 0.1 mile. Turn right onto the road after crossing the bridge, travel around the lake bed of drained Valsetz Lake and proceed along the South Fork of the Siletz River to the junction with North Fork Siletz Road, 8.3 miles. Turn right and drive to a BLM boundary gate, 4.2 miles (watch for orange posts marked VG). Continue to a fork in the road, 2.0 miles. Bear right at the fork and drive to the trailhead for the Natural Area, 0.5 mile, on the right. (See detail map on next page.)

Hiking Instructions: The trail is a scenic loop, 1.8 miles.

Comments: Along the North Fork of the Siletz River, this valley contains the largest Douglas firs in Oregon, some over 700 years old. It is probably a good idea to call to make sure the roads are clear. The river along the way has some good-looking holes, but the water is too cold.

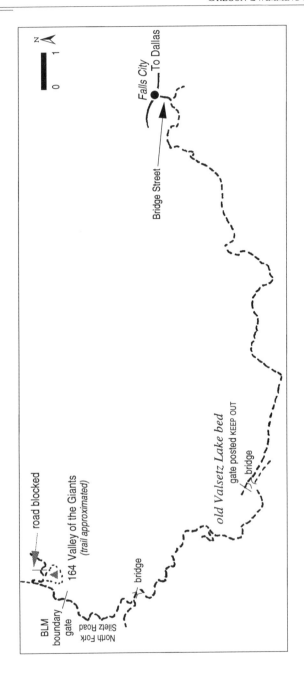

Southwest

Swimming holes in the Southwest are probably the most congenial, overall, in the state. They are generally warmer for longer periods of time than swimming holes in other regions. The climate is warm, even downright hot, without the harshness that may sometimes be experienced in other parts of the state. But poison oak abounds and there are a few rattlesnakes. The hydrology of the region is dominated in the north by the Umpqua River and in the south by the Rogue River. Major portions of both the Rogue and Illinois rivers are designated parts of the National Wild and Scenic River system. Look for Douglas fir and hemlock forests, for madrone trees in the interior lowlands, and for wind-swept shore pine along the coast.

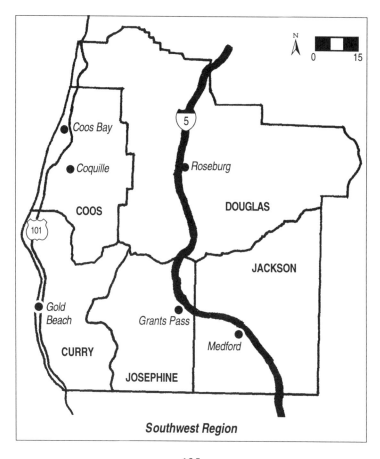

Southwest Region

Coos County
(County Seat: Coquille)

The South Fork of the Coquille River is the primary area for Coos County swimming. Decent, if cool, ocean swimming is also available. Driving instructions begin in Coquille at the intersection of Highway 42 (Adams Street) and Highway 42S (Second Street).

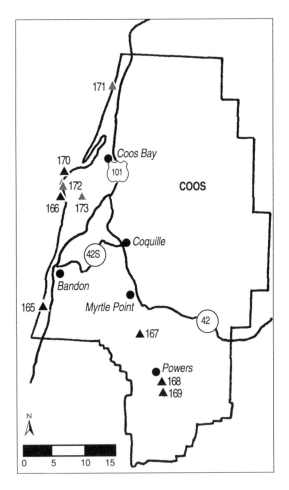

Coos County Swimming Holes

165. Bradley Lake
166. Cape Arago Park, Middle Cove
167. Coquille Myrtle Grove on South Fork Coquille River
168. Orchard Park on South Fork Coquille River
169. South Fork Coquille, near milepost 57

170. Sunset Bay Park

Coos County Points of Interest

171. Oregon Dunes National Recreation Area
172. Shore Acres Park
173. South Slough National Estuarine Reserve

Coos County Swimming Holes

165. Bradley Lake ••••••••••••••••••••••••

Rating:	6
Location:	Private
Water quality:	Good; 7' transparency
Vital statistics:	23 acres; at least 7' deep; 72° F (July); heavy bottom weeds; sand bottom; moderate use
Setting:	Wooded coast at 40'; light to moderate litter
Swim skill:	Moderate
Amenities:	None
Entry fee:	No
Topo:	Bandon 7½'

Driving Instructions: Bradley Lake is 22.5 miles southwest of Coquille. From the intersection of Highways 42 and 42S in Coquille, head west on Highway 42S to Highway 101 in Bandon, 17.5 miles. Proceed south on Highway 101 to Beach Loop Road, 4.2 miles, between mileposts 277 and 278. Turn right and drive to a parking turnout on the left, just before the beginning of a 90-degree turn to the right, 0.8 mile. (See detail map.)

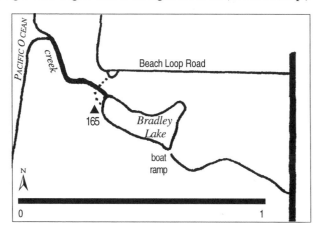

Hiking Instructions: From the parking turnout, a well-used trail through salal crosses a creek to meet a sand dune. Climb up the dune and bear left to the lake, a bit more than 0.1 mile.

Comments: The dunes offer some shelter against the wind at this popular spot. The dark water carries a heavy load of suspended material. A couple of houses and a camp lodge overlook the lake.

166. Cape Arago Park, Middle Cove •••••••••

Rating: 7
Location: State Park
Water quality: Excellent; transparent to bottom
Vital statistics: 280' wide; at least 9' deep within cove; light wave action; 59° F (July); tidal zone aquatic vegetation; boulder and sand bottom; light use
Setting: Wooded coast at sea level; light litter
Swim skill: Moderate to strong
Amenities: Drinking water; flush toilets
Entry fee: No
Topo: Cape Arago 7½'

Driving Instructions: Cape Arago Park, Middle Cove, is 27.7 miles northwest of Coquille. From the intersection of Highways 42 and 42S in Coquille, head northwest on Highway 42 to North Bank Road, 5.0 miles (jog left, then right, out of Coquille), between mileposts 6 and 7. Turn left and drive to East Beaver Hill Road, 2.7 miles. Turn right and go to a stop at Highway 101, 1.7 miles. Turn right and head north to the turnoff for CHARLESTON/SOUTH SLOUGH/STATE PARKS (including Sunset Bay, Shore Acres and Cape Arago state parks), 0.4 mile, between mileposts 252 and 253. Turn left onto West Beaver Hill Road, then right

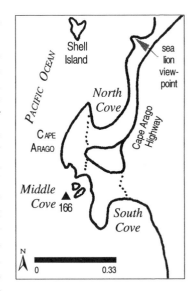

onto Seven Devils Road (in about 6 miles), and drive to a fork in the road, 12.4 miles. Charleston is to the right, state parks are to the left. Bear left to Cape Arago Highway, 0.1 mile. Turn left and drive to the Cape Arago loop, 5.2 miles, past milepost 14. Bear right and go to parking, 0.2 mile. (See detail map.)

Hiking Instructions: The pocket beach of Middle Cove is over the bank at the southwest end of parking and down a steep trail, 300 feet.

Comments: Close offshore rocks and the curvature of the coastline have provided a sheltered cove. There is a 230-foot, very pleasant beach. The swimming is grand, if cool. To the north are viewpoints of sea lions on Simpson Reef.

167. Coquille Myrtle Grove Park on South Fork • • Coquille River

Rating: 6

Location: State Park

Water quality: Excellent; transparent to bottom

Vital statistics: 70′ wide; at least 8′ deep; light current; 78° F (August); moderate algae; gravel on bedrock bottom; moderate use

Setting: Wooded valley at 80′; light litter

Swim skill: Low to moderate

Amenities: No drinking water; pit toilets

Entry fee: No

Topo: Powers 7½′

Driving Instructions: Coquille Myrtle Grove Park is 22.1 miles south of Coquille. From the intersection of Highways 42 and 42S (Second Street) in Coquille, drive west on Second Street and follow signs to Highway 42, about 0.2 mile (turn left, then left again). Turn right and drive south to the turnoff for Powers at Gaylord Road, 11.6 miles. Turn right and drive to the park, 10.3 miles, between mileposts 10 and 11. Turn right into the park.

Hiking Instructions: From near the outhouse, take a short, easy walk on a gravel-and-dirt road to the water.

Comments: At a bend of the river, there is a gravel bar with a little sand. There are plenty of shallows.

168. Orchard Park on South Fork Coquille River • •

Rating: 7

Location: County Park

Water quality: Excellent; transparent to bottom

Vital statistics: 30′ wide; at least 12′ deep; moderate current; 71° F (August); light to moderate algae; pebble and gravel bottom; moderate to heavy use

Setting: Wooded valley at 280′; moderate litter

Swim skill: Moderate

Amenities: No-fee camping; no drinking water; pit toilets

Entry fee: No

Topo: China Flat 7½′

Driving Instructions: Orchard Park is 32.7 miles south of Coquille. Follow the driving instructions for Swimming Hole #167 to the Powers turnoff. Turn right and drive through Powers to the day-use entrance, 20.9 miles, between mileposts 1 and 2, on the right. When going through Powers, there are a couple of turns; follow the signs to Agness. The camping turnoff is 0.2 mile before the day-use parking area.

Comments: The river bends through a gravel bed, creating good deep water around a monolith. There are some shallows, too. There is some sand, but mostly the bank is pebbles and gravel. A five-foot-high diving board has been placed next to the monolith.

169. South Fork Coquille River, near milepost 57• •

Rating:	8
Location:	Siskiyou National Forest
Water quality:	Excellent; transparent to bottom
Vital statistics:	40' wide; at least 9' deep; moderate current; 68° (August); light algae; sand, gravel and boulder bottom; light use
Setting:	Forested valley at 520'; light litter
Swim skill:	Moderate
Amenities:	None
Entry fee:	No
Topo:	China Flat 7½'

Driving Instructions: South Fork Coquille River, near milepost 57, is 37.2 miles south of Coquille. Follow the driving instructions for Swimming Hole #167 to the Powers turnoff. Turn right and drive through Powers, where the road becomes Forest Road 33, to the turnoff for Big Tree Picnic Site, 24.3 miles. When going through Powers, there are a couple of turns; follow the signs to Agness. Continue past Big Tree Picnic Site to a turnout on the right, 1.1 miles, just in front of a SLOW warning sign, between mileposts 57 and 58.

Hiking Instructions: The river is just over the bank. It is a steep clamber down over boulders.

Comments: Beautiful, angular boulders are scattered through a narrow gorge. There are two small pools to either side of a 25-foot-long beach. The downstream pool is surrounds a huge mid-stream boulder. The upstream pool is at the foot of a small rapid. There are sand pockets and lots of shallows.

170. Sunset Bay Park •

Rating:	7
Location:	State Park

Water quality: Good; 6' transparency
Vital statistics: 0.2 mile wide; light wave action; 60° F (July); tidal zone aquatic vegetation; sand bottom; heavy use
Setting: Wooded coast at sea level; light litter
Swim skill: Low to moderate
Amenities: For-fee camping; drinking water; flush toilets
Entry fee: Yes, during summer
Topo: Cape Arago 7½'

Driving Instructions: Sunset Bay Park is 24.9 miles northwest of Coquille. Follow the driving instructions for Swimming Hole #166 to Cape Arago Highway. Turn left and drive to parking at Sunset Bay, 2.6 miles, between mileposts 11 and 12. The day-use area is on the right.

Comments: Sandstone cliffs and beach surround a beautiful bay. There is a reef barrier just beyond the mouth of the bay. There is considerably less wind here than in adjacent coastal locations, and the water is a bit warmer, though it still can be very cold. Rocky ledges provide good clambering.

Coos County Points of Interest

171. Oregon Dunes National Recreation Area ••••
Siuslaw National Forest

Type: Scenic location
Hours: Daily
Fee: No

Driving Instructions: Oregon Dunes National Recreation Area is northwest of Coquille. An unbelievably wonderful 47-mile stretch of sand, the dunes extend along the north coast of Coos County and into Lane and Douglas counties (see #100 and #227).

Comments: A hike through the dunes to an oasis or an isolated, wind-blown beach is a lifetime experience. Be sure to carry water and stay together. Be cautious, particularly at night, of the disorienting effect of the dunes and of the dense belt of trees and shrubs that must be traversed between the dunes and the ocean. Shoes are a must. See Point of Interest #227 for information about the dunes visitor center operated by Siuslaw National Forest.

172. Shore Acres Park •••••••••••••••••••••
State Park

Type: Botanical garden
Hours: Daily, 8 A.M. to dusk

Fee: Yes, during summer

Driving Instructions: Shore Acres Park is 26.3 miles northwest of Coquille. Follow the driving instructions for Swimming Hole #166 to to Cape Arago Highway. Turn left and drive to the park turnoff, 3.7 miles, between mileposts 12 and 13. Turn right and go to parking, 0.3 mile.

Comments: Formal botanical gardens are a treat for those who like flowers and plants to conform to straight lines.

173. South Slough National Estuarine Reserve • • • • •
Seven Devils Road, Charleston; (503) 888-5558

Type: Scenic location
Hours: Daily, 8:30 A.M. to 4:30 P.M. from June to August; Monday through Friday, 8:30 A.M. to 4:30 P.M. from September to May
Fee: No

Driving Instructions: South Slough National Estuarine Reserve is 18.2 miles northwest of Coquille. Follow the driving instructions for Swimming Hole #166 to West Beaver Hill Road. Turn left, then right, onto Seven Devils Road (in about 6 miles), and drive to the slough headquarters turnoff, 8.2 miles. Turn right and go to parking, 0.2 mile.

Comments: Where fresh water meets the sea, South Slough teems with life. The visitor center has interpretive displays, films and information concerning the various trails in the reserve.

Curry County
(County Seat: Gold Beach)

Tucked in the southwest corner of the state, Curry County offers outstanding beaches and startlingly clear swimming streams in close proximity to each other. Myrtlewood and redwood trees join the more usual panoply of coastal vegetation. The best inland swimming on the coast is found here. Numerous pools on the Chetco and Elk rivers are easily accessible from the roads following these rivers and may be chosen from to fit a vast array of swimming desires. Driving instructions begin in Gold Beach at the intersection of Highway 101 and Jerrys Flat Road at the north end of Gold Beach (between Highway 101 mileposts 327 and 328).

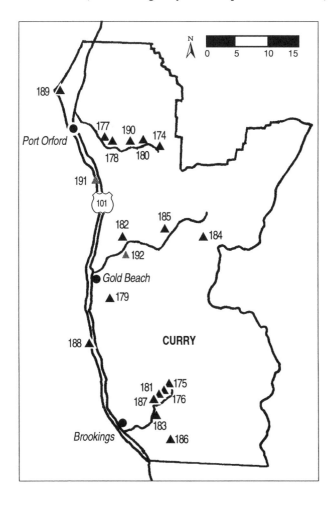

Curry County Swimming Holes

174. Butler Bar on Elk River
175. Chetco River, near milepost 6
176. Elephant Rock on Chetco River
177. Elk River, near milepost 2
178. Elk River, near milepost 4
179. High Bridge Hole on Hunter Creek
180. Jacuzzi Rocks on Elk River
181. Little Redwood on Chetco River
182. Lobster Creek on Rogue River
183. Loeb Park on Chetco River
184. Lower Illinois River
185. Lower Rogue River
186. Ludlum House on Winchuck River
187. Nook Bar on Chetco River
188. Pistol River Park
189. Sixes River and Cape Blanco Park
190. Sunshine Bar on Elk River

Curry County Points of Interest

191. Prehistoric Gardens
192. Shrader Old-Growth Trail

Curry County Swimming Holes

174. Butler Bar on Elk River • • • • • • • • • • • • • • • • •

Rating: 6
Location: Siskiyou National Forest
Water quality: Excellent; transparent to bottom
Vital statistics: 50' wide; at least 11' deep; light current; 68° F (August); light algae; pebble and gravel bottom; moderate to heavy use
Setting: Forested valley at 600'; light litter
Swim skill: Moderate
Amenities: No-fee camping; no drinking water; pit toilets
Entry fee: No
Topo: Father Mountain 7½'

Driving Instructions: Butler Bar is 49.0 miles northeast of Gold Beach. From the intersection of Highway 101 and Jerrys Flat Road, head north on Highway 101 to Elk River Road, 30.0 miles, between mileposts 297 and 298. Turn right and drive to a fork in the road, 18.9 miles (0.3 mile past milepost 11). Bear left at the fork and drive to the turnoff for Butler Bar Campground, less than 0.1 mile.

Hiking Instructions: There is a bridge crossing just past the turnoff into the campground. A spur road on the left-hand, next to the bridge, leads down to the river, 150 feet. It is probably best to hike down the spur.

Comments: The deep water is just downstream of the bridge. Pebbles and bedrock are the dominant bank materials along with some sand. Downstream is a rapids and just beyond it a 7-foot hole.

175. Chetco River, near milepost 6 • • • • • • • • • • •

Rating:	8
Location:	Siskiyou National Forest
Water quality:	Excellent; transparency to bottom
Vital statistics:	110′ wide; at least 20′ deep; light current; 72° F (July); moderate algae; pebble and gravel bottom; light use
Setting:	Forested valley at 120′; light litter
Swim skill:	Moderate
Amenities:	No-fee, primitive camping, no drinking water
Entry fee:	No
Topo:	Bosley Butte 7½′

Driving Instructions: Chetco River, near milepost 6, is 44.1 miles southeast of Gold Beach. From the intersection of Highway 101 and Jerrys Flat Road, head south on Highway 101 to North Bank Chetco River Road turnoff, just past Brookings, 30.0 miles, between mileposts 357 and 358. Turn left and drive to a stop, 0.1 mile. Turn right onto North Bank Road, which becomes Forest Road 1376, and drive to a dirt spur road, 13.9 miles, just past milepost 6. Turn left onto the spur road and go to a primitive camp spot, less than 0.1 mile.

Hiking Instructions: A path leads to the river, generally following a small stream or stream bed, 0.1 mile. Once the river is reached, hike upstream to a spot opposite a rock face, 350 feet. Watch for poison oak.

Comments: Look for big fish at the bottom of the clear pool. Gravel and pebbles compose the bank. There are shallows as well as depth along this lethargic, glassy stream. Salamanders join the swimming, and huckleberries abound.

176. Elephant Rock on Chetco River • • • • • • • • • • •

Rating:	10
Location:	Siskiyou National Forest
Water quality:	Excellent; transparent to bottom

Vital statistics: 100' wide; at least 22' deep; light current; 72° F
(July); heavy algae; boulder and sand bottom; moderate use
Setting: Forested valley at 120'; moderate to heavy litter
Swim skill: Moderate
Amenities: None
Entry fee: No
Topo: Bosley Butte 7½'

Driving Instructions: Elephant Rock is 42.6 miles southeast of Gold
Beach. Follow the driving instructions for Swimming Hole #175 onto
North Bank Road/Forest Road 1376, and drive to a small turnout on the
left, 12.5 miles, between mileposts 4 and 5.

Hiking Instructions: From the turnout, take the steep path down to the
river, 280 feet.

Comments: The path leads to the top of a lava promontory that both
extends into and overlooks the river. The opposite bank is of gravel and
pebbles. There is a rope swing. Salamanders loll languidly at this imposing
place.

177. Elk River, near milepost 2 ● ● ● ● ● ● ● ● ● ● ● ● ● ●

Rating: 7
Location: Siskiyou National Forest
Water quality: Excellent; transparent to bottom
Vital statistics: 40' wide; at least 12' deep moderate current; 67° F
(August); light algae; gravel and boulder bottom; light
to moderate use
Setting: Forested valley at 200'; light litter
Swim skill: Moderate
Amenities: None
Entry fee: No
Topo: Port Orford 7½'

Driving Instructions: Elk River, near milepost 2, is 40.2 miles north
of Gold Beach. Follow the driving instructions for Swimming Hole #174
to Elk River Road. Turn right and drive to an asphalt turnout next to a
grassy bank, 10.2 miles, between mileposts 2 and 3, on the left.

Hiking Instructions: The trail is at the downstream end of the turnout
and is steep and overgrown, 200 feet.

Comments: This is a boulder-strewn jumble between two rapids,
mostly bounded by bedrock shoulders. The deepest hole is at a narrow
place below the upstream rapids. There is a 30-foot sand-and-gravel beach
and some good, large formation rocks for clambering.

178. Elk River, near milepost 4 • • • • • • • • • • • • • •

Rating:	9
Location:	Siskiyou National Forest
Water quality:	Excellent; transparent to bottom
Vital statistics:	30' wide; at least 11' deep; light current; 67° F (August); light algae; sand and bedrock bottom; moderate use
Setting:	Forested valley at 320'; light to moderate litter
Swim skill:	Moderate
Amenities:	No-fee, primitive camping; no drinking water
Entry fee:	No
Topo:	Father Mountain 7½'

Driving Instructions: Elk River, near milepost 4, is 42.5 miles north of Gold Beach. Follow the driving instructions for Swimming Hole #174 to Elk River Road. Turn right and drive to a short dirt spur road, 12.5 miles, between mileposts 4 and 5. Turn left and to a small primitive camp area and parking.

Hiking Instructions: From the camping area, look for a steep pathway down to the river along a granite spine.

Comments: Here is a wonderful, intimate spot, just right for a couple. Listen to Jim Croce's "Time In A Bottle" before climbing down. There is a log across the deep river gorge. The small beach area is of gravel and coarse sand. The feeling is one of seclusion among white granite outcrops.

179. High Bridge Hole on Hunter Creek • • • • • • • •

Rating:	8
Location:	Private
Water quality:	Excellent; transparent to bottom
Vital statistics:	80' wide; at least 8' deep; light current; 72° F (August); light to moderate algae; rock and gravel bottom; moderate use
Setting:	Forested valley at 120'; light litter
Swim skill:	Low to moderate
Amenities:	None
Entry fee:	No
Topo:	Sundown Mountain 7½'

Driving Instructions: High Bridge Hole is 8.4 miles southeast of Gold Beach. From the intersection of Highway 101 and Jerrys Flat Road, head south on Highway 101 to the second Hunter Creek turnoff, 3.3 miles, between mileposts 331 and 332. Turn left, bear to the right and go to the end of the pavement, 4.9 miles. Continue on gravel to the bridge and turnouts over Hunter Creek, 0.2 mile.

Hiking Instructions: After crossing the bridge, access the creek at the upstream side of the bridge. Watch for poison oak.

Comments: This is an amazing place, incongruous in its setting. There are swimmable holes both upstream and downstream of the bridge. There are shallows, too. Salamanders swim along. There are lots of good climbing rocks upstream. A coarse-sand spot is next to the deep hole downstream; otherwise, the beaches are generally gravel and large rocks. A small creek joins upstream.

180. Jacuzzi Rocks on Elk River • • • • • • • • • • • • •

Rating: 10
Location: Siskiyou National Forest
Water quality: Excellent; transparent to bottom
Vital statistics: 90′ wide; at least 13′ deep; light current; 69° F (August); light algae; bedrock and gravel bottom; moderate to heavy use
Setting: Forested valley at 560′; light litter
Swim skill: Moderate
Amenities: None
Entry fee: No
Topo: Father Mountain 7½′

Driving Instructions: Jacuzzi Rocks is 48.9 miles northeast of Gold Beach. Follow the driving instructions for Swimming Hole #174 to Elk River Road. Turn right and drive to a hard-to-see wide gravel shoulder on the left, 18.2 miles (0.6 mile past milepost 10).

Hiking Instructions: From the shoulder a modestly steep trail leads down to the river, 250 feet.

Comments: The river courses through a trench before emptying into a pool. Rapids upstream of the trench bubble though boulders in the streambed, and the bubbling action is the source of the name of the swimming hole. The trench follows a perhaps-220-foot course with a dogleg bend. The place is bedrock-ribbed, with some gravel beach.

181. Little Redwood on Chetco River • • • • • • • • •

Rating: 6
Location: Siskiyou National Forest
Water quality: Excellent; transparent to bottom
Vital statistics: 110′ wide; at least 7′ deep; light current; 72° F (July); moderate algae; pebble and sand bottom; moderate use
Setting: Forested valley at 120′; light litter

Swim skill: Moderate
Amenities: For-fee camping nearby; drinking water; pit toilets
Entry fee: No
Topo: Bosley Butte 7½′

Driving Instructions: Little Redwood is 42.8 miles southeast of Gold Beach. Follow the driving instructions for Swimming Hole #175 onto North Bank Road/Forest Road 1376, and drive to the Little Redwood Picnic Area turnoff, 12.7 miles, between milepost 4 and 5, on the left.

Hiking Instructions: Hike to the river down the easy trail that leads from the turnoff, less than 0.1 mile. Watch for poison oak.

Comments: Watch for huckleberries in August. There are stretches of moderately deep water as one goes upstream toward the campground. The bank is mostly pebbles.

182. Lobster Creek on Rogue River • • • • • • • • • •

Rating: 5
Location: Siskiyou National Forest
Water quality: Good; 9′ transparency
Vital statistics: 310′ wide; at least 15′ deep; moderate current; 78° F (August); light algae and bottom weeds; pebble and sand bottom; heavy use
Setting: Wooded valley at 40′; light litter
Swim skill: Strong
Amenities: No-fee camping; no drinking water; flush toilets
Entry fee: No
Topo: Brushy Bald Mountain 7½′

Driving Instructions: Lobster Creek is 9.8 miles northeast of Gold Beach. From the intersection of Highway 101 and Jerrys Flat Road at the north end of Gold Beach (between Highway 101 mileposts 327 and 328), head northeast on Jerrys Flat Road, which becomes Forest Road 33, to the Lobster Creek Campground turnoff, 9.7 miles, between mileposts 9 and 10. Turn left and go to parking above the boat launch, 0.1 mile.

Comments: This is a place that is okay for a quick swim by better swimmers. There is a huge pebble-and-gravel bar. A shallow bay area is downstream of the boat ramp. While the water is not particularly swift, it is powerful, so stay aware. The current pulls toward a downstream rapids. Be prepared for cross currents and motorboat wakes.

183. Loeb Park on Chetco River • • • • • • • • • • • • •

Rating: 10
Location: State Park
Water quality: Excellent; transparent to bottom

Vital statistics: 100' wide; at least 10' deep; moderate current; 72° F (July); light to moderate algae; pebble bottom; heavy use
Setting: Forested valley at 80'; light to moderate litter
Swim skill: Low to moderate
Amenities: For-fee camping; drinking water; flush toilets
Entry fee: No
Topo: Mount Emily 7½'

Driving Instructions: Loeb Park is 37.7 miles southeast of Gold Beach. Follow the driving instructions for Swimming Hole #175 onto North Bank Road/Forest Road 1376, and drive to the park entrance, 7.5 miles. Turn right to parking on the pebble beach, 0.1 mile.

Comments: Such a spot! The river is banked by pebbles. The indolent sweep of the river includes plenty of shallows. Where the water is deep, it is a steep dropoff to depth. There is an upstream rapids. It is only 0.6 mile beyond the entrance to a satisfying trail among redwood trees in a small chunk of the Siskiyou National Forest.

184. Lower Illinois River ••••••••••••••••••••

Rating: 8
Location: Siskiyou National Forest
Water quality: Excellent; transparent to bottom
Vital statistics: 250' wide; at least ll' deep; light current; 70° F (July); light algae; pebble and boulder bottom; light to moderate use
Setting: Forested valley at 160'; light litter
Swim skill: Moderate
Amenities: No-fee, primitive camping; no drinking water
Entry fee: No
Topo: Agness 7½'

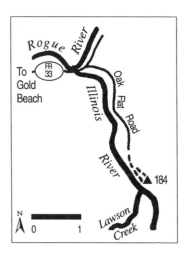

Driving Instructions: Lower Illinois River is 30.7 miles northeast of Gold Beach. From the intersection of Highway 101 and Jerrys Flat Road, head northeast on Jerrys Flat Road/Forest Road 33 to Oak Flat Road, 27.1 miles, between mileposts 27 and 28. This junction is just after passing a viewpoint where the clear and lovely Illinois joins the dirty and rowdy Rogue, and beyond a bridge crossing the Illinois. Turn right and proceed on so-so pavement till the pavement ends, 3.1 miles. Continue on rough gravel to a fork in the road, 0.3 miles. Take either fork, through primitive camping areas, to its end, about 0.2 mile. (See detail map on previous page.)

Hiking Instructions: It is a short walk to the water from either stopping place, a bit farther from the left fork.

Comments: This is just a good straight stretch of easy water. A creek enters from the opposite side. The bank is lined with large pebbles.

185. Lower Rogue River •••••••••••••••••••

Rating: 6
Location: Siskiyou National Forest
Water quality: Good; 11' transparency
Vital statistics: 310' wide; at least 13' deep; swift current; 78° F (August); moderate to heavy algae; sand and pebble bottom; light use
Setting: Wooded valley at 80'; light litter
Swim skill: Moderate to strong
Amenities: No-fee, primitive camping; no drinking water
Entry fee: No
Topo: Quosatana Butte 7½'

Driving Instructions: Lower Rogue River is 16.6 miles northeast of Gold Beach. From the intersection of Highway 101 and Jerrys Flat Road, head northeast on Jerrys Flat Road/Forest Road 33 to a turnoff, 16.5 miles, between mileposts 16 and 17. Turn left and go to parking, less than 0.1 mile.

Hiking Instructions: Hike upstream from the parking through a primitive camping area. There, pick up the trail down to the river, generally along a small stream or stream bed, 300 feet. Then walk downstream to a cove, 200 feet.

Comments: The shoreline is mostly composed of large rocks and small boulders. There is a nice sand area in the cove and a rock outcrop. On the opposite bank is a huge pebble bar. The cove creates a backwater area. Take care in the powerful current farther out and be prepared for boat wakes.

186. Ludlum House on Winchuck River•••••••••

Rating: 6
Location: Siskiyou National Forest
Water quality: Excellent; transparent to bottom
Vital statistics: 60' wide; at least 7' deep; light current; 64° F (August); light algae; gravel and pebble bottom; light to moderate use

Setting: Forested valley at 200'; light litter
Swim skill: Moderate
Amenities: No-fee camping—a bare house is also available for rental; no drinking water; pit toilet
Entry fee: No
Topo: Fourth of July Creek 7½'

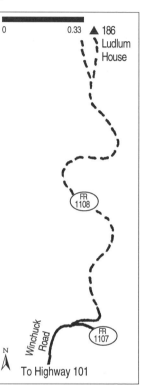

Driving Instructions: Ludlum House is 44.3 miles southeast of Gold Beach. From the intersection of Highway 101 and Jerrys Flat Road, head south on Highway 101 to Winchuck Road, 34.4 miles, between mileposts 362 and 363. Turn left and drive to the Ludlum House turnoff at Wheeler Creek Road/Forest Road 1108, 8.3 miles. Turn left and drive to the end of the pavement, 0.2 mile. Continue on gravel to a turnoff for Ludlum House, 1.2 miles. Turn right and drive to parking, 0.2 mile. (See detail map.)

Hiking Instructions: From the gate at the entrance near the house, follow the path toward Wheeler Creek, which feeds the Winchuck just downstream.

Comments: The hole is at the confluence of a feeder stream and the Winchuck River. While the hole is fairly small, it is very nice. It has a 130-foot gravel bank.

187. Nook Bar on Chetco River • • • • • • • • • • • •

Rating: 7
Location: Siskiyou National Forest
Water quality: Excellent; transparent to bottom
Vital statistics: 60' wide; at least 12' deep; light current; 72° F (July); moderate to heavy algae; pebble and sand bottom; moderate to heavy use
Setting: Forested valley at 120'; light litter
Swim skill: Low to moderate
Amenities: No-fee, primitive camping; no drinking water; pit toilets
Entry fee: No
Topo: Bosley Butte 7½'

Driving Instructions: Nook Bar is 41.9 miles southeast of Gold Beach. Follow the driving instructions for Swimming Hole #175 onto North Bank Road/Forest Road 1376, and drive to the Nook Bar primitive camp turnoff, 11.7 miles, between mileposts 3 and 4. Turn left and drive to the river, 0.1 mile.

Comments: There is a pebble beach with some sand. The water is deepest next to a rock outcrop on the opposite bank where there is a swinging rope. A rapid is upstream.

188. Pistol River Park •

Rating:	9
Location:	State Park
Water quality:	Fair; 5′ transparency
Vital statistics:	300′ wide; at least 7′ deep; moderate current; 72° F (August); moderate algae; sand bottom; moderate use
Setting:	Grassy coast at sea level; light litter
Swim skill:	Low to moderate
Amenities:	None
Entry fee:	No
Topo:	Cape Sebastian 7½′

Driving Instructions: Pistol River Park is 11.5 miles south of Gold Beach. From the intersection of Highway 101 and Jerrys Flat Road, head south on Highway 101 to the park turnoff, 11.4 miles, between mileposts 339 and 340. Turn right and into parking, less than 0.1 mile.

Comments: Here is one of the few swimming spots that are warm, yet have a feel of the ocean. The winds blow a lot and can be cool, but the brackish water is comfortable. The shoreline is fine beach sand. The opposite bank is part of a sand spit between the river and the ocean beyond. Watch for crabs. This is a beautiful place where ocean, sand, easy-flowing river and wind-blown grasses make magic.

189. Sixes River and Cape Blanco Park • • • • • • • •

Rating:	6
Location:	State Park
Water quality:	Good; transparent to bottom
Vital statistics:	200′ wide; at least 11′ deep; light current; 68° F (July); moderate algae and shoreline weeds; rock and silt bottom; moderate use
Setting:	Grassy coast at 20′; light litter
Swim skill:	Moderate
Amenities:	For-fee camping; drinking water; pit and flush toilets

Entry fee: No
Topo: Cape Blanco 7½′

Driving Instructions: Sixes River and Cape Blanco Park is 35.2 miles north of Gold Beach. From the intersection of Highway 101 and Jerrys Flat Road, head north on Highway 101 to the Cape Blanco turnoff, 31.3 miles, between mileposts 296 and 297. Turn left and go to the turnoff for Hughes House, 3.9 miles. Turn right onto gravel and to a fork in the road. Either bear left to the house, 0.2 mile, or right to RV parking by the Sixes River, 0.3 mile. Or, continue past the house turnoff to the campground turnoff, 1.2 miles. Turn left at the campground turnoff and go to the beach turnoff, 0.7 mile. Turn at the beach turnoff and drive to parking, 0.3 mile.

Hiking Instructions: From the RV parking, walk upstream to a rocky outcrop, 200 feet.

Comments: This is a decent place to swim on the Sixes River, but the main attractions are in the surrounding area. Tours at the historic Hughes House, a Victorian home built in 1898, are conducted by volunteers in the summer, Thursday through Monday, 10 A.M. to 5 P.M. (Sunday, noon to 5 P.M.) from May to September. The operating lighthouse is closed to the public but may be opened in the future. The beach, at Oregon's most westerly point, is a place of wonder when the sun sets and shadows play.

190. Sunshine Bar on Elk River • • • • • • • • • • • • • • •

Rating: 7
Location: Siskiyou National Forest
Water quality: Excellent; transparent to bottom
Vital statistics: 80′ wide; at least 8′ deep; light current; 67° F (August); light algae; some sand on rock bottom; moderate to heavy use
Setting: Forested valley at 480′; light to moderate litter
Swim skill: Moderate
Amenities: No-fee, primitive camping; no drinking water; pit toilets
Entry fee: No
Topo: Father Mountain 7½′

Driving Instructions: Sunshine Bar is 45.6 miles north of Gold Beach. Follow the driving instructions for Swimming Hole #174 to Elk River Road. Turn right and drive to the Sunshine Bar Campground turnoff, 15.6 miles, at milepost 8, on the left.

Hiking Instructions: From the campsite nearest the second road entry to the campground, hike to the river on an easy trail, 200 feet.

Comments: There is a 50-foot sand-and-gravel beach along the river. A formation outcrop and lots of shallows add to the scene.

Curry County Points of Interest

191. Prehistoric Gardens •
36848 Highway 101 South, Port Orford; (503) 332-4463

> **Type:** Amusement park
> **Hours:** Daily, 8 A.M. to dusk
> **Fee:** Yes

Driving Instructions: Prehistoric Gardens is 14.5 miles north of Gold Beach. From the intersection of Highway 101 and Jerrys Flat Road, head north on Highway 101 to the gardens turnoff, 14.5 miles, between mileposts 313 and 314, on the left.

Comments: Life-sized replicas of dinosaurs line this walk through prehistory. It is a fun place, particularly with some smaller kids to entertain.

192. Shrader Old-Growth Trail • • • • • • • • • • • • • • •
Siskiyou National Forest

> **Type:** Scenic trail
> **Hours:** Daily
> **Fee:** No

Driving Instructions: Shrader Old-Growth Trail is 11.7 miles northeast of Gold Beach. From the intersection of Highway 101 and Jerrys Flat Road, head northeast on Jerrys Flat Road/Forest Road 33 to the trail turnoff, just past Lobster Creek Campground, 9.7 miles, between mileposts 9 and 10. Turn right, bearing left on the paved road. Drive to the end of pavement, 0.6 mile. Continue on gravel to the trailhead, 1.4 miles. The trailhead is on the right side and parking is on the left.

Comments: This is a well-interpreted trail winding one mile through old-growth Douglas fir and Port Orford cedar trees.

Douglas County
(County Seat: Roseburg)

The richest swimming-hole county in the state, with the Umpqua River and its tributaries, Douglas County offers fantastic delights, including numerous waterfalls. The county park system is the best in the state. Watch for logging trucks. The county does not have its name for nothing, and its Douglas fir is heavily logged. Driving instructions begin in Roseburg at I-5 Exit 125, the exit for Garden Valley Boulevard.

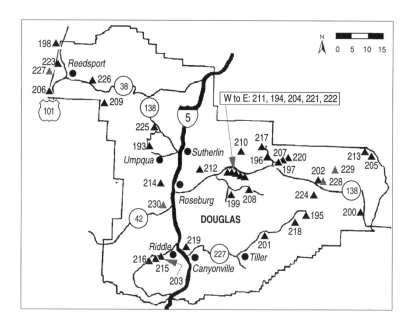

Douglas County Swimming Holes

193. Brown Park on Umpqua River
194. Cable Crossing Park on North Umpqua River
195. Camp Comfort on South Umpqua River
196. Canton Creek Falls
197. Canton Creek on Steamboat Creek
198. Carter Lake
199. Cavitt Falls on Cavitt Creek
200. Diamond Lake at South Shore Picnic Area
201. Dumont Creek on South Umpqua River
202. Eagle Rock on North Umpqua River
203. The Falls on Cow Creek

204. Hill Creek Wayside on North Umpqua River
205. Indigo Lake
206. Lake Marie
207. Little Falls on Steamboat Creek
208. Little River
209. Loon Lake
210. Mill Pond on Rock Creek
211. The Narrows Park on North Umpqua River
212. North Umpqua River at Jackson Wayside and Whistlers Bend Park
213. Opal Lake
214. River Forks Park on Umpqua River
215. The Rock on Cow Creek
216. The Rope on Cow Creek
217. Scared Man Creek on Canton Creek
218. South Umpqua Falls on South Umpqua River
219. Stanton Park on South Umpqua River
220. Steamboat Creek
221. Stick Beach on North Umpqua River
222. Susan Creek on North Umpqua River
223. Threemile Lake
224. Twin Lakes
225. Tyee on Umpqua River
226. Umpqua Wayside on Umpqua River

Douglas County Points of Interest

227. Oregon Dunes National Recreation Area
228. Toketee Falls
229. Umpqua Hot Springs
230. Wildlife Safari

Douglas County Swimming Holes

193. Brown Park on Umpqua River •••••••••••

Rating:	9
Location:	County Park
Water quality:	Good; transparent to bottom
Vital statistics:	0.1 mile wide; at least 8′ deep; moderate to swift current; 77° F (August); moderate algae; bedrock bottom; moderate to heavy use
Setting:	Forested valley at 320′; moderate litter
Swim skill:	Moderate to strong
Amenities:	No drinking water; pit toilets

Entry fee: No
Topo: Tyee 7½'

Driving Instructions: Brown Park is 22.2 miles northwest of Roseburg. From I-5 Exit 125 in Roseburg, head north on I-5 to Exit 136, the exit for Sutherlin and Highway 138, 11.2 miles. Take the exit and drive to a stop, 0.2 mile. Turn left and drive to the Umpqua turnoff, Fort McKay Road, 0.4 mile. Turn left and travel to Tyee Road in Umpqua, 6.1 miles. Turn right and drive to the park entrance, 4.1 miles, between mileposts 4 and 5. Turn left into the parking area. Or continue beyond the entrance to a turnout that gives access to the downstream, more swimmable, end of the park, 0.2 mile.

Comments: Here there is a wonderful deep rapids on the river, chuting through a slab rock channel for about 300 feet. It is exciting tubing. The water through the chute is very swift, but the water is fairly lazy above the chute. There is a 130-foot coarse-sand beach at the downstream end of the park. Below the chute, adjacent to the beach, is a nice backwater pool. Most of the shoreline is slabs of rock. Watch for poison oak.

194. Cable Crossing Park on North Umpqua River • • •

Rating: 10
Location: County Park
Water quality: Excellent; transparency to bottom
Vital statistics: 150' wide; at least 17' deep; swift current; 64° F (August); light algae; pebble and boulder bottom; light to moderate use
Setting: Forested valley at 800'; light to moderate litter
Swim skill: Strong
Amenities: No drinking water; pit toilet
Entry fee: No
Topo: Old Fairview 7½'

Driving Instructions: Cable Crossing Park is 24.5 miles east of Roseburg. From I-5 Exit 125 in Roseburg, head east on Garden Valley Boulevard to the junction with Highway 99, 0.6 mile. Turn right and go to Highway 138/North Umpqua Highway, 1.0 mile. Turn left and head east to the park turnoff, 22.9 miles, between mileposts 22 and 23, on the right. The turnoff is 0.8 mile past Swiftwaters Park.

Hiking Instructions: A short trail leads from the parking area to a rock beach and a fine rapids area. Watch for poison oak.

Comments: There is a nice mix of swift and slow water, great for the skilled swimmer. A pebble bar is a fun place to swim to. Near the bar the water flows upstream. The rapids are good for tubing. About 230 feet downstream is a low, cliff-lined channel about 300 feet long, where the green water flows placidly. It is a swimmer's paradise! The dropoff through the channel is immediate and deep. Be sure to have a plan to get out.

195. Camp Comfort on South Umpqua River • • • •

Rating: 8
Location: Umpqua National Forest
Water quality: Excellent; transparent to bottom
Vital statistics: 30' wide; at least 15' deep; moderate current; 65° F (August); light algae; bedrock bottom; light use
Setting: Forested valley at 2000'; light litter
Swim skill: Moderate
Amenities: No-fee camping; no drinking water; pit toilets
Entry fee: No
Topo: Buckeye Lake 7½'

Driving Instructions: Camp Comfort is 76.4 miles east of Roseburg. From I-5 Exit 125 in Roseburg, head south to Exit 99, the exit for Canyonville, 25.3 miles. Take the exit and drive to a stop, 0.2 mile. Turn left, then quickly right, onto what becomes Main Avenue in Canyonville, and go to the turnoff for Days Creek and Highway 227 at Main Avenue and 3rd Street, 1.2 miles. Turn left and head east to the point where the road forks in Tiller, 23.2 miles. Bear left at the fork onto County Road 46, which becomes Forest Road 28, and travel to the campground turnoff, 26.4 miles, between mileposts 26 and 27. Stay on Forest Road 28 by bearing to the left where the road forks 4.2 miles past South Umpqua Falls. Turn right and drive to parking at the Camp Comfort Trailhead, 0.1 mile.

Hiking Instructions: Take the trail to the confluence of Black Rock and Castle Rock forks, 0.3 mile. Watch for poison oak.

Comments: The bank is bedrock with ledges to the water's edge along an 80-foot channel. The confluence, which marks the beginning of the South Umpqua River, is spectacular, in a secluded and marvelous setting. Lesser holes are downstream.

196. Canton Creek Falls • • • • • • • • • • • • • • • • • •

Rating: 8
Location: Umpqua National Forest
Water quality: Excellent; transparent to bottom
Vital statistics: 70' wide; at least 9' deep; moderate current; 72° F (August); moderate algae; pebble and boulder bottom; light use
Setting: Forested valley at 1200'; light litter

Swim skill: Moderate
Amenities: None
Entry fee: No
Topo: Steamboat 7½′

Driving Instructions: Canton Creek Falls is 42.0 miles east of Roseburg. From I-5 Exit 125 in Roseburg, head east on Garden Valley Boulevard to the junction with Highway 99, 0.6 mile. Turn right and go to Highway 138/North Umpqua Highway, 1.0 mile. Turn left and head east to the Steamboat Creek turnoff, Forest Road 38, 38.7 miles, between mileposts 38 and 39. Turn left and drive to the Canton Creek Road turnoff, 0.6 mile. Turn left and drive to a turnout on the left, along Canton Creek, 1.1 miles.

Comments: A cozy spot, the hole is at the base of 5-foot falls. The bank is mostly large rocks and small boulders. There are many shallows, but also sharp dropoffs to deep water. The rocks are very accessible for clambering, if a bit slippery. There are crawdads. Here, as on all of Steamboat Creek and its tributaries, angling is forbidden; it is a protected spawning stream.

197. Canton Creek on Steamboat Creek • • • • • •

Rating: 6
Location: Umpqua National Forest
Water quality: Good; transparency to bottom
Vital statistics: 60′ wide; at least 13′ deep; moderate current; 68° F (July); light algae; bedrock bottom; moderate use
Setting: Forested valley at 1160′; light litter
Swim skill: Moderate
Amenities: For-fee camping; drinking water; pit toilets
Entry fee: No
Topo: Steamboat 7½′

Driving Instructions: Canton Creek is 40.8 miles east of Roseburg. Follow the driving instructions of Swimming Hole #196 to Forest Road 38. Turn left and drive to Canton Creek Campground, 0.4 mile. Turn right into the campground and park, 0.1 mile.

Hiking Instructions: From parking, follow Steamboat Creek upstream a short way to its confluence with Canton Creek. Watch for poison oak.

Comments: At the confluence, near the bridge over Canton Creek, is a decent hole amid formation rock. Both creeks course through rapids before dumping into their joint pool. There are gravel and rock beach spots. There are crawdads. Here, as on all of Steamboat Creek and its tributaries, angling is forbidden; it is a protected spawning stream.

198. Carter Lake •••••••••••••••••••••••••

Rating: 7
Location: Siuslaw National Forest
Water quality: Good; 12′ transparency
Vital statistics: 30 acres; 30′ deep; 76° F (July); moderate bottom weeds; sand and silt bottom; light to moderate use
Setting: Wooded coast at 80′; light litter
Swim skill: Low to moderate
Amenities: For-fee camping; drinking water; flush toilets
Entry fee: No
Topo: Tahkenitch 7½′

Driving Instructions: Carter Lake is 85.3 miles northwest of Roseburg. From I-5 Exit 125 in Roseburg, head north on I-5 to Exit 136, the exit for Sutherlin and Highway 138, 11.2 miles. Take the exit and drive to a stop, 0.2 mile. Turn left and drive to the junction in Elkton with Highway 38, about 24 miles. Turn left and drive to Highway 101 in Reedsport, 36.5 miles. Turn right and drive to the turnoff for the lake, 12.8 miles, between mileposts 198 and 199. Turn left and follow the campground road to parking by the lake, 0.6 mile.

Comments: The tea-brown lake is part of the Oregon Dunes National Recreation Area. A sandy beach fronts the lake. There are lots of huckleberries and many shore pines. Traffic sounds come from the highway. It is a short but steep walk to be in lovely dunes.

199. Cavitt Falls on Cavitt Creek •••••••••••••

Rating: 9
Location: Bureau of Land Management
Water quality: Good; transparent to bottom
Vital statistics: 90′ wide; at least 7′ deep; moderate current; 69° F (August); light algae; sand and gravel bottom; moderate use
Setting: Forested valley at 1080′; light litter
Swim skill: Moderate
Amenities: For-fee camping; drinking water; pit toilets
Entry fee: No
Topo: Lane Mountain 7½′

Driving Instructions: Cavitt Falls is 28.2 miles east of Roseburg. Follow the driving instructions of Swimming Hole #194 to Highway 138/North Umpqua Highway. Turn left and head east to Little River Road, just before Glide, 16.4 miles. Turn right and drive to Cavitt Creek Covered Bridge, 6.8 miles, between mileposts 17 and 18. Bear right across the bridge onto County Road 82 and drive to the Cavitt Falls turnoff, 3.3 miles.

Turn left and drive to picnic parking, 0.1 mile (bear right where the road forks).

Hiking Instructions: The access is easy, down a staircase from the parking area. Watch for poison oak.

Comments: The 8-foot falls and pool are encased by solid rock. Crawdads abound at this wondrous place.

200. Diamond Lake at South Shore Picnic Area • •

Rating: 5
Location: Umpqua National Forest
Water quality: Good; 13' transparency
Vital statistics: 3214 acres; 52' deep; 71° F (August); moderate bottom weeds; sand and silt bottom; moderate to heavy use
Setting: Forested mountains at 5383'; light litter
Swim skill: Low to moderate
Amenities: For-fee camping is around the lake; drinking water; flush toilets
Entry fee: No
Topo: Diamond Lake 7½'

Driving Instructions: Diamond Lake at South Shore Picnic Area is 85.5 miles east of Roseburg. Follow the driving instructions of Swimming Hole #194 to Highway 138/North Umpqua Highway. Turn left and head east to the turnoff for the lake, 79.8 miles, between mileposts 79 and 80. Turn right and follow the road clockwise around the lake to the turnoff for South Shore Picnic Area, 3.8 miles. Turn right and drive to the parking turnoff, 0.3 mile, on the right.

Comments: Here is a 150-foot by 80-foot roped area. It is necessary to go beyond the rope to get to swimmable depth. There is a narrow, sandy margin along the bank. Boats and noise are present, but the lake is big, with a pretty view of Mount Thielsen to the east.

201. Dumont Creek on South Umpqua River • • • •

Rating: 8
Location: Umpqua National Forest
Water quality: Excellent; transparent to bottom
Vital statistics: 40' wide; at least 10' deep; moderate current; 74° F (August); light algae; gravel and rock bottom; light use
Setting: Forested valley at 1360'; light to moderate litter
Swim skill: Moderate
Amenities: No-fee camping; no drinking water; pit toilets
Entry fee: No

Topo: Dumont Creek 7½′

Driving Instructions: Dumont Creek is 61.7 miles southeast of Roseburg. Follow the driving instructions for Swimming Hole #195 to County Road 46/Forest Road 28, and travel to the campground turnoff, 11.8 miles, between mileposts 11 and 12, on the right.

Hiking Instructions: From the upstream end of the campground, walk upstream to the beach along the river, 190 feet. Watch for poison oak.

Comments: There is a 100-foot-long sand-and-gravel beach, with good, low climbing rocks. At both ends of the placid pool are nonthreatening rapids.

202. Eagle Rock on North Umpqua River • • • • • •

Rating: 6
Location: Umpqua National Forest
Water quality: Excellent; transparent to bottom
Vital statistics: 80′ wide; at least 8′ deep; moderate current; 60° F (August); light algae; rock and gravel bottom; light use
Setting: Forested valley at 1600′; light to moderate litter
Swim skill: Strong
Amenities: None
Entry fee: No
Topo: Illahee Rock 7½′

Driving Instructions: Eagle Rock is 52.6 miles east of Roseburg. Follow the driving instructions for Swimming Hole #194 to Highway 138/North Umpqua Highway. Turn left and head east to the second large turnout at the base of Eagle Rock, 51.0 miles, at milepost 51, on the left, 0.7 mile beyond Eagle Rock Campground.

Hiking Instructions: Hike down to the river on a decent path that begins at the downstream end of the turnout, 250 feet.

Comments: Here is a beautiful pool at the end of a powerful rapid, for better swimmers. Another rapid is downstream. Eagle Rock towers majestically above. Large rocks cover the bank, and rock monoliths are on the opposite bank. The slack water on the near side is not strongly affected by the rapid, though it has an upstream drift that may draw the swimmer into the current. The upstream rapid slams into rock on the opposite bank, so it is vital to have a plan to exit. Also, the water is colder here than downstream.

203. The Falls on Cow Creek • • • • • • • • • • • • • • • •

Rating: 7
Location: Bureau of Land Management
Water quality: Excellent; transparent to bottom

Vital statistics: 140' wide; at least 10' deep; light current; 70° F (July); light to moderate algae; sand and gravel bottom; moderate to heavy use
Setting: Wooded valley at 720'; moderate to heavy litter
Swim skill: Moderate
Amenities: None
Entry fee: No
Topo: Nickel Mountain 7½'

Driving Instructions: The Falls is 29.6 miles south of Roseburg. From I-5 Exit 125 in Roseburg, head south on I-5 to Exit 103, the exit for Riddle, 22.0 miles. Take the exit and go to a stop, 0.2 mile. Turn right onto Riddle Bypass, which becomes Cow Creek Road, and drive to a spur road, 7.2 miles (ignore the first two milepost-1 markers along the way; stay left at the nickel plant entry). The spur road is at the third milepost-1 marker. Turn left and drive on rough gravel and dirt to parking near the hole, 0.2 mile.

Comments: Though there is no falls, a 100-foot sand beach is adjacent to a very nice place to swim. A stretch of myriad rapids is downstream along with some low formation-rock banks and pockets of sand. Unfortunately, graffiti mar the beauty of the place.

204. Hill Creek Wayside on North Umpqua River • •

Rating: 8
Location: County Park
Water quality: Excellent; transparent to bottom
Vital statistics: 200' wide; at least 11' deep; moderate current; 64° F (August); light algae; rock and sand bottom; moderate use
Setting: Forested valley at 800'; light litter
Swim skill: Moderate
Amenities: No drinking water; pit toilet
Entry fee: No
Topo: Old Fairview 7½'

Driving Instructions: Hill Creek Wayside is 24.8 miles northeast of Roseburg. Follow the driving instructions for Swimming Hole #194 to Highway 138/North Umpqua Highway. Turn left and head east to the wayside turnoff, 23.2 miles, between mileposts 23 and 24, 1.1 miles past the Swiftwaters Park turnoff. The short spur road to parking is to the right.

Hiking Instructions: The best trail down to the river is across from the pit toilet.

Comments: A strong current feeds a downstream rapid. There are pools upstream near a rock ledge and next to a 40-foot sand beach. The beach pool has a rope swing.

205. Indigo Lake ●

Rating: 7
Location: Willamette National Forest
Water quality: Excellent; 33′ transparency
Vital statistics: 20 acres; 35′ deep; 63° F (July); light shoreline weeds; sand, rock and silt bottom; light use
Setting: Forested mountains at 5913′; light litter
Swim skill: Moderate
Amenities: No-fee camping; no drinking water; pit toilets
Entry fee: No
Topo: Cowhorn Mountain 7½′

Driving Instructions: Indigo Lake is 93.8 miles east of Roseburg. Follow the driving instructions for Swimming Hole #194 to Highway 138/North Umpqua Highway. Turn left and head east to the turnoff for Lemolo Lake and Forest Road 2610, 72.7 miles, between mileposts 72 and 73. Turn left and drive to Forest Road 2614, 3.1 miles. Turn right and travel to Forest Road 2612, 2.7 miles. Turn right, toward Forest Road 60, and drive to Forest Road 700/Kelsay-Calamut Road, 0.7 mile. Turn left and drive on gravel to a fork in the road, 3.9 miles. Bear right and go to Forest Road 770/Warm Springs Butte Road, 1.8 miles. Bear left, and head to Forest Road 2154/Timpanogas Road, 3.7 miles. Turn right and drive to the Timpanogas Lake turnoff, 3.1 miles. Turn right and go to a trailhead turnoff at Timpanogas Lake, 0.4 mile (bear right at 0.1 mile). Turn right and go to parking at the trailhead, 0.1 mile. (See detail map on next page.)

Hiking Instructions: Now hike in to the lake on an easy, well-marked trail, 1.9 miles.

Comments: Part of the Oregon Cascades Recreation Area, and at the base of Sawtooth Mountain, the lake is dazzling. There is minor log fall, but the lake is open and accessible.

206. Lake Marie ●

Rating: 5
Location: State Park
Water quality: Good; 16′ transparency
Vital statistics: 15 acres; 30′ deep; 69° F (August); moderate bottom weeds; sand bottom; heavy use
Setting: Wooded coast at 40′; light litter
Swim skill: Low to moderate
Amenities: For-fee camping; drinking water; flush toilets
Entry fee: No
Topo: Winchester Bay 7½′

Driving Instructions: Lake Marie is 77.6 miles northwest of Roseburg.

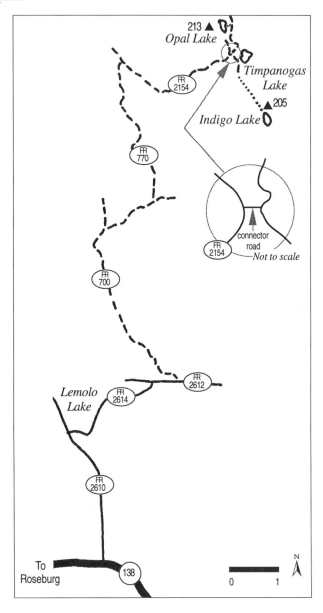

Follow the driving instructions for Swimming Hole #198 to Highway 101
in Reedsport. Turn left and drive to the turnoff for Umpqua Lighthouse
State Park, 5.1 miles, between mileposts 216 and 217. Turn right and go
to parking by the lake, 0.6 mile (bear right at the fork).

Comments: The lake's swimming area is hugely popular. There is a
ton of kids in a small, sandy nook. The rest of the tea-brown lake is

generally inaccessible due to thick vegetation. The lighthouse is not open to the public.

207. Little Falls on Steamboat Creek ••••••••••

Rating: 9
Location: Umpqua National Forest
Water quality: Excellent; transparent to bottom
Vital statistics: 60' wide; at least 15' deep; moderate current; 70° F (August); moderate algae; boulder on bedrock bottom; moderate to heavy use
Setting: Forested valley at 1160'; moderate litter
Swim skill: Moderate
Amenities: None
Entry fee: No
Topo: Steamboat 7½'

Driving Instructions: Little Falls is 41.7 miles east of Roseburg. Follow the driving instructions for Swimming Hole #196 to Forest Road 38. Turn left and drive to the dirt turnout at Little Falls, 1.4 miles, on the right. The falls are fully visible from the turnout.

Comments: Little Falls is a wonderful spot. Several cascades drop into a beautiful hole. The 8-foot falls are surrounded by rock cliffs. Many folks jump and dive into the water, though just paddling around at the base of the falls is pleasure enough. But beware of the jumpers. Dropoffs to deep water are sheer. Here, as on all of Steamboat Creek and its tributaries, there is no angling. It is a protected spawning stream.

208. Little River •••••••••••••••••••••••••••

Rating: 6
Location: Umpqua National Forest
Water quality: Good; transparent to bottom
Vital statistics: 60' wide; at least 14' deep; light current; 70° F (August); light algae; boulder and bedrock bottom; moderate use
Setting: Forested valley at 1120'; moderate to heavy litter
Swim skill: Moderate
Amenities: None
Entry fee: No
Topo: Red Butte 7½'

Driving Instructions: Little River is 29.8 miles east of Roseburg. Follow the driving instructions of Swimming Hole #194 to Highway 138/North Umpqua Highway. Turn left and head east to Little River Road, just before Glide, 16.4 miles. Turn right and drive to a turnout, 11.8 miles, between mileposts 22 and 23, on the right, 0.7 mile after the Umpqua National Forest sign.

Comments: Despite the litter and a few suds, this is a pleasant spot with bedrock banks. There are a swinging rope and some sand. Watch for poison oak.

209. Loon Lake ••••••••••••••••••••••••

Rating:	6
Location:	Bureau of Land Management
Water quality:	Fair; 5′ transparency
Vital statistics:	294 acres; 105′ deep; 73° F (July); heavy bottom weeds; sand bottom; heavy use
Setting:	Forested foothills at 392′; light litter
Swim skill:	Low to moderate
Amenities:	For-fee camping; drinking water; flush toilets
Entry fee:	Yes
Topo:	Loon Lake 7½′

Driving Instructions: Loon Lake is 65.3 miles northwest of Roseburg. Follow the driving instructions for Swimming Hole #198 to Highway 38. Turn left and drive to the lake turnoff, about 23 miles, between mileposts 13 and 14. Turn left and drive to the entrance to parking, 6.9 miles.

Comments: The tea-colored lake has a 0.1-mile fine-sand beach front which is mostly marked off for swimming.

210. Mill Pond on Rock Creek •••••••••••••••

Rating:	6
Location:	Bureau of Land Management
Water quality:	Good; transparent to bottom
Vital statistics:	60′ wide; at least 7′ deep; light current; 72° F (August); light algae; pebble and gravel bottom; moderate use
Setting:	Forested valley at 1080′; light litter
Swim skill:	Low to moderate
Amenities:	For-fee camping; drinking water; pit toilets
Entry fee:	No
Topo:	Harrington Creek 7½′

Driving Instructions: Mill Pond is 28.9 miles northeast of Roseburg. Follow the driving instructions for Swimming Hole #194 to Highway 138/ North Umpqua Highway. Turn left and head east to the Mill Pond turnoff at Rock Creek Road, 22.2 miles, between mileposts 22 and 23. Turn left and go to Mill Pond, 5.1 miles.

Hiking Instructions: At the campground end of the day-use parking lot, there is an asphalt path which leads to a sand and mud bank along the creek, less than 0.1 mile.

Comments: The water appears shallow, but deepens gradually toward the rocks on the opposite side of the creek.

211. The Narrows Park on North Umpqua River • •

Rating:	9
Location:	County Park
Water quality:	Excellent; 23′ transparency
Vital statistics:	250′ wide; at least 30′ deep; swift current; 68° F (August); light algae; bedrock bottom; moderate use
Setting:	Forested valley at 760′; moderate litter
Swim skill:	Strong
Amenities:	No drinking water; pit toilet
Entry fee:	No
Topo:	Glide 7½′

Driving Instructions: The Narrows Park is 23.1 miles northeast of Roseburg. Follow the driving instructions for Swimming Hole #194 to Highway 138/North Umpqua Highway. Turn left and head east to the park turnoff, 21.5 miles, between mileposts 21 and 22. Turn right.

Hiking Instructions: The paths to the river are short and steep, the best one being behind the pit toilet. Watch for poison oak.

Comments: Two agreeable pools are above and below a rapid and a narrow, approximately 300-foot chute. The river is completely encased in rock, and the rock may be very slippery. This is a good place for tubing and for better swimmers only. It is necessary to have a plan to exit. Dropoffs to deep water are sheer.

212. North Umpqua River at Jackson Wayside • • • and Whistlers Bend Park

Rating:	7
Location:	County Park
Water quality:	Good; transparent to bottom
Vital statistics:	180′ wide; at least 14′ deep; swift current; 64° F (July); moderate shoreline weeds and algae; pebble and bedrock bottom; light to moderate use
Setting:	Wooded valley at 600′; light litter
Swim skill:	Moderate to strong
Amenities:	For-fee camping on Whistlers Bend side; drinking water at Whistlers Bend; pit toilets

Entry fee: No
Topo: Oak Creek Valley 7½′

Driving Instructions: North Umpqua River at Jackson Wayside and Whistlers Bend Park is 17.2 miles northeast of Roseburg. From I-5 Exit 125 in Roseburg, head north on I-5 to Exit 129, the exit for Wilbur and Winchester, 4.2 miles. Take the exit and go to a stop at Highway 99, 0.2 miles. Turn left and drive to North Bank Road, 2.0 miles. Turn right and proceed to the wayside, 10.8 miles, between mileposts 10 and 11, on the right. Or, follow the driving instructions for Swimming Hole #194 to Highway 138/North Umpqua Highway. Turn left and head east to Whistlers Bend turnoff, 11.7 miles, between mileposts 11 and 12. Turn left and go to the picnic parking turnoff, 3.3 miles. Turn right and find parking, 0.3 mile. (See detail map.)

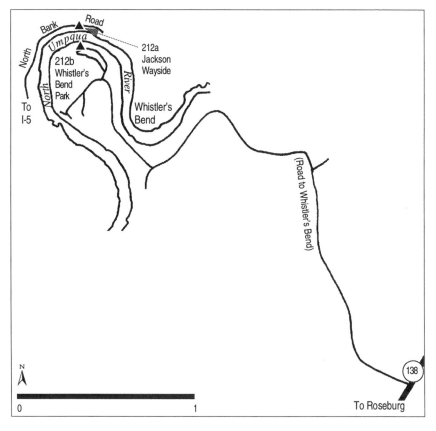

Comments: The parks are near the apex of mushroom-shaped Whistlers Bend. Jackson Wayside is lightly used, Whistlers Bend Park is moderately used. Swimmers can enjoy both sides. The bank is bedrock and large pebbles. There is some sand on the Whistlers Bend side. While there are areas of slack water and shallows, there are also precipitous drops to deep, swift water. A small playground is on the Whistlers Bend side. Watch for poison oak.

213. Opal Lake ••••••••••••••••••••••••

Rating: 8
Location: Willamette National Forest
Water quality: Excellent; transparency to bottom
Vital statistics: 12 acres; 30' deep; 73° F (August); moderate bottom and shoreline weeds; sand and silt bottom; light use
Setting: Forested mountains at 5353'; light to moderate litter
Swim skill: Moderate
Amenities: No drinking water; pit toilets
Entry fee: No
Topo: Cowhorn Mountain 7½'

Driving Instructions: Opal Lake is 94.0 miles east of Roseburg. Follow the driving instructions for Swimming Hole #194 to Highway 138/ North Umpqua Highway. From there, follow the driving instructions for Swimming Hole #205 to the Timpanogas Lake turnoff. Turn right and, still on Forest Road 2154, proceed to Opal Lake Trailhead, 0.7 mile (bear left at 0.1 mile). (See detail map for Swimming Hole #205.)

Hiking Instructions: Hike down to the lake and to a rock fall on an easy trail, counterclockwise around the lake, 0.2 mile.

Comments: It is a long way here, but worth it. The lake sparkles and the rock fall provides a good place for entry and a superb post for perching or clambering.

214. River Forks Park on Umpqua River ••••••••

Rating: 7
Location: County Park
Water quality: Good; transparent to bottom
Vital statistics: 170' wide; at least 8' deep; moderate current; 71° F (August); light to moderate algae; pebble and sand bottom; moderate to heavy use
Setting: Wooded valley at 360'; moderate litter
Swim skill: Low to moderate
Amenities: Drinking water; flush toilets
Entry fee: No
Topo: Garden Valley 7½'

Driving Instructions:
River Forks Park is 6.7 miles northwest of Roseburg. From I-5 Exit 125 in Roseburg, head northwest on Garden Valley Boulevard to Old Garden Valley Road, 4.6 miles. Turn left and drive to River Forks Road, 1.6 miles. Turn left and go to the turnoff for picnic area parking, 0.5 mile, on the left. (See detail map.)

Hiking Instructions: Take the short trail, in the vicinity of the playground, down to the river.

Comments: This is the confluence of the North and South forks of the Umpqua River. The manicured lawns on the high bank yield to a 230-foot beach of coarse sand and large pebbles along the river. After the joining of the two streams, the Umpqua is a straight channel by the park.

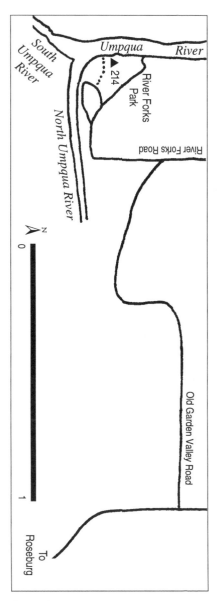

215. The Rock on Cow Creek ●●●●●●●●●●●●●●●

Rating: 8
Location: Bureau of Land Management
Water quality: Excellent; transparent to bottom
Vital statistics: 40′ wide; at least 13′ deep; moderate current; 70° F

(July); moderate algae; pebble bottom; moderate use
Setting: Wooded valley at 720'; moderate litter
Swim skill: Moderate
Amenities: No-fee, primitive camping down the spur road; no drinking water
Entry fee: No
Topo: Nickel Mountain 7½'

Driving Instructions: The Rock is 30.4 miles south of Roseburg. Follow the driving instructions for Swimming Hole #203 to Riddle Bypass/Cow Creek Road, and drive to a paved turnout, 8.2 miles, just before milepost 2, on the left just before a spur road. Ignore the first two milepost-1 markers along the way; stay left at the nickel plant entry. Park at the turnout.

Hiking Instructions: Find the short, but steep, trail at the downstream end of the turnout. Watch for poison oak.

Comments: At this very nice place, deep water pools around the base of an asphalt-like, conglomerate monolith which fronts the creek. A small sandy beach is 130 feet downstream, and upstream is a rapid.

216. The Rope on Cow Creek •••••••••••••••••

Rating: 6
Location: Bureau of Land Management
Water quality: Excellent; transparent to bottom
Vital statistics: 150' wide; at least 14' deep; light current; 70° F (July); light algae; sand and gravel bottom; light to moderate use
Setting: Wooded valley at 720'; moderate litter
Swim skill: Moderate
Amenities: None
Entry fee: No
Topo: Nickel Mountain 7½'

Driving Instructions: The Rope is 32.3 miles south of Roseburg. Follow the driving instructions for Swimming Hole #203 to Riddle Bypass/Cow Creek Road, and drive to a small gravel turnout at a curve, 10.1 miles, just before milepost 4, on the left. Ignore the first two milepost-1 markers along the way; stay left at the nickel plant entry.

Hiking Instructions: From the turnout it is a short, steep trail down to the water. Watch for poison oak.

Comments: A cable has been strung across the creek, and a rope swing is on the opposite shore. There are boulders and some sand on the bank.

217. Scared Man Creek on Canton Creek • • • • •

Rating: 6
Location: Bureau of Land Management
Water quality: Good; transparent to bottom
Vital statistics: 30′ wide; at least 8′ deep; light current; 70° (August); light algae; gravel and rock bottom; light to moderate use
Setting: Forested valley at 1360′; light litter
Swim skill: Moderate
Amenities: No-fee camping; drinking water; pit toilets
Entry fee: No
Topo: Scared Man Creek 7½′

Driving Instructions: Scared Man Creek is 44.0 miles east of Roseburg. Follow the driving instructions for Swimming Hole #196 to Canton Creek Road. Turn left and drive to Scared Man Creek Campground, 3.1 miles. Turn left into the parking area that is just past the bridge and the campground turnoff.

Hiking Instructions: Take the short trail from the parking area to the swimming hole, 200 feet. The hole is upstream of the bridge.

Comments: There are small sand-and-gravel pockets in the bedrock bank. A bit of a rapid is upstream. Here, as on all of Steamboat Creek and its tributaries, angling is forbidden; it is a protected spawning stream.

218. South Umpqua Falls on South Umpqua River

Rating: 8
Location: Umpqua National Forest
Water quality: Excellent; transparent to bottom
Vital statistics: 150′ wide; at least 10′ deep; swift current; 70° F (August); moderate algae; bedrock and gravel bottom; heavy use
Setting: Forested valley at 1680′; moderate to heavy litter
Swim skill: Moderate to strong
Amenities: No drinking water; pit toilets
Entry fee: No
Topo: Acker Rock 7½′

Driving Instructions: South Umpqua Falls is 67.8 miles east of Roseburg. Follow the driving instructions for Swimming Hole #195 onto County Road 46/Forest Road 28, and travel to the falls parking area, 19.9 miles, between mileposts 19 and 20, on the right.

Hiking Instructions: The falls are downstream of the parking area.

Comments: The river flows here over a wide bedrock sheet which, at the site of the 15-foot falls, drops off abruptly to a pool below. There is an annoying fish ladder to one side, but still the falls are an impressive sight. The rocks are very slippery, and therein lies much of the pleasure, but also much of the danger, of the place. Respect the slipperiness of the rock and the heights around the falls. Sliding from the top of the falls, from a sitting position, into the pool below is a blast. Watch for jumpers when swimming. Beyond the pool at the base of the falls is a large, flat rock ledge that serves as a beach area.

219. Stanton Park on South Umpqua River • • • • • •

Rating: 7
Location: County Park
Water quality: Good; transparent to bottom
Vital statistics: 110' wide; at least 11' deep; light current; 72° F (July); light to moderate algae; bedrock and pebble bottom; heavy use
Setting: Forested valley at 680'; light litter
Swim skill: Moderate
Amenities: For-fee camping; drinking water; flush toilets
Entry fee: No
Topo: Canyonville 7½'

Driving Instructions: Stanton Park is 25.5 miles south of Roseburg. From I-5 Exit 125 in Roseburg, head south on I-5 to Exit 101, the exit for Riddle and Stanton Park, 23.6 miles, between mileposts 101 and 102. Take the exit and drive to a stop at Highway 99, 0.3 mile. Turn right and go to the park turnoff, 1.5 miles. Turn left and park as near the end of the camping area as possible, 0.1 mile.

Hiking Instructions: From parking, a short trail leads downhill to the river.

Comments: A pebble and coarse-sand beach lies along a 300-foot stretch of the river. Water quality has been a problem. The DEQ 305(b) Report identifies this part of the South Umpqua as partially water-quality limited. Otherwise, it is a beautiful place to swim. There is a playground in the park.

220. Steamboat Creek •

Rating: 8
Location: Umpqua National Forest
Water quality: Excellent; transparent to bottom
Vital statistics: 70' wide; at least 8' deep; moderate current; 71° F (August); light algae; sand, rock and boulder bottom; light to moderate use
Setting: Forested valley at 1240'; moderate litter

Swim skill: Low to moderate
Amenities: No-fee, primitive camping; no drinking water
Entry fee: No
Topo: Steamboat 7½′

Driving Instructions: Steamboat Creek is 42.4 miles east of Roseburg. Follow the driving instructions for Swimming Hole #196 to Forest Road 38. Turn left and drive to a gravel road turnoff, 1.9 miles (0.5 mile past Little Falls). Turn right and go to parking, 0.2 mile.

Hiking Instructions: At the entry into the parking lot, take the trail to the creek, 230 feet. Watch for poison oak.

Comments: On a nice curve in the creek, there is a 60-foot sandy beach. A gravel bank is opposite. The current is relaxed, with a small upstream rapid. Crowds are considerably lighter here than at Little Falls, downstream. Here, as on all of Steamboat Creek and its tributaries, angling is forbidden; it is a protected spawning stream.

221. Stick Beach on North Umpqua River • • • • • •

Rating: 8
Location: Bureau of Land Management
Water quality: Excellent; transparent to bottom
Vital statistics: 90′ wide; at least 12′ deep; moderate current; 65° F (August); light algae; pebble and boulder bottom; moderate use
Setting: Forested valley 840′; moderate litter
Swim skill: Moderate
Amenities: None
Entry fee: No
Topo: Old Fairview 7½′

Driving Instructions: Stick Beach is 26.5 miles east of Roseburg. Follow the driving instructions for Swimming Hole #194 to Highway 138/North Umpqua Highway. Turn left and head east to a spur road that leads to a parking area, 24.9 miles (1.7 miles past Hill Creek Wayside), between mileposts 24 and 25, on the right.

Hiking Instructions: Take the short, easy trail from the parking area to the river.

Comments: A 170-foot coarse-sand and gravel beach awaits, probably the best sand beach on the river. A shallow rapid is upstream.

222. Susan Creek on North Umpqua River • • • • •

Rating: 10
Location: Bureau of Land Management

"Small but wonderful" aptly describes this playful twosome as well as Swimming Hole #134, Canyon Creek on Little North Fork Santiam River.

A Portfolio of. . .

(Left) **Cold creek, scalding springs: Point of Interest #97, McCredie Springs.**

(Below) **Point of Interest #99, McKenzie River Hot Springs, is tucked into a ferny bank right next to the roaring McKenzie River.**

. . .Oregon Hot Springs

**Eight broad, shallow, hot-spring pools and a nearby cool pool
welcome a family at Swimming Hole #90, Rider Creek Arm of
Cougar Reservoir and Terwilliger Hot Springs.**

Down the creek with a whoop and a holler at Swimming Hole #147, Three Pools on Little North Fork Santiam River.

(Right) **Top-notch Swimming Hole #207, Little Falls on Steamboat Creek, offers several cascades and a beautiful pool.**

(Below) **Sandstone cliffs frame this tranquil, inviting beach at Swimming Hole #170, Sunset Bay Park.**

At Swimming Hole #250, Seats Dam on Rough and Ready Creek, the fine pool below the dam calls for a big, splashing jump.

Swimming Hole #176, Elephant Rock on Chetco River, is the embodiment of peace and quiet. . .
(see right)

Swim those urban stresses away at placid Swimming Hole #204, Hill Creek Wayside on North Umpqua River.

(from left)
. . .until someone grabs the rope overhanging the river and turns into Tarzan!

**A forested valley and a rocky bank cradle lovely
Swimming Hole #231, Applegate River, near milepost 5.**

Water quality: Excellent; transparent to bottom
Vital statistics: 170' wide; at least 17' deep; swift current; 64° F (July); moderate algae; gravel, rock and sand bottom; moderate use
Setting: Forested valley at 920'; light litter
Swim skill: Moderate to strong
Amenities: For-fee camping; drinking water; flush toilets
Entry fee: No
Topo: Old Fairview 7½'

Driving Instructions: Susan Creek is 30.0 miles east of Roseburg. Follow the driving instructions for Swimming Hole #194 to Highway 138/ North Umpqua Highway. Turn left and head east to the Susan Creek Picnic Area turnoff, 28.4 miles, between mileposts 28 and 29, on the right. The Susan Creek Campground turnoff is beyond the picnic area, 0.5 mile.

Hiking Instructions: A pleasant trail, through stands of Douglas fir and cedar, connects the picnic area to the campground, 0.6 mile.

Comments: At the picnic area, there is a nice swim spot with a gravel beach. At about the halfway point along the trail is a wondrous spot where a solid rock shelf, 120 feet by 120 feet, extends about two-thirds out into the river before dropping off precipitously into the main river channel. One foot or so of water flushes over the shelf. There are plenty of large rocks for sunning and a small sand-and-gravel spot. At the campground, behind Site 4, there is a short trail to the river. Two small rapids dump into a pool beside a bank composed of large rocks and gravel. Watch for poison oak.

223. Threemile Lake •••••••••••••••••••••••

Rating: 6
Location: Siuslaw National Forest
Water quality: Good; 13' transparency
Vital statistics: 63 acres; 33' deep; 69° F (August); light bottom weeds; sand and mud bottom; light use
Setting: Wooded coast at 37'; light litter
Swim skill: Moderate
Amenities: No-fee, primitive camping; no drinking water
Entry fee: No
Topo: Tahkenitch Creek 7½'

Driving Instructions: Threemile Lake is 78.3 miles northwest of Roseburg. Follow the driving instructions for Swimming Hole #198 to Highway 101 in Reedsport. Turn right and drive to Sparrow Park Road, 4.1 miles, between mileposts 207 and 208. Turn left and drive on gravel to a small turnout by the trailhead to the lake, 2.3 miles, on the right. (The road

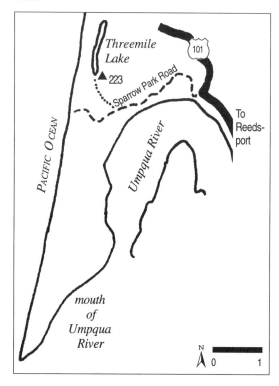

continues to parking beside where the dunes meet the coastline, 0.6 mile beyond.) (See detail map.)

Hiking Instructions: Hike the easy trail from parking to the lake, 0.9 mile. Along the way, bear right across a log bridge, then left at the fork after the bridge (the bridge and fork are not shown on the detail map).

Comments: The trail comes out at an open beach area at the south end of the tea-brown lake, which is part of the Oregon Dunes National Recreation Area. The beach is mostly compact sand with gravel.

224. Twin Lakes •••••••••••••••••••••••••••

Rating: 6
Location: Umpqua National Forest
Water quality: Excellent; transparent to bottom
Vital statistics: Big Twin—14 acres, 50' deep; Little Twin—6 acres, 30' deep; 71° F (August); light bottom and shoreline weeds; silt bottom; light use
Setting: Forested mountains at 5230'; light litter
Swim skill: Moderate
Amenities: No-fee, primitive camping; no drinking water
Entry fee: No
Topo: Twin Lakes Mountain 7½'

Driving Instructions: Twin Lakes is 60.5 miles east of Roseburg. Follow the driving instructions for Swimming Hole #194 to Highway 138/ North Umpqua Highway. Turn left and head east to Forest Road 4770/

Wilson Creek Road, just after crossing Marsters Bridge, 49.7 miles, between mileposts 49 and 50. Turn right and drive on gravel to the Twin Lakes Trailhead, 9.2 miles. (See detail map.)

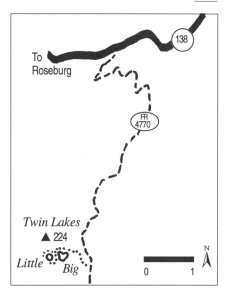

Hiking Instructions: The trail to Big Twin Lake is well-marked and pleasant, 1.2 miles. Hike counterclockwise around the lake to a huge rock, 0.3 mile. This is the best place to access the water for Big Twin Lake and is where the connecting trail to Little Twin Lake begins. From there, hike to Little Twin Lake, 0.1 mile (bear left at the footbridge).

Comments: Both lakes are quite lovely. Little Twin Lake is 10 feet higher than Big Twin. There is some log fall, particularly at Little Twin. Both lakes have accessible dirt shorelines. At each, one must swim some distance out into the lake to find deep water. A trail circles both lakes. Rhododendrons are profuse.

225. Tyee on Umpqua River ••••••••••••••••

Rating: 7
Location: Bureau of Land Management
Water quality: Good; transparent to bottom
Vital statistics: 0.1 mile wide; at least 10′ deep; moderate current; 78° (August); light algae; boulder and bedrock bottom; light to moderate use
Setting: Wooded valley at 200′; light litter
Swim skill: Moderate
Amenities: For-fee camping; drinking water; pit toilets
Entry fee: No
Topo: Tyee Mountain 7½′

Driving Instructions: Tyee is 22.9 miles north of Roseburg. Follow the driving instructions for Swimming Hole #198 to the stop after the Sutherlin/Highway 138 exit. Turn left and drive to Bullock Road, 10.9 miles, between mileposts 13 and 14. Turn left, turn right after crossing the bridge, and turn right again into the campground, 0.6 mile.

Comments: The river is mostly set in low bedrock, with dirt and sand banks back of that. Deep-water pockets are scattered and the current is surprisingly strong in places, so it is necessary to stay alert. There is a small rapid downstream.

226. Umpqua Wayside on Umpqua River • • • • • •

Rating: 5
Location: State Park
Water quality: Good; transparent to bottom
Vital statistics: 0.2 mile wide; at least 8′ deep; light current; 73° F (July); light bottom weeds; gravel and mud bottom; moderate use
Setting: Wooded valley at 40′; light litter
Swim skill: Moderate
Amenities: No drinking water; pit toilet
Entry fee: No
Topo: Deer Head Peak 7½′

Driving Instructions: Umpqua Wayside is 62.7 miles northwest of Roseburg. Follow the driving instructions for Swimming Hole #198 to Highway 38. Turn left and drive to the wayside turnoff, 27.3 miles, between mileposts 9 and 10, on the right.

Comments: This is a straight stretch of water next to a 50-foot gravel beach. Considerable road noise comes from the highway.

Douglas County Points of Interest

227. Oregon Dunes National Recreation Area • • • •

Siuslaw National Forest Visitor Center; 855 Highway Avenue, Reedsport; (503) 271-3611

Type: Scenic location
Hours: Daily; visitor center hours Monday through Friday, 8 A.M. to 4:30 P.M.; from Memorial Day to Labor Day visitor center open to 6 P.M. and on weekends 9 A.M. to 5 P.M.
Fee: No

Driving Instructions: Oregon Dunes National Recreation Area is over 70 miles northwest of Roseburg. Follow the driving instructions for Swimming Hole #198 to Highway 101 in Reedsport. Continue straight across the intersection to the Oregon Dunes Forest Service Visitor Center, immediately on the left.

Comments: The dunes are an unbelievably wonderful 47-mile stretch of sand. The visitor center is a jumping-off place for the dunes. While having only minimal interpretation, it does have lots of brochures and a film on dune history and ecology. The dunes extend all along the length of the Douglas County coastline and beyond—south into Coos County (Point of Interest #171) and north into Lane County (Point of Interest #100). A hike through the dunes to an oasis or an isolated, wind-blown beach is a lifetime experience. Be sure to carry water and stay together. Be cautious, particularly at night, of the disorienting effect of the dunes and of the dense belt of trees and shrubs that must be traversed between the dunes and the ocean. Shoes are a must.

228. Toketee Falls •
Umpqua National Forest

> **Type:** Scenic location
> **Hours:** Daily
> **Fee:** No

Driving Instructions: Toketee Falls is 60.5 miles east of Roseburg. Follow the driving instructions for Swimming Hole #194 to Highway 138/ North Umpqua Highway. Turn left and head east to Toktee Lake turnoff, Toketee-Rigdon Road/Forest Road 34, 58.6 miles, between mileposts 56 and 57. Turn left and go to Toketee Falls Viewpoint turnoff, 0.2 mile (bear left across the bridge). Turn left and drive on gravel to the trailhead, 0.1 mile.

Hiking Instructions: A pleasant hike leads to a platform overlook of the falls, 0.3 mile.

Comments: The view is exalting. Toketee Falls provides perhaps the best falls scene in the state. But do not try to swim here. The water is cold, 53° F (August), at its warmest, and the access is treacherous. Pit toilets are at the trailhead.

229. Umpqua Hot Springs • • • • • • • • • • • • • • • • • • •
Umpqua National Forest

> **Type:** Natural hot springs
> **Hours:** Daily
> **Fee:** No

Driving Instructions: Umpqua Hot Springs is 64.6 miles east of Roseburg. Follow the driving instructions for Swimming Hole #194 to Highway 138/North Umpqua Highway and then the driving instructions for Point of Interest #228 to Toketee Lake turnoff. Turn left and go to the turnoff for Umpqua Hot Springs, Forest Road 3401/Thorn Prairie Road, 2.4 miles. Turn right and drive on gravel to the parking area on the left, 2.0 miles. (See detail map.)

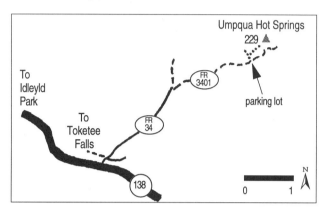

Hiking Instructions: Walk over the bridge next to the parking lot and hike to the hot springs, 0.3 mile. Bear right where the trail forks, generally following the North Umpqua River upstream. The trail is steep in spots.

Comments: The view of the North Umpqua River below is very nice. There are two oval pools for soaking at 2640 feet elevation. The larger pool is covered. The upper, smaller pool is 4 by 5 feet and 112° F; the lower, larger pool is 5 by 8 feet and 110° F. Both pools are 2—3 feet deep and floored with coarse sand. Expect nudity. There are pit toilets. No-fee, primitive camping is along the river downstream.

230. Wildlife Safari •
Safari Road, Winston; (503) 679-6761

    Type: Wildlife park
   Hours: Daily, 8:30 A.M. to 8 P.M. during the summer; 9 A.M. to dusk the rest of the year
    Fee: Yes

Driving Instructions: Wildlife Safari is 8.5 miles southwest of Roseburg. From I-5 Exit 125 in Roseburg, head south on I-5 to Exit 119, the exit for Winston, 5.6 miles. Take the exit onto Highway 42, heading southwest, to Lookingglass Road, 2.7 miles. Turn right and go to Safari Road, 0.2 mile. Turn right and go to the park entrance and parking, 1.8 miles.

Comments: The safari consists of self-guided drive-through tours, plus exhibits and programs. Animals of Africa, Asia and North America mostly roam free in a 600-acre park.

Jackson County
(County Seat: Medford)

This is Oregon's banana belt. Though it is the Rogue River which is preeminent in the economy and the lore of the county, it is the Applegate River, a tributary of the Rogue, which provides the best swimming holes. Driving instructions begin in Medford at Exit 30, the I-5 junction with Highway 62.

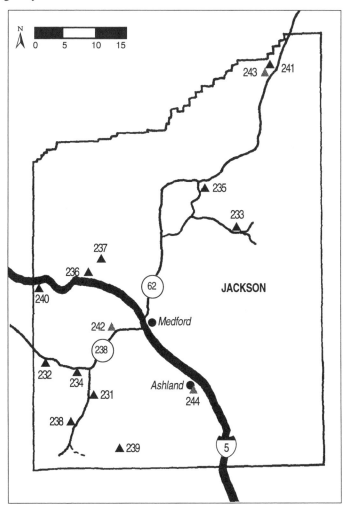

Jackson County Swimming Holes

231. Applegate River, near milepost 5

232. Applegate Wayside on Applegate River
233. Butte Falls on South Fork Big Butte Creek
234. Cantrall-Buckley Park on Applegate River
235. Crowfoot Falls on Big Butte Creek
236. Gold Hill Beach Park on Rogue River
237. Gold Nugget on Rogue River
238. Jackson Picnic Ground on Applegate River
239. Lovely Lady Lake
240. Savage Rapids Park on Rogue River
241. Union Creek on Upper Rogue River

Jackson County Points of Interest

242. Jacksonville National Historic Landmark Town
243. Natural Bridge Scenic Area
244. Oregon Shakespeare Festival

Jackson County Swimming Holes

231. Applegate River, near milepost 5 • • • • • • • • •

Rating:	6
Location:	Private
Water quality:	Good; transparent to bottom
Vital statistics:	50′ wide; at least 11′ deep; moderate current; 63° F (August); light algae; bedrock bottom; light to moderate use
Setting:	Wooded valley at 1480′; moderate to heavy litter
Swim skill:	Moderate
Amenities:	None
Entry fee:	No
Topo:	Ruch 7½′

Driving Instructions: Applegate River, near milepost 5, is 20.0 miles southwest of Medford. From Exit 30 in Medford at the I-5 junction with Highway 62, head southwest on Highway 62 to Highway 99, 0.4 mile. Following signs to Jacksonville and Highway 238, continue straight onto Highway 99, which becomes Central Avenue, to 4th Street, 1.2 miles. Turn right and drive to Front Street, less than 0.1 mile. Turn left and proceed to Highway 238/Main Street, 0.2 mile. Turn right and travel to Jacksonville at California Street, 5.2 miles. Turn right, still on Highway 238, and drive to Applegate Road in Ruch, 7.8 miles, between mileposts 25 and 26. Turn left and go to a turnout, 5.1 miles, just beyond milepost 5, on the left.

Comments: A formation rock bank makes this a nice spot with a pleasant backwater.

232. Applegate Wayside on Applegate River • • •

Rating: 8
Location: Private
Water quality: Good; 9' transparency
Vital statistics: 50' wide; at least 11' deep; moderate current; 72° F
(August); light algae; gravel bottom; heavy use
Setting: Wooded valley at 1280'; light to moderate litter
Swim skill: Moderate
Amenities: No drinking water; pit toilets
Entry fee: No
Topo: Applegate 7½'

Driving Instructions: Applegate Wayside is 22.4 miles west of Medford. Follow the driving instructions for Swimming Hole #231 to Jacksonville at California Street. Turn right and drive to the wayside in the town of Applegate, 15.3 miles, between mileposts 18 and 19, on the left.

Comments: This lovely spot is the property of Randi and Sue Lummis, who own the adjacent business. The opposite bank, owned by others, is posted against trespassing. Gravel beaches nestle between rocky outcrops that lie alongside the river.

233. Butte Falls on South Fork Big Butte Creek • • •

Rating: 7
Location: Private
Water quality: Good; transparent to bottom
Vital statistics: 130' wide; at least 9' deep; moderate current; 68° F
(August); moderate algae; rock and boulder bottom;
moderate use
Setting: Forested valley at 2360'; moderate litter
Swim skill: Strong
Amenities: None
Entry fee: No
Topo: Butte Falls 7½'

Driving Instructions: Butte Falls is 30.2 miles northeast of Medford. From Exit 30 in Medford at the I-5 junction with Highway 62, head northeast on Highway 62 to Butte Falls Road, 14.1 miles, between mileposts 14 and 15, taking care to stay on Highway 62 through Eagle Point. Turn right and drive to a gravel road turnoff, 15.5 miles (look for a cattle guard shortly before reaching town; the turnoff is 0.2 mile past the cattle guard, 0.5 mile past milepost 15). (If you miss the turnoff, you will reach a flashing light in Butte Falls at the intersection of Fir Avenue and Broad Avenue. Simply backtrack west to the turnoff, 0.2 mile.) Turn left onto the gravel road and drive to a split in the road, 0.6 mile. Stay straight at the split and then park. (See detail map.)

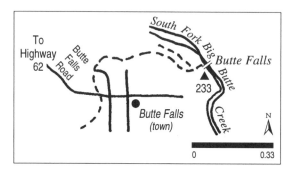

Hiking Instructions: Listen for the sound of the falls and walk to it, 125 feet. The access down to the pool is a little tricky. It is necessary to clamber down a ledge upstream and across from the falls, then work down the creek bed. Take care around the swift water at the outlet of the pool.

Comments: The land the falls is on is owned by Medford Corporation, a timber outfit. The large pool at the base of the 13-foot falls is pretty placid, though the current drifts persistently toward the outlet. The brushy bank is lined with large rocks and boulders.

234. Cantrall-Buckley Park on Applegate River • •

Rating:	7
Location:	County Park
Water quality:	Good; transparent to bottom
Vital statistics:	80' wide; at least 9' deep; moderate current; 69° F (August); light algae; gravel and pebble bottom; moderate to heavy use
Setting:	Wooded valley at 1400'; moderate litter
Swim skill:	Low to moderate
Amenities:	For-fee camping; drinking water; flush toilets
Entry fee:	Yes
Topo:	Ruch 7½'

Driving Instructions: Cantrall-Buckley Park is 17.5 miles southwest of Medford. Follow the driving instructions for Swimming Hole #231 to Jacksonville at California Street. Turn right and drive past Ruch to Hamilton Road, 9.2 miles, between mileposts 24 and 25. Turn left and drive to the park turnoff 0.9 mile. Turn right, cross a bridge, and go to the park entrance, 0.2 mile. Turn right and go to parking, 0.1 mile.

Hiking Instructions: From parking, walk a short way downhill to the river. Watch for poison oak.

Comments: The deepest hole is along the rocks on the opposite side. There are lots of low climbing rocks and gravel beach areas.

235. Crowfoot Falls on Big Butte Creek • • • • • • • •

Rating:	8
Location:	State Department of Fish and Wildlife
Water quality:	Good; transparent to bottom
Vital statistics:	70' wide; at least 8' deep; moderate current; 62° F (July); moderate algae; rock on bedrock bottom; moderate use
Setting:	Wooded valley at 1560'; moderate to heavy litter
Swim skill:	Moderate
Amenities:	None
Entry fee:	No
Topo:	McLeod 7½'

Driving Instructions: Crowfoot Falls is 29.6 miles northeast of Medford. From Exit 30 in Medford at the I-5 junction with Highway 62, head northeast on Highway 62 to Crowfoot Road, 28.9 miles, between mileposts 29 and 30, taking care to stay on Highway 62 through Eagle Point. Turn right and drive to the turnouts alongside the creek, 0.7 mile, on the left.

Comments: A 6-foot fall drops into a luscious pool. The bank is bedrock. There are some suds. Watch for poison oak.

236. Gold Hill Beach Park on Rogue River • • • • • •

Rating:	6
Location:	City Park
Water quality:	Fair; 10' transparency
Vital statistics:	240' wide; at least 28' deep; light current; 60° F (July); light bottom weeds; sand bottom; moderate use
Setting:	Wooded valley at 1080'; light to moderate litter
Swim skill:	Moderate
Amenities:	None
Entry fee:	No
Topo:	Gold Hill 7½'

Driving Instructions: Gold Hill Beach Park is 11.1 miles northwest of Medford. From Exit 30 in Medford at the I-5 junction with Highway 62, head northwest on I-5 to Exit 40, the exit for Gold Hill, 10.4 miles. Take the exit and drive to a stop, 0.2 mile. Turn right and go to a second stop at Highway 234, 0.3 mile. Turn left, cross the bridge and park in the gravel turnout immediately to the left, 0.2 mile.

Hiking Instructions: There is a staircase that leads from the turnout down to the river, 400 feet.

Comments: There is a 90-foot, hard-packed sand beach. The beach and water are shared with ducks and geese. A rapid is downstream. The DEQ 305(b) Report identifies this stretch of the Rogue as partially water-quality limited.

237. Gold Nugget on Rogue River •••••••••••

Rating:	5
Location:	Bureau of Land Management
Water quality:	Fair; 6′ transparency
Vital statistics:	180′ wide; at least 7′ deep; swift current; 70° F (August); light algae; gravel and rock bottom; moderate use
Setting:	Wooded valley at 1080′; light litter
Swim skill:	Strong
Amenities:	Drinking water sometimes; pit toilets sometimes
Entry fee:	No
Topo:	Gold Hill 7½′

Driving Instructions: Gold Nugget is 13.4 miles northwest of Medford. Follow the driving instructions for Swimming Hole #236 to Highway 234. Turn left and, curving to the right through Gold Hill, drive to the middle turnoff at Gold Nugget, 2.5 miles, between mileposts 4 and 5, on the right. There are three turnoffs into picnic parking in a 0.5 mile stretch.

Comments: Rafters abound. Between the second and third turnouts is an extensive rapids area, Nugget Falls, which is probably best avoided. A pleasant float may be had from the middle picnic area to the one farthest downstream. It is a fairly fast, but fun, float. The two downstream picnic areas are connected by a trail. There is no slack water, so be sure to have a plan to get out. The DEQ 305(b) Report identifies this stretch of the Rogue as partially water-quality limited. Watch for poison oak.

238. Jackson Picnic Ground on Applegate River

Rating:	5
Location:	Rogue River National Forest
Water quality:	Good; transparent to bottom
Vital statistics:	60′ wide; at least 6′ deep; moderate current; 60° F (August); light algae; gravel and bedrock bottom; moderate use
Setting:	Wooded valley at 1640′; light to moderate litter

Swim skill: Low to moderate
Amenities: For-fee camping; drinking water; flush toilets
Entry fee: No
Topo: Lovely Lady Lakes 7½'*

Driving Instructions: Jackson Picnic Ground is 24.7 miles southwest of Medford. Follow the driving instructions for Swimming Hole #231 to Applegate Road in Ruch. Turn left and drive to the picnic ground, 9.8 miles, between mileposts 9 and 10, on the right.

Hiking Instructions: From parking, follow the short path down, through a split-rail fence, to the river. Watch for poison oak.

Comments: The river has a sand-and-gravel beach. There is not enough water for an extensive swim, but what water there is, is fine. A lightly traveled road on the opposite shore detracts some.

239. Lovely Lady Lake* •

Rating: 8
Location: Rogue River National Forest
Water quality: Excellent; 20' transparency
Vital statistics: 46 acres; 121' deep; 75° F (August); moderate bottom and shoreline weeds; gravel and silt bottom; moderate use
Setting: Forested foothills at 3019'; light litter
Swim skill: Moderate
Amenities: For-fee camping (reservations for camping are required; call Star Ranger Station (503) 899-1812); drinking water; pit toilets
Entry fee: No
Topo: Lovely Lady Lakes 7½'*

Driving Instructions: Lovely Lady Lake* is 38.0 miles southwest of Medford. Follow the driving instructions for Swimming Hole #231 to Applegate Road in Ruch. Turn left onto Applegate Road, which becomes Forest Road 10, and drive to the Lovely Lady Lake* turnoff, 14.9 miles, between mileposts 14 and 15. Turn left, across the dam, onto Forest Road 1075 and go to the end of the pavement, 2.4 miles. Continue on gravel to the parking lot at Big Lovely Lady Lake*, 5.8 miles. (See detail map on next page.)

Hiking Instructions: Hike to the lake from the Forest Service sign at the split-rail trail entrance, 0.2 mile.

Comments: While a hike to Little Lovely Lady Lake* is okay, it is only the big, or lower, lake that offers good swimming. The bank is gravel

---

*"Lovely Lady" is not the name used on the topo or on any other map or reference to these lakes. The name used elsewhere is a sexist and racist term for "Native American woman," and I refuse to use it in this book. — *R.C.*

and dirt. Considerable suspended silica catches the light and makes the water sparkle. The lake is open and accessible from the south end, where there are reasonable gravel beach areas along the shore. Both of the long sides of the lake are steep. A popular swimming area toward the northeast corner of the lake is equipped with a rope for swinging off of tree roots.

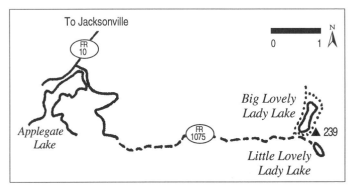

240. Savage Rapids Park on Rogue River • • • • • •

           Rating: 5
         Location: County Park
    Water quality: Fair; transparent to bottom in roped area
   Vital statistics: 0.1 mile wide; at least 7′ deep; light current in roped
                       area; 73° F (August); moderate bottom weeds; sand
                       and silt bottom; heavy use
          Setting: Wooded valley at 1000′; light litter
       Swim skill: Moderate
        Amenities: No drinking water; pit toilets
        Entry fee: No
             Topo: Rogue River 7½′

Driving Instructions: Savage Rapids Park is 21.5 miles northwest of Medford. From Exit 30 in Medford at the I-5 junction with Highway 62, head northwest on I-5 to Exit 48, the exit for City of Rogue River, 18.2 miles. Exit and drive to a stop, 0.3 mile. Turn left and go across a bridge to a stop sign on Highway 99, 0.1 mile. Turn right and drive to the park, 2.9 miles, on the right.

Comments: There is a roped area with a sandy strip between the water and a grassy bank. Disadvantages are the noise from boats on one side, cars on the other and the crowded nature of the place.

241. Union Creek on Upper Rogue River • • • • • • •

           Rating: 6
         Location: Rogue River National Forest

Water quality: Good; transparent to bottom
Vital statistics: 60' wide; at least 7' deep; swift current; 58° F (August); light algae; gravel and silt bottom; moderate use
Setting: Forested valley at 3280'; light litter
Swim skill: Strong
Amenities: For-fee camping; drinking water; pit toilets
Entry fee: No
Topo: Union Creek 7½'

Driving Instructions: Union Creek is 55.7 miles northeast of Medford. From Exit 30 in Medford at the I-5 junction with Highway 62, head northeast on Highway 62 to the campground turnoff, 55.3 miles, between mileposts 55 and 56, taking care to stay on Highway 62 through Eagle Point. Turn left and find access to the confluence of Union Creek with the Rogue River on either side of the creek behind Sites 20 or 85, 0.4 to 0.5 mile.

Comments: This pretty spot does not attract a lot of swimmers. But with its cold, clear water it is in contrast to the Rogue's other swimmable places much farther downstream. The bank is sandy gravel and dirt.

Jackson County Points of Interest

242. Jacksonville National Historic Landmark Town
Jacksonville Museum, 206 North 5th Street, Jacksonville; (503) 773-6536

Type: Historic community
Hours: The museums are open daily, 10 A.M. to 5 P.M. from Memorial Day to Labor Day; they are open the same hours, but closed Monday, the rest of the year
Fee: Yes, for the museums

Driving Instructions: Jacksonville National Historic Landmark Town is 7.1 miles west of Medford. Follow the driving instructions for Swimming Hole #231 to Jacksonville at California Street. The museums are on the left just before reaching California Street.

Comments: The Jacksonville Museum, Children's Museum and well-preserved downtown buildings combine to make this the most interesting historic small town in the state.

243. Natural Bridge Scenic Area • • • • • • • • • • • • •
Rogue River National Forest

Type: Scenic location
Hours: Daily
Fee: No

Driving Instructions: Natural Bridge Scenic Area is 55.0 miles northeast of Medford. From Exit 30 in Medford at the I-5 junction with Highway 62, head northeast on Highway 62 to the Natural Bridge turnoff, 54.3 miles, between mileposts 54 and 55, taking care to stay on Highway 62 through Eagle Point. Turn left and drive to parking, 0.7 mile.

The Rogue River Gorge Overlook turnoff is beyond the Natural Bridge turnoff, 1.3 miles, between mileposts 56 and 57. Turn left and go to parking, 0.1 mile.

Comments: Overdeveloped but still neat, the infant Rogue River charges through a lava tube and potholes. The Rogue River Gorge Overlook also provides a worthwhile spectacle.

244. Oregon Shakespeare Festival • • • • • • • • • • • •
15 South Pioneer Street, Ashland; (503) 482-2111

> **Type:** Professional theater
> **Hours:** February to October
> **Fee:** Yes

Driving Instructions: The Oregon Shakespeare Festival is 13.9 miles southeast of Medford. From Exit 30 in Medford at the I-5 junction with Highway 62, head southeast on I-5 to Exit 19, the exit for Ashland, 11.0 miles. Exit and drive to a stop, 0.2 mile. Turn right onto Valley View Road and drive to Highway 99, which becomes Main Street through Ashland, 0.4 mile. Turn left and drive to the Shakespeare Center turnoff at Pioneer Street, 2.2 miles. Turn right and drive to the center, less than 0.1 mile, on the right.

Comments: Outdoor performances of three of Shakespeare's plays are offered during the summer at this world-famous theater. Several other plays are performed indoors during the year. A number of different theater groups perform "Off Bardway" throughout the year.

Josephine County
(County Seat: Grants Pass)

Swimming in Josephine County is at its best along the Illinois River, an exquisitely beautiful river that cradles the warmest, most magnificent swimming holes in the state. Driving instructions begin in Grants Pass at the intersection of I-5 and Highway 99 at Exit 58, the exit for Grants Pass, at the junction with Highway 99.

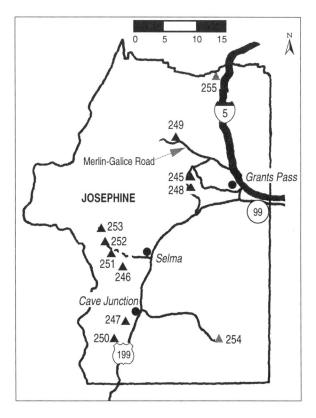

Josephine County Swimming Holes

245. Griffin Park on Rogue River
246. Illinois River Bridge
247. Illinois River Park
248. Matson Park on Rogue River
249. Rainbow on Rogue River
250. Seats Dam on Rough and Ready Creek
251. Sixmile on Illinois River

252. Store Gulch on Illinois River
253. Swinging Bridge and Illinois River Falls on Illinois River

Josephine County Points of Interest

254. Oregon Caves National Monument
255. Wolf Creek Tavern

Josephine County Swimming Holes

245. Griffin Park on Rogue River •••••••••••••

Rating:	7
Location:	County Park
Water quality:	Fair; transparent to bottom
Vital statistics:	150' wide; at least 7' deep; moderate current; 74° F (August); moderate bottom weeds; pebble bottom; moderate to heavy use
Setting:	Wooded valley at 840'; moderate litter
Swim skill:	Moderate
Amenities:	For-fee camping; drinking water; pit toilets
Entry fee:	No
Topo:	Wilderville 7½'

Driving Instructions: Griffin Park is 16.4 miles west of Grants Pass. From I-5 Exit 58, head south on Highway 99 (6th Street, heading south) to Highway 199/Redwood Highway, 2.6 miles (after crossing the bridge, stay right toward Cave Junction). Turn right and go to Riverbanks Road, 7.0 miles, at milepost 7. Turn right and drive to Griffin Road, 6.1 miles, between mileposts 16 and 17. Turn right and find parking, 0.7 mile. (See detail map on next page.)

Comments: This park has a playground and a nicely landscaped upper park area. The bank is composed mostly of large pebbles, except for a 50-foot by 200-foot sandy beach area. The DEQ 305(b) Report says this stretch of the Rogue is partially water-quality limited.

246. Illinois River Bridge ••••••••••••••••••••

Rating:	7
Location:	Siskiyou National Forest
Water quality:	Good to excellent; transparent to bottom
Vital statistics:	100' wide; at least 9' deep; light current; 80° F (August); moderate to heavy algae; rock bottom; light use
Setting:	Forested valley at 1200'; moderate litter
Swim skill:	Moderate

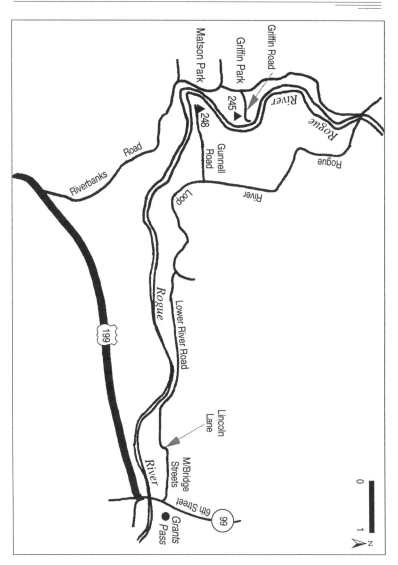

Amenities: No-fee, primitive camping on either side of the river;
no drinking water

Entry fee: No

Topo: Cave Junction 7½′

Driving Instructions: Illinois River Bridge is 29.4 miles southwest of
Grants Pass. Follow the driving instructions for Swimming Hole #245 to
Highway 199/Redwood Highway. Turn right and go to a flashing orange

light in Selma, 20.2 miles. Continue on Highway 199 to Eight Dollar Road, which becomes Forest Road 4201, 3.7 miles, between mileposts 23 and 24. Turn right and drive to a bridge across the Illinois River, 2.9 miles. Park at the turnout on the right just before crossing the bridge. (See detail map.)

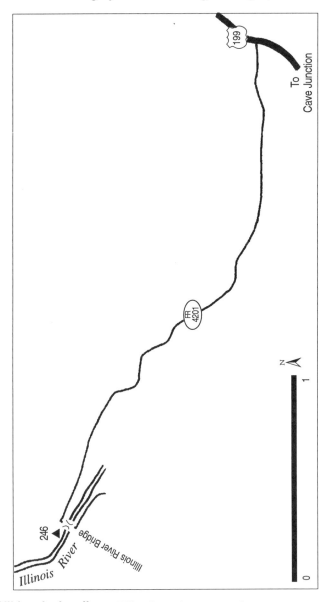

Hiking Instructions: Hike from the turnout downstream to a rock outcrop, 350 feet.

Comments: Check out the beautiful, but sharp, metamorphic rocks that line the shore on the hike downstream. The Siskiyous are the oldest geologic region in Oregon, and the rocks are brilliant and colorful. Away from the pool, the water is shallow. The DEQ 305(b) Report says this stretch of the Illinois is partially water-quality limited.

247. Illinois River Park ••••••••••••••••••••••

Rating:	7
Location:	State Park
Water quality:	Good to excellent; transparent to bottom
Vital statistics:	140′ wide; at least 7′ deep; light current; 78° F (August); light algae; gravel and silt bottom; moderate use
Setting:	Forested valley at 1280′; light litter
Swim skill:	Moderate
Amenities:	Drinking water; flush toilets
Entry fee:	No
Topo:	Cave Junction 7½′

Driving Instructions: Illinois River Park is 32.8 miles southwest of Grants Pass. Follow the driving instructions for Swimming Hole #245 to Highway 199/Redwood Highway. Turn right and go to Cave Junction at the intersection with Highway 46, 28.9 miles. Continue past the intersection, still on Highway 199, to the park turnoff, 0.6 mile, between mileposts 29 and 30. Turn right and go to parking, 0.7 mile.

Hiking Instructions: Walk to a small beach area downstream from the parking lot, 200 feet.

Comments: The water moves languidly through this beautiful spot along a 30-foot gravel bank. The DEQ 305(b) Report says this stretch of the Illinois is partially water-quality limited.

248. Matson Park on Rogue River •••••••••••

Rating:	6
Location:	County Park
Water quality:	Fair; transparent to bottom
Vital statistics:	140′ wide; at least 8′ deep; moderate current; 74° F (August); moderate to heavy algae and bottom weeds; pebble and gravel bottom; moderate use
Setting:	Wooded valley at 840′; moderate to heavy litter
Swim skill:	Moderate
Amenities:	No drinking water; pit toilet
Entry fee:	No
Topo:	Wilderville 7½′

Driving Instructions: Matson Park is 11.8 miles west of Grants Pass. From I-5 Exit 58, head south on Highway 99 (6th Street, heading south) to "M" Street, 2.2 miles. Turn right onto "M" Street, which becomes Bridge Street, and go to Lincoln Lane, 1.8 miles. Turn left and head to Lower River Road, 0.1 mile. Turn right and go to the junction with Rogue River Loop Road, 3.0 miles. Turn left onto and drive to the park turnoff at Gunnell Road, 2.7 miles. Turn left and go to parking, 2.0 miles. (See detail map for Swimming Hole #245.)

Comments: The river makes a giant bend around a large bar of pebbles and gravel. It is a nice float around the bar. Homes and a road on the opposite bank are negative but not prohibitive features. The DEQ 305(b) Report says this stretch of the Rogue is partially water-quality limited.

249. Rainbow on Rogue River ● ● ● ● ● ● ● ● ● ● ● ● ●

Rating: 9
Location: Bureau of Land Management
Water quality: Good; 6' transparency
Vital statistics: 110' wide; at least 15' deep; swift current; 73° F (August); moderate bottom weeds; gravel, sand and silt bottom; light to moderate use
Setting: Wooded valley at 720'; moderate litter
Swim skill: Moderate to strong
Amenities: No drinking water; pit toilet
Entry fee: No
Topo: Galice 7½'

Driving Instructions: Rainbow is 15.2 miles northwest of Grants Pass. From I-5 Exit 58, head northwest on I-5 to Exit 61, the exit for Merlin, approximately 3.5 miles. Exit and go to a stop, 0.3 mile. Turn left onto Merlin-Galice Road and travel to the Rainbow turnoff, 11.3 miles (this is 0.6 mile past Indian Mary County Park). Turn right and go to parking, 0.1 mile.

Hiking Instructions: An easy trail leads to the river from the parking area, 0.1 mile. Watch out for poison oak.

Comments: One of the nicest places on the river, Rainbow is lightly used relative to the heavily crowded places above and below. Although quite a few driftboaters pass by, they are a happy, noninterfering lot who do not stage here. The trail leads to a splendid backwater cove and a small gravel beach. A large rock outcropping on the opposite bank makes a nice swimming objective for better swimmers.

250. Seats Dam on Rough and Ready Creek ● ● ● ●

Rating: 8
Location: Siskiyou National Forest

Water quality: Excellent; transparent to bottom
Vital statistics: 60' wide; at least 10' deep; light current; 77° F (August); light to moderate algae; pebble bottom; moderate to heavy use
Setting: Forested valley at 1460'; moderate litter
Swim skill: Low to moderate
Amenities: None
Entry fee: No
Topo: O'Brien 7½'

Driving Instructions: Seats Dam is 38.0 miles southwest of Grants Pass. Follow the driving instructions for Swimming Hole #245 to Highway 199/Redwood Highway. Turn right and go to Cave Junction at the intersection with Highway 46, 28.9 miles. Continue past the intersection, still on Highway 199, to Airport Drive, 4.0 miles, between mileposts 32 and 33. Turn right and go on gravel to a rocky dirt road, 2.2 miles (it may be hard to see, so stay sharp; if you encounter a private road, backtrack less than 0.1 mile). Turn left and go to parking near the dam, 0.3 mile (stay to the right when the road branches). (See detail map.)

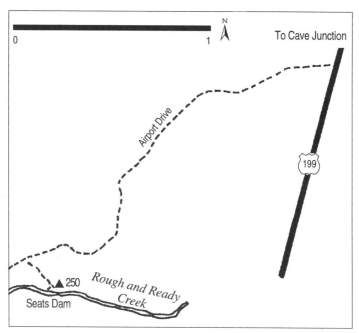

Comments: The 5-foot dam is a small, concrete affair with an earthen extension. Above the dam, the bank is composed of large rocks. Mostly the water is not over 4 or 5 feet deep, but there is a 10-foot hole in a rocky outcrop area 120 feet upstream. Below the dam is a pool which abuts a beach of gravel and small stones. There is a five-inch-thick wood slab tethered to the dam for diving into the pool. Watch out for poison oak.

251. Sixmile on Illinois River •••••••••••••••••

Rating: 10
Location: Siskiyou National Forest
Water quality: Good to excellent; transparent to bottom
Vital statistics: 100' wide; at least 14' deep; light current; 80° F (August); moderate algae; sand, gravel and boulder bottom; moderate to heavy use
Setting: Forested valley at 1120'; moderate litter
Swim skill: Low to moderate
Amenities: No-fee, primitive camping; no drinking water; pit toilet
Entry fee: No
Topo: Eight Dollar Mountain 7½'

Driving Instructions: Sixmile is 30.7 miles southwest of Grants Pass. Follow the driving instructions for Swimming Hole #245 to Highway 199/Redwood Highway. Turn right and go to a flashing orange light in Selma, 20.2 miles. Turn right onto Illinois River Road, which becomes Forest Road 4103, and drive to a turnout just before the bridge over Sixmile Creek, 7.9 miles, on the left.

Hiking Instructions: It is a short walk to the river by a trail from the turnout. Watch for poison oak.

Comments: Swimming does not get better than this. On the river, upstream of the entry of Sixmile Creek, is a rare and delicate swimming hole. Small rapids are both upstream and downstream. A huge rock shoulder on the opposite bank is a fun place to jump from. The water meanders beside boulders along the shore and there is some sand on the bank, including a 50-foot beach. There are shallows, too. Here is a stupendous spot that is marred only by litter and overlogging. The DEQ 305(b) Report says this stretch of the Illinois is partially water-quality limited.

252. Store Gulch on Illinois River ••••••••••••

Rating: 10
Location: Siskiyou National Forest
Water quality: Good to excellent; transparent to bottom
Vital statistics: 100' wide; at least 14' deep; light current; 82° F (August); light algae; sand and gravel bottom; moderate to heavy use

Setting: Forested valley at 1040'; light to moderate litter
Swim skill: Moderate
Amenities: No-fee camping; no drinking water; pit toilet
Entry fee: No
Topo: Pearsoll Peak 7½'

Driving Instructions: Store Gulch is 32.0 miles southwest of Grants Pass. Follow the driving instructions for Swimming Hole #245 to Highway 199/Redwood Highway. Turn right and go to flashing orange light in Selma, 20.2 miles. Turn right onto Illinois River Road/Forest Road 4103, and drive to the end of the pavement, 8.0 miles. Continue on a packed gravel/asphalt road to the campground, 1.2 miles. Parking is on the left.

Hiking Instructions: Hike down to the river on a well-maintained trail from the parking area, less than 0.2 mile. Watch for poison oak.

Comments: Driving along the Illinois River, Bach's *Air on the G String* is just right. A fantastic pool around a huge monolith awaits. Angular boulders, coarse sand, and gravel line the pool. There are benign rapids both upstream and downstream. It must be noted that the Illinois River on either side of Store Gulch is like a shopping aisle of swimming holes. From Sixmile to 1.1 miles past Store Gulch, where the road hikes up the hill leaving the river below, there are wonderful, easily accessible small pools at virtually every bend. The DEQ 305(b) Report says this stretch of the Illinois is partially water-quality limited.

253. Swinging Bridge and Illinois River Falls ● ● ● ● ●
on Illinois River

Rating: 10
Location: Siskiyou National Forest
Water quality: Good to excellent; transparent to bottom
Vital statistics: 200' wide; at least 49' deep; moderate current; 80° F (August); light to moderate algae; gravel and bedrock bottom; light to moderate use
Setting: Forested valley at 1000'; light litter
Swim skill: Moderate to strong
Amenities: None
Entry fee: No
Topo: Pearsoll Peak 7½'

Driving Instructions: Swinging Bridge and Illinois River Falls are 34.3 miles southwest of Grants Pass. Follow the driving instructions for Swimming Hole #245 to Highway 199/Redwood Highway, then those for Swimming Hole #251 to Illinois River Road/Forest Road 4103, and drive to the end of the pavement, 8.0 miles. Continue on a packed gravel/asphalt road to the turnoff for McCaleb Ranch, a Boy Scout operation, 3.1 miles (do not proceed on the main road unless prepared for a very bumpy ride; the packed gravel ends here). Turn left and drive on rough gravel to a small turnout above the swinging bridge, 0.4 mile. (See detail map.)

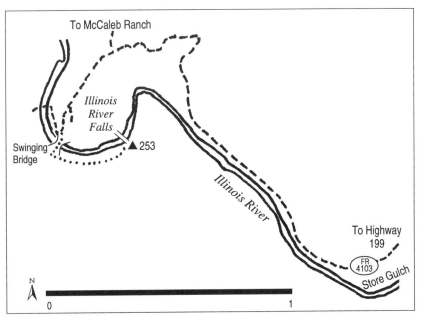

Hiking Instructions: The trail to the 15-foot falls is on the opposite bank. Cross the bridge and hike upstream, 0.4 mile. Watch for poison oak.

Comments: Anywhere along this rocky and irregular stretch of shoreline is superb swimming. It may be disappointing to find that there is an easy trail to the falls. Hiking on the untrailed shoreline or swimming up the channel may provide a greater opportunity for adventure. Look for the beautifully striped bedrock below the falls. The DEQ 305(b) Report says this stretch of the Illinois is partially water-quality limited.

Josephine County Points of Interest

254. Oregon Caves National Monument •••••••••
National Park Service; (503) 592-3400

> **Type:** Scenic location
> **Hours:** Daily, 8 A.M. to 7 P.M. during the summer; 8:30 A.M. to 4 P.M. during the winter
> **Fee:** Yes

Driving Instructions: Oregon Caves National Monument is 51.0 miles south of Grants Pass. Follow the driving instructions for Swimming

Hole #245 to Highway 199/Redwood Highway. Turn right and go to Cave Junction at the intersection with Highway 46, 28.9 miles, between mileposts 28 and 29. Turn left and drive to parking at the monument, 19.5 miles.

Comments: Children under six may not enter the caves, but a sitting service is provided. One of three national monuments in Oregon, the cave preserves beautiful marble decorations created over vast reaches of time.

255. Wolf Creek Tavern •••••••••••••••••••••
Wolf Creek, (503) 866-2474

> **Type:** Historic site
> **Hours:** Monday through Saturday, 11 A.M. to 8:30 P.M. (9 P.M. during the summer); Sunday, 10 A.M. to 8 P.M.
> **Fee:** No

Driving Instructions: Wolf Creek Tavern is 18.5 miles north of Grants Pass. From I-5 Exit 58, head north on I-5 to Exit 76, the exit for Wolf Creek, 17.8 miles, between mileposts 75 and 76. Exit, then curve to the left and to the right to the tavern, 0.7 mile, on the left.

Comments: This is a reconstructed and operating inn from the stagecoach days of the late 1800s. Owned by the state park system, it is run by a concessionaire. It is an agreeable place for a stop.

Central

High in elevation and subject to the whims of the elements, this region sees the transition from high mountain wilderness to the stark radiance of the desert. Look for pine forests in the mountains and for juniper and sage in the high desert. It is always necessary to travel wisely, to carry water, and to be prepared for extremes of temperature within a day that are greater than anywhere else in the state. Oregon's only poisonous snake, the rattlesnake, is found east of the Cascades, though it generally makes itself scarce. There are ticks and thus the danger of Lyme disease, so take care to check body and clothing after jaunts.

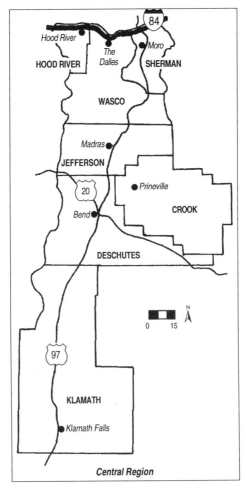

Central Region

204

Crook County
(County Seat: Prineville)

Crook County, in addition to its losing its status as the last bellwether county of the nation in predicting the outcome of presidential elections, is hurting for swimming holes. At least there is one. Driving instructions begin in Prineville at the intersection of Highway 26 (3rd Street) and Main Street.

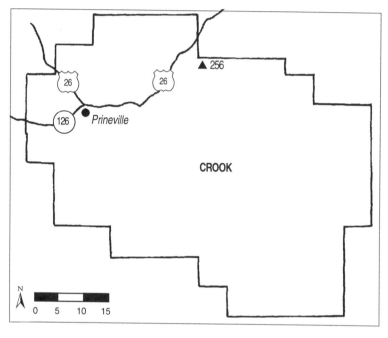

Crook County Swimming Hole

256. Walton Lake

Crook County Swimming Hole ● ● ● ● ● ● ● ● ● ● ● ● ● ●

256. Walton Lake

Rating: 5
Location: Ochoco National Forest
Water quality: Fair; 9' transparency
Vital statistics: 18 acres; 21' deep; 68° F (August); moderate suspended algae; sandy bottom in swim area; moderate to heavy use

Setting: Forested mountains at 5156'; light litter
Swim skill: Low to moderate
Amenities: For-fee camping; drinking water; pit toilets
Entry fee: No
Topo: Ochoco Butte 7½'

Driving Instructions: Walton Lake is 32.5 miles east of Prineville. From the intersection of Highway 26 and Main Street in Prineville, head east on Highway 26 to Ochoco Creek Road, 16.7 miles, between mileposts 34 and 35. Turn right and go to Forest Road 22, 8.7 miles. Turn left and drive to the Walton Lake turnoff, 6.9 miles. Turn left and go to where the road splits three ways, 0.1 mile. Take the middle fork to the beach spot on the lake, 0.1 mile. (See detail map.)

Comments: This artificial lake has a prepared sandy shoulder. The beach is 75 feet wide.

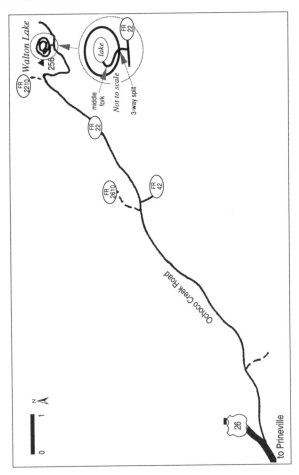

Deschutes County
(County Seat: Bend)

Deschutes County is lake country. It is the most prolific swimming-hole location east of the Cascades—despite the fact that the Deschutes River is generally too swift or too shallow for swimming. There is a ton of lakes to choose from, many unique and glorious. Permits are required in the Three Sisters Wilderness. Day-use permits are at trailheads; overnight permits are obtained at Forest Service stations and recreation establishments. Driving instructions begin in Bend at the joining of Highways 20 and 97 at Greenwood Avenue and 3rd Street.

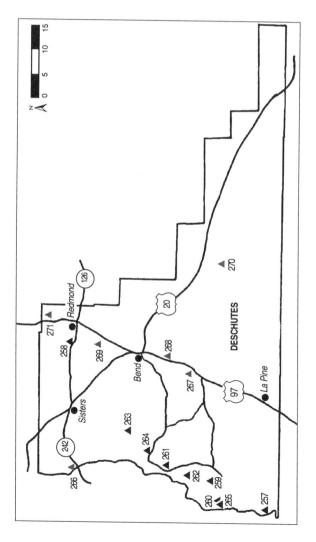

Deschutes County Swimming Holes

257. Bobby Lake
258. Cline Falls on Deschutes River
259. Cultus Lake
260. East Hanks Lake
261. Elk Lake at Beach Picnic Area
262. Lucky Lake
263. Three Creek Lake
264. Todd Lake
265. West Hanks Lake

Deschutes County Points of Interest

266. McKenzie Pass
267. Newberry National Volcanic Monument
268. Oregon High Desert Museum
269. Petersen's Rock Garden
270. Pine Mountain Observatory
271. Smith Rock Park

Deschutes County Swimming Holes

257. Bobby Lake •

Rating:	10
Location:	Deschutes National Forest
Water quality:	Excellent; 45′ transparency
Vital statistics:	91 acres; 59′ deep; 64° F (June); light algae; sand and silt bottom; light use
Setting:	Forested mountains at 5408′; light litter
Swim skill:	Moderate
Amenities:	No-fee, primitive camping, no drinking water
Entry fee:	No
Topo:	The Twins 7½′

Driving Instructions: Bobby Lake is 78.4 miles southwest of Bend. From the joining of Highways 20 and 97 in Bend, head south on Highway 97 to Crescent Road (unmarked, at a flashing orange light) in Crescent, 46.9 miles. Turn right and drive to Highway 58, 12.3 miles. Turn right and go to the Waldo Lake turnoff, Forest Road 5897, 13.7 miles, between mileposts 58 and 59. Turn right and proceed to the Bobby Lake trailhead, 5.5 miles, between mileposts 5 and 6, on the right. (See detail map for Swimming Hole #75.)

Hiking Instructions: From the trailhead, a well-used trail leads to the lake, 2.5 miles (pass by the Gold Lake trail, shown as the first fork on the detail map; where the trail crosses the Pacific Crest Trail in 2.1 miles, stay straight). At the lake, take the lakeshore trail counterclockwise for 0.2 mile, to the point where a huge rock face enters the water.

Comments: The place is gorgeous. Be careful of the slippery rock when entering the water at this magical spot.

258. Cline Falls on Deschutes River •••••••••

Rating:	7
Location:	Central Oregon Irrigation District
Water quality:	Good; transparent to bottom
Vital statistics:	35' wide; at least 10' deep; light current; 79° F (August); light algae; boulder and bedrock bottom; moderate use
Setting:	Scrub desert at 3020'; moderate to heavy litter
Swim skill:	Moderate
Amenities:	No-fee, primitive camping; no drinking water (available at nearby state park)
Entry fee:	No
Topo:	Cline Falls 7½'

Driving Instructions: Cline Falls is 21.3 miles north of Bend. From the joining of Highways 20 and 97 in Bend, head north on Highway 97 to the Sisters and Cline Falls turnoff in Redmond at Highway 126, 16.8 miles (bear right, staying on Highway 97 toward Redmond, when Highway 20 splits to the left, 2.5 miles north of Bend). Turn left and proceed to 71st Street, 4.1 miles (the Cline Falls State Park entrance is 0.2 mile too far), at milepost 108. Turn right and go to the point where the road is blocked at the entry to an abandoned bridge, 0.4 mile.

Comments: The best swimming is upstream of the abandoned bridge. The river, in channeling through a layer of basalt, has cut a deep trench between the abandoned bridge to nearly under the presently used bridge, high overhead. There are shallows both above and below the deep water. Cline Falls, such as it is, is downstream, near a gauging station. There is some noise from the highway.

259. Cultus Lake •••••••••••••••••••••••••

Rating:	7
Location:	Deschutes National Forest
Water quality:	Excellent; 56' transparency
Vital statistics:	791 acres; 211' deep; 72° F (July); light algae; sand and rock bottom; moderate to heavy use
Setting:	Forested mountains at 4668'; light litter

Swim skill: Low to moderate
Amenities: For-fee camping; drinking water; pit toilets
Entry fee: No
Topo: Irish Mountain 7½'

Driving Instructions: Cultus Lake is 49.6 miles southwest of Bend. From the joining of Highways 20 and 97 in Bend, head south on Highway 97 to Franklin Avenue (which becomes Louisiana Avenue), 0.3 mile. Turn right and go to Tumalo Avenue (which becomes Galveston Avenue), 1.2 miles. Turn right and drive to 14th Street, 0.4 mile. Turn left onto 14th Street (which becomes Century Drive, Cascade Lakes Highway and Forest Road 46) and head to the Cultus Lake turnoff, Forest Road 4635, 45.8 miles, between mileposts 45 and 46; be sure to stay to the right between mileposts 19 and 20. Turn right and go to the designated swim area at the lake, 1.9 miles, on the left. (See detail map.)

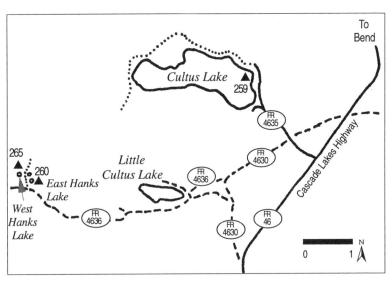

Comments: This is a pretty lake with several sand or gravel beaches, nice ones, on the east and west ends of the lake. The 460-foot beach at the swim area is sand and gravel. Motorboats are a significant presence.

260. East Hanks Lake •

Rating: 8
Location: Deschutes National Forest
Water quality: Excellent; transparent to bottom
Vital statistics: 0.1 mile wide; at least 20' deep; 70° F (July); moderate shoreline weeds; sand and rock bottom; light use

Setting: Forested mountains at 5379'; light litter
Swim skill: Moderate
Amenities: No-fee, primitive camping; no drinking water
Entry fee: No
Topo: Irish Mountain 7½'

Driving Instructions: East Hanks Lake is 57.1 miles southwest of Bend. Follow the driving instructions for Swimming Hole #259 to the Cultus Lake turnoff. Turn right and go to the turnoff for Little Cultus Lake and Forest Road 4630, 0.8 mile.

Turn left and drive on gravel to Forest Road 4636, 1.7 miles. Continue straight onto Forest Road 4636, and drive to the Many Lakes Trailhead, 6.9 miles, as follows: bear left, then right around the south end of Little Cultus Lake; bear left 0.4 mile past Little Cultus Lake to stay on Forest Road 4636. The last 4 miles are sometimes very rough; it may be best to

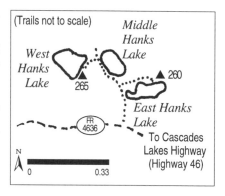

hike. The trailhead is on the right. (See detail maps here and for Swimming Hole #259.)

Hiking Instructions: From the trailhead hike the main trail to a point where a path branches to the right, 0.2 mile. Take the path to a rock outcrop overlooking the lake, 0.1 mile.

Comments: From the trailhead there is a three-lake complex within a 0.5-mile stretch. All are uncrowded, with only an occasional angler or hiker. The lake closest to the road, East Hanks Lake, is very nice. At night, it is a lovely place to see the stars and their reflections in the lake. An aesthetically pleasing rock outcropping is on the north side, a place to sun and dry between plunges.

261. Elk Lake at Beach Picnic Area • • • • • • • • • • •

Rating: 7
Location: Deschutes National Forest
Water quality: Excellent; 33' transparency
Vital statistics: 405 acres; 62' deep; 74° F (August); light algae; sand and gravel bottom; moderate to heavy use
Setting: Forested mountains at 4884'; light litter
Swim skill: Low to moderate
Amenities: For-fee camping; drinking water; pit toilets

Entry fee: No
Topo: Elk Lake 7½'

Driving Instructions: Elk Lake is 36.3 miles west of Bend. Follow the driving instructions of Swimming Hole #259 onto 14th Street and head to the turnoff for the picnic area, 34.2 miles (be sure to stay to the right between mileposts 19 and 20), between mileposts 34 and 35. Turn left and go to parking, 0.2 mile. (See detail map.)

Comments: Beach Picnic Area is the best spot on the lake to swim. Other identified swim areas around the lake are at Sunset View, Little Fawn and Point. Beach Picnic Area offers—surprise—a large, coarse-sand and gravel beach. To the north is South Sister. Motorboats are a significant presence.

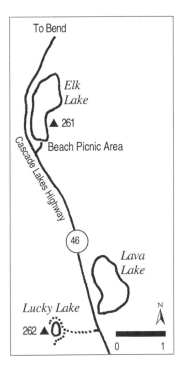

262. Lucky Lake •

Rating: 6
Location: Deschutes National Forest
Water quality: Excellent; transparent to bottom
Vital statistics: 30 acres; at least 10' deep; 72° F (August); light shoreline weeds; gravel, sand and silt bottom; light to moderate use
Setting: Forested mountains at 5200'; light litter
Swim skill: Moderate
Amenities: No-fee, primitive camping; no drinking water; pit toilet at trailhead
Entry fee: No
Topo: Elk Lake 7½'

Driving Instructions: Lucky Lake is 40.5 miles southwest of Bend. Follow the driving instructions of Swimming Hole #259 onto 14th Street and head to the trailhead turnoff for Lucky Lake, 38.5 miles (be sure to stay to the right between mileposts 19 and 20), between mileposts 38 and 39. Turn right and find parking at the trailhead, 0.1 mile. (See detail map for Swimming Hole #261.)

Hiking Instructions: Hike on a moderately ascending trail to the point where the trail forks, 1.4 miles. To get to the beach, take the right fork and hike counterclockwise around the lake, 0.5 mile.

Comments: The lake is clear and inviting. There are occasional sandy spots interspersed in the grassy banks. Fallen logs adorn the edges. The beach, when the water is not so high as to submerge it, is 230 feet long.

263. Three Creek Lake ••••••••••••••••••••

Rating:	7
Location:	Deschutes National Forest
Water quality:	Excellent; transparent to bottom
Vital statistics:	75 acres; 30′ deep; 63° F (July); light algae; sand and rock bottom; moderate use
Setting:	Forested mountains at 6560′; light litter
Swim skill:	Moderate
Amenities:	No-fee camping; no drinking water; pit toilets
Entry fee:	No
Topo:	Tumalo Falls 7½′

Driving Instructions: Three Creek Lake is 37.9 miles west of Bend. From the joining of Highways 20 and 97 in Bend, head north on Highway 20 to the lake turnoff in Sisters, 21.6 miles (bear left, staying on Highway 20 toward Sisters, when Highway 97 splits to the right, 2.5 miles north of Bend). Turn left onto the road that becomes Forest Road 16 and drive to the end of the pavement, 14.2 miles. Continue on gravel to parking by the lake, near the campground, 2.1 miles, on the right.

Comments: Beautiful cinnamon-barked ponderosa pine is along the way. The lake is accessible and picture-perfect, with a mountain peak above the south shore. There is a sandy beach next to the campground.

264. Todd Lake ••••••••••••••••••••••••••

Rating:	6
Location:	Deschutes National Forest
Water quality:	Excellent; 23′ transparency
Vital statistics:	29 acres; 60′ deep; 66° F (August); light shoreline weeds; sand and gravel bottom; moderate to heavy use
Setting:	Forested mountains at 6160′; light litter
Swim skill:	Moderate
Amenities:	No-fee, primitive camping; no drinking water; pit toilets
Entry fee:	No

Topo: Broken Top 7½'

Driving Instructions: Todd Lake is 26.2 miles west of Bend. Follow the driving instructions of Swimming Hole #259 onto 14th Street and head to the turnoff to Todd Lake, 23.7 miles (be sure to stay to the right between mileposts 19 and 20), between mileposts 23 and 24. Turn right and go to parking, 0.6 mile. (See detail map.)

Hiking Instructions: Walk on a well-used trail from parking to the lake, less than 0.2 mile. Go either way around the lake to find places to swim.

Comments: The lake is open, with an almost-too-regular shoreline. Sand and gravel spots intermingle with the grassy banks. A nice stream flows out of the lake near the point where the trail reaches the lake.

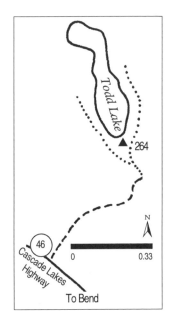

265. West Hanks Lake •

Rating:	8
Location:	Deschutes National Forest
Water quality:	Excellent; transparent to bottom
Vital statistics:	0.1 mile wide; at least 11' deep; 71° F (July); moderate shoreline weeds; rock and silt bottom; light use
Setting:	Forested mountains at 5400'; light litter
Swim skill:	Moderate
Amenities:	None
Entry fee:	No
Topo:	Irish Mountain 7½'

Driving Instructions: West Hanks Lake is 57.1 miles southwest of Bend. Follow the driving instructions for Swimming Hole #259 to the Cultus Lake turnoff. Continue, following the driving instructions of Swimming Hole #260, to the Many Lakes Trailhead. (See detail maps for Swimming Holes #259 and #260.)

Hiking Instructions: Once at the trailhead, hike on the main trail, past the side trail to East Hanks Lake (to the right), to a path which splits off to the left, 0.4 mile. This fork is after East Hanks Lake and just at the end of Middle Hanks Lake. Take the path to West Hanks Lake, crossing a marshy area, less than 0.1 mile.

Comments: From the trailhead there is a three-lake complex within a 0.5-mile stretch. The third from the road, West Hanks Lake, is remarkable for its beautiful outcropping on the north end. Remnants of a lava dike jut out about 50 feet into the water above the surface, and continue under the surface nearly across the lake. There is a small island near the point where the trail reaches the lake. There are many downed trees on the banks around the lake. On the west side is a high ridge that, for a fairly easy climb up, gives a great view of the lake and of the surrounding area. The Three Sisters and Broken Top are to the north.

Deschutes County Points of Interest

266. McKenzie Pass •
Deschutes National Forest

> **Type:** Scenic drive
> **Hours:** Daily
> **Fee:** No

Driving Instructions: McKenzie Pass is 36.6 miles northwest of Bend. From the joining of Highways 20 and 97 in Bend, head north on Highway 20 to the far side of Sisters where Highway 242 begins, 21.8 miles (bear left, staying on Highway 20 toward Sisters, when Highway 97 splits to the right, 2.5 miles north of Bend). Bear left onto Highway 242, the McKenzie Highway, and drive to the summit and to overlook parking at Wright Observatory, 14.8 miles, between mileposts 77 and 78.

Comments: Topping out at 5325 feet elevation, this is an impressive scenic drive to Wright Observatory, which overlooks a landscape of lava flows and imposing mountains. Listen to a Kenny G tape on the drive through this wonderland. The road is closed by snow in the winter. See Point of Interest #98 for the western approach to McKenzie Pass, which passes through landscape scenically quite different from the east side.

267. Newberry National Volcanic Monument • • • •
Deschutes National Forest; (503) 593-2421

> **Type:** Scenic location
> **Hours:** Daily; visitor center hours are daily, 9 A.M. to 5 P.M.
> from March to October; dates and hours may vary
> **Fee:** For some attractions (see below)

Driving Instructions: Newberry National Volcanic Monument is 11.2 miles south of Bend. From the joining of Highways 20 and 97 in Bend, head south on Highway 97 to the Lava Lands Visitor Center turnoff, 11.1 miles, between mileposts 149 and 150. Turn right and go to parking, 0.1 mile.

Comments: The monument encompasses Newberry Crater, Lava

Butte, Lava River Cave (there is an entry fee for this, the longest lava tube in Oregon), Paulina Peak, Lava Cast Forest, Big Obsidian Flow, Paulina and East Lakes, and much more. This is a marvelous setting for learning about the volcanic origins of the region. The visitor center, operated by the Forest Service, is the logical beginning place for orientation to the area.

268. Oregon High Desert Museum •••••••••••••
59800 South Highway 97, Bend; (503) 382-4754

    Type: Desert museum
    Hours: Daily, 9 A.M. to 5 P.M.; closed major holidays
    Fee: Yes

Driving Instructions: Oregon High Desert Museum is 7.2 miles south of Bend. From the joining of Highways 20 and 97 in Bend, head south on Highway 97 to the museum turnoff, 6.7 miles, between mileposts 145 and 146. Turn left and go to parking, 0.5 mile.

Comments: This is a great place for learning more about the desert environment and its natural and cultural history.

269. Petersen's Rock Garden ••••••••••••••••••
Southwest 77th Street, Redmond; (503) 382-5574

    Type: Rock garden
    Hours: Daily, 8 A.M. to 6 P.M. from mid-May to September (grounds open till dusk); 9 A.M. to 4 P.M. the rest of the year
    Fee: Yes

Driving Instructions: Petersen's Rock Garden is 11.6 miles north of Bend. From the joining of Highways 20 and 97 in Bend, head north on Highway 97 to 61st Street, 9.1 miles, between mileposts 128 and 129, bearing right and staying on Highway 97 toward Redmond when Highway 20 splits to the left 2.5 miles north of Bend. Turn left and drive to Young Avenue, 1.1 miles. Turn left and go to 77th Street, 0.9 mile. Turn right and drive to the Petersen's entrance, 0.5 mile, on the right.

Comments: Elaborate works of art create a beautiful effect here. Peacocks and chickens roam freely. There are a rock shop and a display area.

270. Pine Mountain Observatory ••••••••••••••
University of Oregon, Friends of Pine Mountain Observatory; (503) 382-8331

    Type: Observatory
    Hours: Friday and Saturday, 9 P.M. to whenever from Memorial Day to Labor Day; weekdays by appointment

Fee: No; donation requested

Driving Instructions: Pine Mountain Observatory is 32.7 miles southeast of Bend. From the joining of Highways 20 and 97 in Bend, head east on Highway 20 to the observatory turnoff, just past Millican, 24.6 miles, between mileposts 26 and 27. Turn right, onto gravel, and drive to parking near the observatory, 8.1 miles.

Comments: A volunteer group gives tours of this research facility of the University of Oregon. Watching astronomy presentations and viewing through three large telescopes are engaging activities. A no-fee Deschutes National Forest campground adjoins the observatory.

271. Smith Rock Park •
State Park

> **Type:** Scenic location
> **Hours:** Daily
> **Fee:** Yes, during summer

Driving Instructions: Smith Rock Park is 26.0 miles north of Bend. From the joining of Highways 20 and 97 in Bend, head north on Highway 97 to "B" Avenue, Smith Rock Way, in Terrebonne, 22.7 miles, between mileposts 115 and 116, bearing right and staying on Highway 97 toward Redmond when Highway 20 splits to the left 2.5 miles north of Bend. Turn right and go to 1st Street (which becomes Wilcox Avenue), 0.6 mile. Turn left and proceed to Crooked River Drive, 2.0 miles. Turn left and drive to the park, 0.7 mile (the park may not be signed at Crooked River Drive; there is a sign that says JUNIPER JUNCTION).

Hiking Instructions: A hike down to the river is almost a must in this state park. The trail is easy to find from the parking area.

Comments: A beautiful canyon was created where the Crooked River cut through colorful volcanic sediments. Though a favorite spot for serious rock climbers, this is not much of a place to swim.

Hood River County
(County Seat: Hood River)

The river from which the county takes its name is a disappointment for swimming: it is too shallow. But there is consolation in the nice places that the county does provide. Driving instructions begin in Hood River at I-84 Exit 63, the exit for City Center.

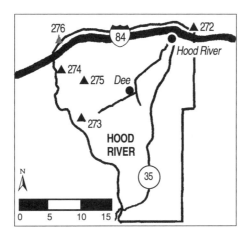

Hood River County Swimming Holes

272. Koberg Beach on Columbia River
273. Lost Lake
274. Punch Bowl Falls on Eagle Creek
275. Wahtum Lake

Hood River County Point of Interest

276. Sternwheeler Tours

Hood River County Swimming Holes

272. Koberg Beach on Columbia River • • • • • • • •

Rating: 7
Location: State Park
Water quality: Fair; 6′ transparency
Vital statistics: 0.6 mile wide; at least 43′ deep; light current; 73° F (August); moderate bottom weeds; gravel bottom; moderate use
Setting: Wooded valley at 120′; moderate litter

Swim skill: Moderate
Amenities: Drinking water; flush toilets
Entry fee: No
Topo: White Salmon 7½'

Driving Instructions: Koberg Beach is 10.2 miles east of Hood River. From I-84 Exit 63 in Hood River, head east on I-84 to Exit 69, the exit for Mosier, 5.6 miles, between mileposts 69 and 70. Take the exit and go to a stop, 0.2 mile. Turn left and drive to the entrance for the freeway heading west, 0.2 mile. Drive on I-84, to the Koberg Beach and Rest Area exit, 4.0 miles, at milepost 66. Go to parking, 0.2 mile.

Hiking Instructions: Access to the beach is by trail from the downriver end of parking, 250 feet. Watch for poison oak.

Comments: A 180-foot sand-and-gravel beach lies along the Columbia, adjacent to high rock cliffs upriver. This is a somewhat protected cove area. The freeway can be heard, but the place is still very pleasant.

273. Lost Lake •

Rating: 6
Location: Mount Hood National Forest
Water quality: Excellent; 40' transparency
Vital statistics: 231 acres; 175' deep; 65° F (August); light algae; silt bottom; moderate to heavy use
Setting: Forested foothills at 3143'; light litter
Swim skill: Moderate
Amenities: For-fee camping; drinking water; pit toilets
Entry fee: No
Topo: Bull Run Lake 7½'

Driving Instructions: Lost Lake is 26.9 miles southwest of Hood River. From I-84 Exit 63 in Hood River, head south on the freeway connector street to Oak Street, 0.1 mile. Turn right and go to 13th Street, at a flashing yellow light, 0.6 mile. Turn left onto 13th Street (which successively becomes 12th Street, Tucker Road and Hood River Highway) and drive to the turnoff for Dee and Lost Lake, 11.5 miles, between mileposts 11 and 12 (turn left at 3.1 miles to stay on the main road). Turn right and go to a fork in the road, 0.2 mile. Bear left onto Lost Lake Road, which becomes Forest Road 13, and drive to a stop sign at the lake, 14.4 miles. Turn right and go to parking, 0.1 mile.

Comments: Though complete with a large campground and resort which together cause the lake to be crowded, this is still a pleasant place to be, with a nice view of Mount Hood. Occasional small gravel openings to the water are along the trail that circles the lake.

274. Punch Bowl Falls on Eagle Creek ••••••••

Rating: 7
Location: Mount Hood National Forest
Water quality: Excellent; transparent to bottom
Vital statistics: 130' wide; at least 15' deep; moderate current; 63° F (August); light algae; pebble bottom; heavy use
Setting: Forested valley at 400'; light litter
Swim skill: Strong
Amenities: For-fee camping near trailhead; drinking water at trailhead; flush toilets at trailhead
Entry fee: No
Topo: Tanner Butte 7½'

Driving Instructions: Punch Bowl Falls is 26.0 miles west of Hood River. From I-84 Exit 63 in Hood River, head west on I-84 to Exit 40, the exit for Bonneville Dam, 23.5 miles. Take the exit to a stop, 0.3 mile. Turn left and drive under the freeway and back onto I-84, heading east, 0.2 mile. Drive to Exit 41, the exit for Eagle Creek Recreation Area, 1.2 miles, between mileposts 41 and 42. Take Exit 41 and go to a stop sign, 0.3 mile. Turn right and follow signs to parking at the trailhead, 0.5 mile. (See detail map on next page.)

To get back on the freeway heading west, head east to Exit 44, where you can leave the freeway and then reenter it heading in the opposite direction, 1.7 miles.

Hiking Instructions: The trailhead is at the upstream end of the parking area. Hike to the point where the Lower Punch Bowl Falls trail forks to the right, 1.7 miles. (From here, it is a short way on the main trail to the overlook of Punch Bowl Falls, 0.2 mile.) Take the Lower Punch Bowl Falls trail down into the canyon to the lower falls, 0.2 mile. Beyond the lower falls, walk upstream 300 feet over the pebbles that line the bank to get to a clear view of Punch Bowl Falls. The trail is easy and wide, with dramatic vistas.

Comments: In the Columbia Wilderness, Punch Bowl Falls is a vision of loveliness. Lower Punch Bowl Falls, 11 feet high, is downstream. Eagle Creek courses through a channel between the pools of the two falls. The pool below Punch Bowl Falls is encircled by sheer rock walls which create the cauldron into which the falls majestically plunge. No other falls in Oregon, with perhaps the exception of Toketee Falls (Point of Interest #228), matches the raw beauty of Punch Bowl Falls. To get to the base of the falls one must actually swim the channel upstream. The water becomes shallow at the entry into the cauldron, with the pile-up of pebbles and large rocks, then drops off again. There is considerable turbulence near the falls. This is no place for any but the most experienced swimmer. Here there is an awesome exhilaration. For a less formidable swim, Lower Punch Bowl

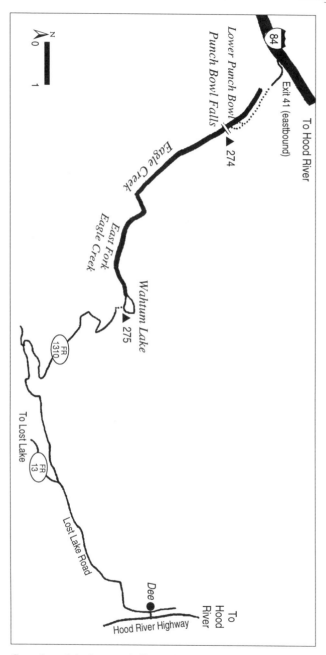

is just fine, though its bottom is littered with beer cans. It is a bit tricky to get to over the rocks. Care is required. The whole scene through the Eagle Creek Gorge is spectacular. A profusion of fern and Oregon grape dominates the forest floor.

275. Wahtum Lake •••••••••••••••••••••

         Rating: 6
      Location: Mount Hood National Forest
   Water quality: Excellent; 35′ transparency
   Vital statistics: 62 acres; 184′ deep; 70° F (August); moderate shore-
                line weeds; rock and gravel bottom; moderate use
        Setting: Forested foothills at 3732′; light litter
    Swim skill: Moderate
    Amenities: No-fee camping; no drinking water; pit toilets
    Entry fee: No
        Topo: Wahtum Lake 7½′

Driving Instructions: Wahtum Lake is 27.6 miles southwest of Hood River. Follow the driving instructions for Swimming Hole #273 onto Lost Lake Road/Forest Road 13 and drive to a fork in the road, 4.9 miles. Bear right and go to Forest Road 1310, 4.4 miles. Bear right and proceed to the campground at Wahtum Lake, 5.9 miles. (See detail map for Swimming Hole #274.)

    Hiking Instructions: From parking next to the campground, take the steep trail down to the lake, 0.2 mile.

    Comments: The lake is in the Columbia Wilderness. There are small gravel pockets providing entry to the water along an otherwise brushy shoreline.

Hood River County Point of Interest

276. Sternwheeler Tours •••••••••••••••••••
   Cascade Locks; (503) 374-8427

        Type: Boat ride
     Hours: Mid-June through most of September
        Fee: Yes

Driving Instructions: Sternwheeler Tours is 20.0 miles west of Hood River. From I-84 Exit 63 in Hood River, head west on I-84 to Exit 44, the exit for Cascade Locks, 18.6 miles. Take the exit onto Wanapa Street and drive to the sternwheeler turnoff, 1.1 miles. Turn right, bear right after an underpass and proceed to parking, 0.3 mile.

    Comments: The sternwheeler "Columbia Gorge" cruises the Columbia River. Along the way, passengers are treated to splendid scenery and to historic tales of the river.

Jefferson County
(County Seat: Madras)

Jefferson County has some nice lakes to choose from. Driving instructions begin in Madras at the intersection of Highways 26 and 97 (4th Street, heading south; 5th Street, heading north) with "D" Street.

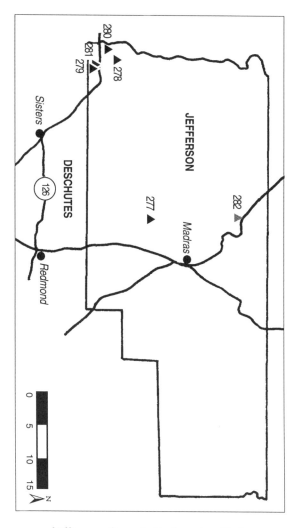

Jefferson County Swimming Holes

277. Cove Palisades Park on Lake Billy Chinook
278. Round Lake

279. Scout Lake
280. Square Lake
281. Suttle Lake

Jefferson County Point of Interest

282. The Museum at Warm Springs

Jefferson County Swimming Holes

277. Cove Palisades Park on Lake Billy Chinook • •

        Rating: 5
     Location: State Park
  Water quality: Good; 15′ transparency
   Vital statistics: 3916 acres; 415′ deep; 77° F (August); moderate to
               heavy suspended algae; sand and boulder bottom;
               heavy use
       Setting: Scrub desert at 1945′; light to moderate litter
    Swim skill: Moderate
   Amenities: For-fee camping nearby; drinking water; flush toilets
    Entry fee: Yes, during summer
        Topo: Round Butte Dam 7½′

Driving Instructions: Cove Palisades Park is 12.0 miles southwest of
Madras. From the intersection of Highways 26 and 97 and "D" Street in
Madras, head southwest on "D" Street (which becomes Culver Highway),
following signs for The Cove, to Gem Lane, 7.7 miles, between mileposts
7 and 8. Turn right, continue following signs for The Cove State Park
through turns onto Frazier Drive and Peck Road, and drive down a steep
incline to day-use parking on the Crooked River arm of the lake, 4.3 miles.
The turnoff to another day-use area on the Deschutes River arm is beyond,
clockwise around the lake, 3.5 miles. Turn right and find parking, 0.5 mile.

Comments: There are stretches of sandy beach, set in juniper and
sage and marked for swimming. For a reservoir, these are okay places
despite the crowds and the noise and smell of boats. The Crooked River
Petroglyph is 0.2 mile before reaching the Deschutes River arm turnoff.

278. Round Lake •

        Rating: 6
     Location: Deschutes National Forest
  Water quality: Excellent; transparent to bottom
   Vital statistics: 0.3 mile wide; at least 25′ deep; 73° F (August); light
               shoreline weeds; sand and silt bottom; light to moder-
               ate use

Setting: Forested foothills at 4285'; light litter
Swim skill: Low to moderate
Amenities: No-fee camping; no drinking water; pit toilets
Entry fee: No
Topo: Three Fingered Jack 7½'

Driving Instructions: Round Lake is 64.5 miles southwest of Madras. From the intersection of Highways 26 and 97 and "D" Street in Madras, head south on Highway 97 to Highway 126 in Redmond, about 26 miles. Turn right and drive to Highway 20, 19.0 miles. Continue onto Highway 20 through Sisters to Jack Lake Road/Forest Road 12, 12.8 miles, between mileposts 88 and 89. Turn right and go to the second turnoff for Forest Road 1210, 1.1 miles. Turn left and drive to the end of the pavement, 0.2 mile. Proceed on gravel to the lake campground turnoff, 5.4 miles. Turn right and go to the lake, 0.1 mile. (See detail map.)

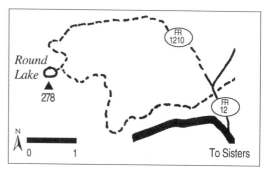

Comments: With Three Fingered Jack on the horizon, this lake provides a good, packed-sand entry from the campground. Much of the rest of the shoreline is brushy, with some log fall.

279. Scout Lake •

Rating: 8
Location: Deschutes National Forest
Water quality: Excellent; 19' transparency
Vital statistics: 8 acres; 34' deep; 74° F (August); light bottom weeds; gravel and silt bottom; moderate to heavy use
Setting: Forested foothills at 3650'; light to moderate litter
Swim skill: Low to moderate
Amenities: For-fee camping; drinking water; pit toilets
Entry fee: No
Topo: Black Butte 7½'

Driving Instructions: Scout Lake is 60.8 miles southwest of Madras. Follow the driving instructions for Swimming Hole #278 onto Highway 20. Continue through Sisters to the turnoff for Suttle Lake and Forest Road 2070, 13.8 miles, between mileposts 87 and 88. Turn left and go to Forest

Road 2066, 1.3 miles. Turn left and drive to parking at the junction with the lake road, 0.7 mile. (See detail map.)

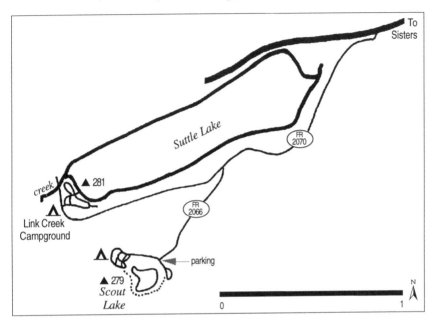

Comments: This lake is dedicated to swimming. It is apparently the only one in Oregon accorded that treatment. It is a very acceptable lake, too, in a pleasant setting. Two-thirds of the shoreline is gravel beach. Wouldn't it be nice for a few more lakes to be wrested from the blast of motors, to put swimming on a par with motorboating?

280. Square Lake ●

Rating:	6
Location:	Deschutes National Forest
Water quality:	Excellent; transparent to bottom
Vital statistics:	0.4 mile wide; at least 8' deep; 66° F (August); moderate shoreline weeds; sand and silt bottom; light use
Setting:	Forested mountains at 4800'; light litter
Swim skill:	Moderate
Amenities:	No-fee, primitive camping; no drinking water
Entry fee:	No
Topo:	Three Fingered Jack 7½'

Driving Instructions: Square Lake is 66.1 miles southwest of Madras. Follow the driving instructions for Swimming Hole #278 onto Highway

20. Continue through Sisters to a Pacific Crest Trail turnoff at Santiam Pass, 20.7 miles, between mileposts 80 and 81. Turn right and go to parking at the trailhead, 0.4 mile. (See detail map.)

Hiking Instructions: Heading north on the Pacific Crest Trail, hike to the Square Lake turnoff, 0.2 mile. Turn right and hike on an easy-to-moderate trail to a couple of large boulders where the trail splits, 1.6 miles. Three Fingered Jack can be seen in the distance. Bear right at this split and walk downhill to the lake, 0.2 mile. Go counterclockwise to a beach spot, less than 0.1 mile.

Comments: The lake has a pretty view and some nice sand spots. The dark sand is hard-packed and gives a good entry to the lake.

281. Suttle Lake ••••••••••••••••••••••••

Rating: 5
Location: Deschutes National Forest
Water quality: Good; 10′ transparency
Vital statistics: 253 acres; 75′ deep; 70° F (August); moderate shore-line and bottom weeds; gravel bottom; heavy use
Setting: Forested foothills at 3438′; light litter
Swim skill: Moderate
Amenities: For-fee camping; drinking water; pit toilets
Entry fee: No
Topos: Black Butte and Three Fingered Jack 7½′

Driving Instructions: Suttle Lake is 61.2 miles southwest of Madras. Follow the driving instructions for Swimming Hole #278 onto Highway 20. Continue through Sisters to the turnoff for Suttle Lake and Forest Road 2070, 13.8 miles, between mileposts 87 and 88. Turn left and go to the Link Creek Campground turnoff, 2.2 miles. Turn right and find Site 20, bearing left around the pay station, 0.2 mile. (See detail map for Swimming Hole #279.)

Hiking Instructions: The trail to the lake, 200 feet away, starts next to Site 20.

Comments: There is a narrow, 200-foot gravel beach. Buoys furnish some protection from the motorboats.

Jefferson County Point of Interest

282. The Museum at Warm Springs ••••••••••••
Warm Springs; (503) 553-3331

Type: Native American museum
Hours: Daily, 10 A.M. to 5 P.M.
Fee: Yes

Driving Instructions: The Museum at Warm Springs is 14.8 miles northwest of Madras. From the intersection of Highways 26 and 97 and "D" Street in Madras, head northwest on Highway 26 to the museum turnoff at Warm Springs, 14.8 miles (stay left when Highway 97 splits to the right at 0.4 mile), between mileposts 104 and 105, on the left.

Comments: Conceived and operated by The Confederated Tribes of the Warm Springs Reservation of Oregon, the museum houses a comprehensive, tribally owned artifact collection and presents a survey of the history and culture of the tribal groups represented on the reservation.

Klamath County
(County Seat: Klamath Falls)

Some of the most agreeable lakes are found in a cluster in the northwest corner of the county. All driving instructions begin in Klamath Falls at the intersection of Highway 97 and Main Street (Business Highway 97).

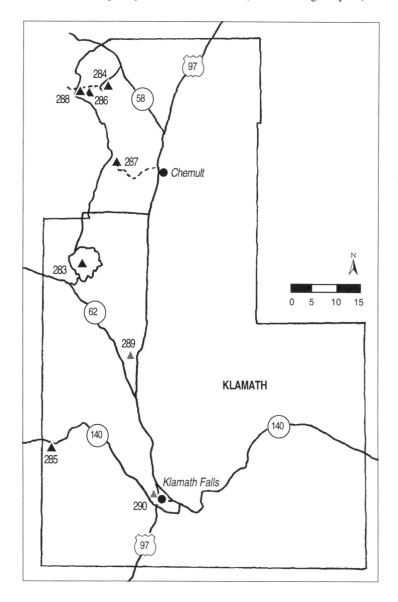

Klamath County Swimming Holes

283. Crater Lake National Park
284. Crescent Lake
285. Lake of the Woods
286. Meek Lake
287. Miller Lake
288. Summit Lake

Klamath County Points of Interest

289. Collier Park and Logging Museum
290. Favell Museum of Western Art and Indian Artifacts

Klamath County Swimming Holes

283. Crater Lake National Park • • • • • • • • • • • • •

Rating: 7
Location: National Park; (503) 594-2211
Water quality: Excellent; 95′ transparency
Vital statistics: 13,139 acres; 1932′ deep; 59 ° F (July); light algae; gravel and boulder bottom; heavy use
Setting: Forested mountains at 6178′; light litter
Swim skill: Strong
Amenities: For-fee camping; drinking water; pit and flush toilets
Entry fee: Yes
Topos: Crater Lake East and Crater Lake West 7½′

Driving Instructions: Crater Lake National Park is 60.1 miles north of Klamath Falls. From Highway 97 at Main Street in Klamath Falls, head north on Highway 97 to its junction with Highway 62 at the turnoff for Crater Lake, 23.6 miles, between mileposts 251 and 252. Turn left and drive to the park connector road, 29.8 miles. Turn right and go to Rim Drive, 6.7 miles. For a swim or, probably better, a boat ride at Cleetwood Cove, turn left and go to Rim Drive East, 6.0 miles. Bear right and continue clockwise around the lake to the turnoff for parking at the Cleetwood Cove trail, 4.6 miles.

Hiking Instructions: Descend steeply to the cove, 1.0 mile.

Comments: Here is Oregon's only national park and perhaps its loveliest place. The fanfare from Richard Strauss' *Also Sprach Zarathustra* would provide a brief, fitting backdrop on the approach to the rim. Crater Lake is the deepest lake in the United States. It is too cold and austere to be a really comfortable swimming hole (mean August temperature in 1991 was 61° F, with a high of 63° F). Snow often lingers well into July. However, the profoundly blue waters have a riveting attractiveness and the setting is unrivaled. As a spectacle, the lake is a "twenty" on a scale of one to ten! While the swimming is not that good, the temptation to swim may be irresistible. From June to September the visitor center and Sinnott Overlook are open from 8 A.M. to 7 P.M. and 9 A.M. to 6 P.M., respectively.

284. Crescent Lake ••••••••••••••••••••••

Rating: 10
Location: Deschutes National Forest
Water quality: Excellent; 43' transparency
Vital statistics: 4547 acres; 265' deep; 68° (August); moderate bottom weeds; sand bottom; moderate use
Setting: Forested mountains at 4839'; light litter
Swim skill: Moderate to strong
Amenities: No-fee camping; drinking water at two campgrounds; pit toilets
Entry fee: No
Topo: Crescent Lake 7½'

Driving Instructions: Crescent Lake is 99.5 miles north of Klamath Falls. From Highway 97 at Main Street in Klamath Falls, head north on Highway 97 to its junction with Highway 58, 80.3 miles. Turn onto Highway 58 and follow it to the turnoff for Crescent Lake, 17.0 miles, between mileposts 69 and 70. Turn left and travel to Forest Road 60, 2.2 miles. From this point, going either right or straight ahead leads to wonderful places. To the right leads to Tranquil Cove, 4.2 miles, and the turnoff to Contorta Point, 3.7 miles beyond Tranquil Cove (the last 2.6 miles to Contorta Point are on gravel). Along the way are Tandy Bay, the Windy-Oldenburg Lakes Trailhead and Spring Campground, where the paved road ends. Straight ahead leads to Simax Beach. Drive on a gravel road to a fork, 0.4 mile. Go left at the fork and travel to parking at Simax Beach, 0.5 mile. Extensions of the beach are 0.7 mile and 1.0 mile beyond, where the road ends. (See detail map on next page.)

Comments: With its gorgeously clear water, its marvelous beaches and its magnificent setting, Crescent Lake fulfills the meaning of exquisite. It is not perfect, though. It is a natural lake with a dam, and it suffers from deficient forest-management practices. 'Tis is a pity it cannot be a pristine place, free of development and motorboats. But in spite of all this, the lake manages to be exquisite. With Diamond Peak rising high to the west, the lake glows with beauty as a swimmer's paradise. At Tranquil Cove there is an almost tropical effect, with a small island (or peninsula, depending on the water level) just offshore. Both Simax Beach and the beach at Contorta Point are wide and long, composed of fine volcanic sand, and populated by sandpipers.

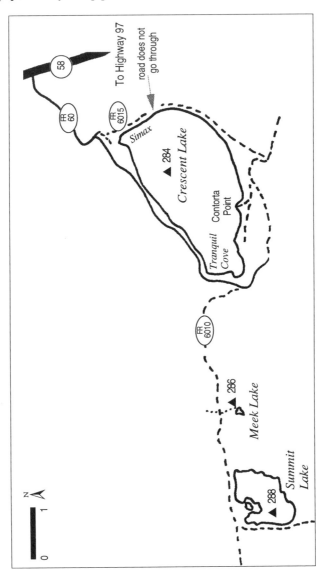

285. Lake of the Woods •

Rating: 6
Location: Winema National Forest
Water quality: Excellent; 28' transparency

Vital statistics:	1146 acres; 55′ deep; 73° F (August); light algae; sand bottom; heavy use
Setting:	Forested mountains at 4953′; light litter
Swim skill:	Low to moderate
Amenities:	For-fee camping; drinking water; flush toilets
Entry fee:	No
Topos:	Lake of the Woods North and Lake of the Woods South 7½′

Driving Instructions: Lake of the Woods is 35.4 miles northwest of Klamath Falls. From Highway 97 at Main Street in Klamath Falls, head south to the exit for Highways 66 and 140 and for Lake of the Woods, 1.9 miles, between mileposts 276 and 277. Take the exit and drive to the turnoff for Lake of the Woods and Highway 140, 0.4 mile. Turn right and drive to the Lake of the Woods turnoff, 32.5 miles, between mileposts 36 and 37. Turn left. There are roped swimming areas at Aspen Point (0.6 mile from the turnoff), Rainbow Bay (1.0 mile from the turnoff), and Sunset Campground (2.2 miles from the turnoff). All are on the right.

Comments: Despite the resort and motorboats, this is a very pretty lake. All the swimming spots are about the same, with a slight edge to Aspen Point. The banks are gravel and sand. Deep water is beyond the ropes.

286. Meek Lake ••••••••••••••••••••••••••

Rating:	8
Location:	Deschutes National Forest
Water quality:	Excellent; transparent to bottom
Vital statistics:	0.2 mile wide; at least 19′ deep; 69° F (July); light shoreline weeds; gravel, rock and silt bottom; light use
Setting:	Forested mountains at 5572′; light litter
Swim skill:	Low to moderate
Amenities:	No-fee, primitive camping; no drinking water
Entry fee:	No
Topo:	Cowhorn Mountain 7½′

Driving Instructions: Meek Lake is 108.4 miles north of Klamath Falls. Follow the driving instructions for Swimming Hole #284 to the Crescent Lake turnoff. Turn left and travel to Forest Road 60, 2.2 miles. Turn right and go to the Summit Lake turnoff, 5.0 miles. Turn right, onto Forest Road 6010, and go on a sand and dirt road to the trailhead for Meek and Snell lakes, 3.9 miles. (See detail map for Swimming Hole #286.)

Hiking Instructions: Take the trail to Meek Lake on the left-hand, 0.5 mile. Do not mistake a marshy lake along the trail for Meek Lake!

Comments: There is a marvelous rocky point where the trail comes to Meek Lake at the east end. The bank and entry are rock and sandy gravel. There is some log fall. The lake is in the Oregon Cascades Recreation Area.

287. Miller Lake ••••••••••••••••••••••••••••

Rating: 5
Location: Winema National Forest
Water quality: Excellent; over 9′ transparency
Vital statistics: 566 acres; 145′ deep; 61° F (June); light bottom and shoreline weeds; sand and silt bottom; moderate use
Setting: Forested mountains at 5630′; light to moderate litter
Swim skill: Moderate
Amenities: For-fee camping; drinking water; flush toilets
Entry fee: No
Topo: Miller Lake 7½′

Driving Instructions: Miller Lake is 85.2 miles north of Klamath Falls. From Highway 97 at Main Street in Klamath Falls, head north on Highway 97 to the Miller Lake turnoff, just past Chemult, 72.9 miles, between mileposts 202 and 203. Turn left, onto Forest Road 9772, and drive on gravel to the lake, 12.0 miles. To get to the marked-off swimming area at Digit Point, bear left past the boat launch and camping turnoffs, 0.3 mile (follow the picnic table signs).

Comments: The shore is sandy. There is a swimming platform.

288. Summit Lake ••••••••••••••••••••••••••••

Rating: 8
Location: Deschutes National Forest
Water quality: Excellent; 39′ transparency
Vital statistics: 482 acres; 63′ deep; 69° F (July); light shoreline weeds; sand, silt and bedrock bottom; light to moderate use
Setting: Forested mountains at 5553′; light litter
Swim skill: Low to moderate
Amenities: No-fee camping; no drinking water; pit toilets
Entry fee: No
Topo: Cowhorn Mountain 7½′

Driving Instructions: Summit Lake is 109.9 miles north of Klamath Falls. Follow the driving instructions for Swimming Hole #284 to the Crescent Lake turnoff. Turn left and travel to Forest Road 60, 2.2 miles. Turn right and go to the Summit Lake turnoff, 5.0 miles. Turn right, onto Forest Road 6010, and go on sand and dirt to the lake, 5.4 miles. (See detail map for Swimming Hole #284.)

Comments: The lake has a varied shoreline, worthy of exploration. A narrow 380-foot sand beach is 0.3 mile counterclockwise from the camping area first encountered. The lake is part of the Oregon Cascades Recreation Area.

Klamath County Points of Interest

289. Collier Park and Logging Museum • • • • • • • • •
State Park; (503) 783-2471

> **Type:** Logging museum
> **Hours:** Daily
> **Fee:** No

Driving Instructions: Collier Park and Logging Museum is 31.2 miles north of Klamath Falls. From Highway 97 at Main Street in Klamath Falls, head north on Highway 97 to the Collier Museum turnoff, 31.2 miles, between mileposts 244 and 245. Turn left.

Comments: While the expressed sentiments for logging and the pioneer spirit are a bit overblown, this outdoor museum is a good way to see historic logging implements, both huge and small. It also includes relocated pioneer buildings, down to the privies, in a pine and big-sage setting.

290. Favell Museum of Western Art • • • • • • • • • •
and Indian Artifacts
125 West Main Street, Klamath Falls; (503) 882-9996

> **Type:** History museum
> **Hours:** Monday through Saturday, 9:30 A.M. to 5:30 P.M.
> **Fee:** Yes

Driving Instructions: From Highway 97 at Main Street in Klamath Falls, drive west on Main Street to the museum, less than 0.1 mile, on the right.

Comments: Though lacking in interpretive power and sometimes highlighting the trivial, this museum holds one of the state's better displays of Native American items.

Sherman County
(County Seat: Moro)

Mostly, Sherman County raises grain—soft winter wheat and barley. There is not a lot to do, although a drive through miles and miles of rolling wheat fields is interesting. Good swimming holes are hard to find. Driving instructions begin in Moro at the intersection of Highway 97 and Main Street.

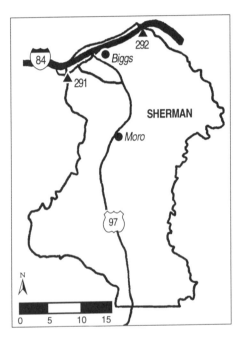

Sherman County Swimming Holes

291. Deschutes River Recreation Area
292. LePage Park on John Day River

Sherman County Swimming Holes

291. Deschutes River Recreation Area • • • • • • • •

Rating: 6
Location: State Park
Water quality: Fair; 4′ transparency
Vital statistics: 0.1 mile wide; at least 7′ deep; moderate current; 67° F (August); light algae; boulder and bedrock bottom; moderate use
Setting: Scrub valley at 200′; light litter

Swim skill: Moderate
Amenities: For-fee camping; drinking water; flush toilets
Entry fee: No
Topo: Wishram 7½′

Driving Instructions: Deschutes River Recreation Area is 20.8 miles northwest of Moro. From the intersection of Highway 97 and Main Street in Moro, head north on Highway 97 to its junction with Highway 206, 9.1 miles, between mileposts 8 and 9. Turn left and drive to the turnoff for the recreation area, 9.9 miles. Turn left and go to the park entrance, 1.6 miles. Turn left and go to parking, 0.2 mile. (Or take I-84 Exit 97 and follow signs to the park.)

Comments: The river here widens before its merger with the Columbia River. It is really best as a place to float, except for an area adjacent to a row of poplars in the camping area, where there is a decent hole. There are lots of shallows. The banks are generally grassy, with sand and rock at the water's edge. Despite considerable traffic noise, it is a nice freeway stop.

292. LePage Park on John Day River • • • • • • • • •

Rating: 5
Location: Army Corps of Engineers
Water quality: Fair; 4′ transparency
Vital statistics: 0.2 mile wide; at least 15′ deep; light current; 79° F (August); moderate to heavy algae and bottom weeds; gravel and rock bottom; heavy use
Setting: Scrub valley at 280′; light to moderate litter
Swim skill: Moderate
Amenities: No-fee, close-quarter camping; drinking water; flush toilets
Entry fee: No
Topo: Rufus 7½′

Driving Instructions: LePage Park is 28.4 miles north of Moro. From the intersection of Highway 97 and Main Street in Moro, head north on Highway 97 to the I-84 entrance at Biggs, approximately 18 miles. Enter I-84, heading east, to Exit 114, the exit for the John Day River Recreation Area, about 10 miles. Take the exit and go to the end of pavement, 0.3 mile. Following signs to the campground, drive on gravel to parking by the marked swim area, 0.1 mile.

Comments: This recreation site is on Lake Umatilla, the backwaters of the John Day Dam. The swim area, next to a gravel and sand beach, is okay for a quick cool-off stop. There is a swimming platform. Boat and freeway noise are constant, but acceptable.

Wasco County
(County Seat: The Dalles)

Wasco County is probably best known for the now-not-very-interesting site of the defunct Rancho Rajneesh, former home of the Bhagwan Shree Rajneesh, east of Antelope. Swimming holes are rare. Driving instructions begin in The Dalles at the intersection of I-84 and Highway 197.

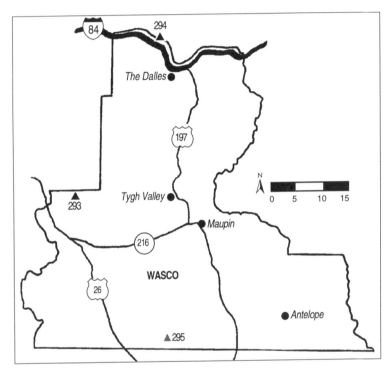

Wasco County Swimming Holes

293. Boulder Lake
294. West Mayer Park

Wasco County Point of Interest

295. Kahneeta Resort

Wasco County Swimming Holes

293. Boulder Lake ●

Rating: 5
Location: Mount Hood National Forest

Water quality: Excellent; transparent to bottom

Vital statistics: 340' wide; at least 15' deep; 63° F (July); moderate shoreline weeds; sand bottom; light use

Setting: Forested mountains at 4560; light litter

Swim skill: Moderate

Amenities: No-fee, primitive camping; no drinking water

Entry fee: No

Topo: Badger Lake 7½'

Driving Instructions: Boulder Lake is 57.0 miles southwest of The Dalles. From I-84 Exit 87 at the intersection with Highway 197 in The Dalles, head south on Highway 197 to the first Tygh Valley/Wamic turnoff, 28.4 miles, between mileposts 33 and 34. Turn right and go to Wamic Market Road, 0.4 mile. Turn right and drive to the Mount Hood National Forest boundary, 10.2 miles (bear left at a fork in Wamic, onto Rock Creek Dam Road, 5.5 miles along the way). Now on Forest Road 48, drive to Forest Road 4880, about 11.5 miles. Turn right and drive on gravel to a fork in the road, 2.4 miles. Bear right, still on Forest Road 4880, and drive to the trailhead for the lake, 4.1 miles, on the left. (See detail map.)

Hiking Instructions: The hike to the lake is on an easy, steadily ascending trail, 0.4 mile.

Comments: A high bluff, fronted by a huge rock fall, is on the side opposite the trail entry. The deep water is along that edge of the lake. There is some log fall.

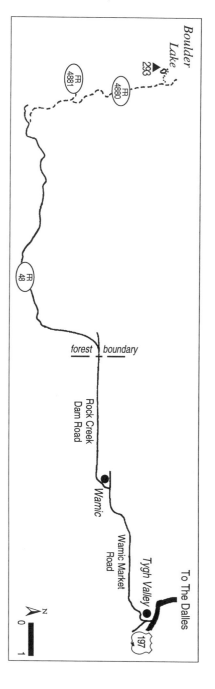

294. West Mayer Park ••••••••••••••••••••

Rating: 6
Location: State Park
Water quality: Fair; 3′ transparency
Vital statistics: 0.1 mile wide; at least 20′ deep; 79° F (August); light algae; sand and silt bottom; moderate use
Setting: Wooded valley at 120′; moderate litter
Swim skill: Low to moderate
Amenities: Drinking water; flush toilets
Entry fee: No
Topo: Lyle 7½′

Driving Instructions: West Mayer Park is 11.7 miles northwest of The Dalles. From I-84 Exit 87 at the intersection with Highway 197 in The Dalles, head west on I-84 to Exit 76, the exit for Mayer State Park and Rowena, 10.1 miles, between mileposts 76 and 77. Take the exit and go to Rowena R Road, 0.3 mile. Turn left and drive to a stop at Highway 30, 0.2 mile (avoid returning to the freeway). Turn right and drive to the park turnoff, 0.4 mile, at milepost 9. Turn right and proceed to the park entrance, 0.6 mile. Pass by the entrance, which is on the right, and park just beyond it at a gravel turnout on the left, 0.1 mile.

Hiking Instructions: An asphalt path leads from the turnout to the beach, 330 feet. Watch for poison oak.

Comments: There is a sandy beach beside a small lake. There is noise from both trains and the freeway.

Wasco County Point of Interest

295. Kahneeta Resort ••••••••••••••••••••••
Warm Springs Reservation; (503) 553-1112 or 1-800-831-0100

Type: Commercial hot springs
Hours: Daily, 10 A.M. to 7 P.M. (10 P.M. during the summer)
Fee: Yes

Driving Instructions: Kahneeta Resort is 70.4 miles south of The Dalles. From I-84 Exit 87 at the intersection with Highway 197 in The Dalles, head south on Highway 197 to Highway 216, heading west, 35.4 miles. Turn right and drive to Reservation Highway 3, 7.2 miles. Turn left and go to the resort turnoff, 26.4 miles, between mileposts 10 and 11. Turn left and proceed to an entry booth, 1.1 miles. Turn right alongside the booth, then turn to the right past it and proceed to a bridge crossing where the road curves back to pool parking, 0.3 mile.

Comments: Owned and operated by The Confederated Tribes of the Warm Springs Reservation of Oregon, the resort has a huge mineral-heated pool and saunas. The pool is maintained at 95° F.

Northeast

The Northeast contains the rugged, conifer-forested Wallowa and Blue mountains, the hill region of the Columbia River, and sage-covered desert. Swimming holes are far apart and generally require some travel on scenic backways. The remoteness of the land requires vigilance by the traveler. Oregon's only poisonous snake, the rattlesnake, is found east of the Cascades, though it generally makes itself scarce. There are ticks and hence the danger of Lyme disease, so take care to check body and clothing after jaunts. Folks in many rural parts of Eastern Oregon are "wavers": they wave at passersby—a friendly habit to be encouraged by waving back.

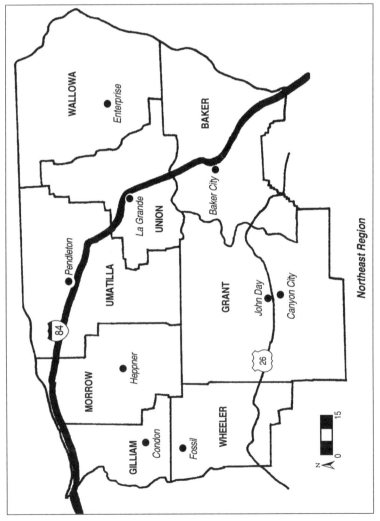

Baker County
(County Seat: Baker City)

Baker is the county with the state's most active gold mining and pioneer traditions. It also sports some decent places to swim. Driving instructions begin in Baker City at I-84 Exit 304, the freeway intersection with Highway 7/Campbell Street.

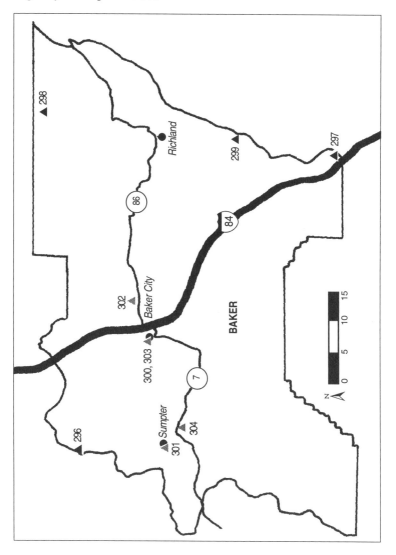

Baker County Swimming Holes

296. Anthony Lake
297. Farewell Bend Park on Snake River
298. Fish Lake
299. Snake River Turnouts

Baker County Points of Interest

300. Gold Display
301. Gold Dredge
302. National Historic Oregon Trail Interpretive Center
303. Oregon Trail Regional Museum
304. Sumpter Valley Railroad Steam Train

Baker County Swimming Holes

296. Anthony Lake •

Rating: 6
Location: Wallowa-Whitman National Forest
Water quality: Excellent; 18' transparency
Vital statistics: 22 acres; 32' deep; 61° F (July); moderate bottom and shoreline weeds; silt and rock bottom; moderate to heavy use
Setting: Forested mountains at 7131'; light litter
Swim. skills: Moderate
Amenities: For-fee camping; drinking water; pit toilets
Entry fee: No
Topo: Anthony Lake 7½'

Driving Instructions: Anthony Lake is 35.8 miles northwest of Baker City. From I-84 Exit 304 in Baker City, head west on Campbell Street to 10th Street/Highway 30, 1.5 miles. Turn right and drive to Elkhorn Drive in Haines, 10.3 miles, between mileposts 40 and 41. Turn left and go to the turnoff for the lake, 23.8 miles, between mileposts 9 and 10. Turn left and find picnic parking by the lake, 0.2 mile.

Comments: Outstanding views of the peaks of the Elkhorn Mountains, a sub-range of the Blue Mountains, are to the south. A profusion of granite boulders gleams along the shore. There is a charming irregularity to the lake shoreline. Clockwise around the lake there are boulders that provide good swimming access. The coolness of the water make this more a scenic masterpiece than a place for a lengthy swim. A trail circles the lake.

297. Farewell Bend Park on Snake River • • • • • • •

Rating: 5
Location: State Park
Water quality: Fair; 1' transparency
Vital statistics: 0.6 mile wide; at least 14' deep in roped area; light current; 72° F (July); light algae; gravel bottom; moderate to heavy use
Setting: Wooded valley at 2080'; light litter
Swim. skills: Moderate
Amenities: For-fee camping; drinking water; flush toilets
Entry fee: Yes, during summer
Topo: Olds Ferry 7½'

Driving Instructions: Farewell Bend Park is 50.0 miles southeast of Baker City. From I-84 Exit 304 in Baker City, head southeast to Exit 353, the exit for Farewell Bend, 48.7 miles. Exit and drive to a stop, 0.3 mile. Turn left and drive to the park turnoff, 1.0 mile. Turn right into the park.

Hiking Instructions: The swim area is a bit upstream from parking by the restrooms.

Comments: This is a place for a necessity stop only. There is a lot of boat and traffic noise. But the park is grassy and green, though the beach is covered with stones. The barrel-marked swim area is next to a split-rail fence.

298. Fish Lake •

Rating: 7
Location: Wallowa-Whitman National Forest
Water quality: Excellent; 16' transparency
Vital statistics: 67 acres; 49' deep; 64° F (July); light shoreline weeds; mud bottom; light to moderate use
Setting: Forested mountains at 6664'; light litter
Swim. skills: Moderate
Amenities: No-fee camping; drinking water; pit toilets
Entry fee: No
Topo: Deadman Point 7½'

Driving Instructions: Fish Lake is 74.2 miles northeast of Baker City. From I-84 Exit 304 in Baker City, head north on I-84 to Exit 302, the exit for Richland and Hells Canyon, 1.1 miles. Take the exit to a stop sign, 0.3 mile. Turn right onto Highway 86 and drive to the first turnoff for Halfway, 51.0 miles, between mileposts 53 and 54. Turn left and take this unmarked road which becomes Main Street through Halfway to unmarked Fish Lake

Road, 1.6 miles. Turn right and
drive to the end of the pavement,
3.4 miles. Turn left at this point
onto gravel, which becomes Forest Road 66, and drive to the Fish
Lake turnoff, 16.7 miles, at milepost 15. Along the way, bear right
at 4.1, 5.5, 6.1 and 10.3 miles; the
objective is to stay on the main
road, Forest Road 66. Turn left
and find parking at Site 2 of the
lake campground, 0.1 mile. (See
detail map, which does not show
all the side roads.)

Comments: This is an accessible natural lake with a dam. It
has a varied dirt and rock bank,
punctuated by granite boulders
strewn throughout the vicinity.
There are nice climbing outcrops.
Two islands make good swimming
objectives. There are occasional
stumps in the water.

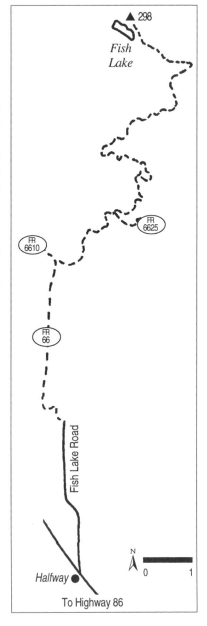

299. Snake River Turnouts • • • • • • • • • • • • • • • • •

Rating: 5
Location: Bureau of Land Management
Water quality: Fair; 5' transparency
Vital statistics: 0.6 mile wide; at least 19' deep; 71° F (July); light algae; gravel and rock bottom; light to moderate use
Setting: Scrub valley at 2120'; moderate litter
Swim. skills: Moderate
Amenities: No-fee, primitive camping at first spot, up a draw next to cove; no drinking water
Entry fee: No
Topos: Sturgill Creek and Conner Creek 7½'

Driving Instructions: Snake River Turnouts are 55.7 miles southeast of Baker City. From I-84 Exit 304 in Baker City, head north on I-84 to Exit 302, the exit for Richland and Hells Canyon, 1.1 miles. Take the exit to a stop sign, 0.3 mile. Turn right onto Highway 86 and drive to Richland at the intersection of First Street and Main Street, 39.7 miles, between mileposts 42 and 43. Turn right onto First Street, which becomes Snake River Road, and drive to the end of the pavement, 4.0 miles. Continue on gravel to a cove turnout, 10.6 miles (0.9 mile past Swede's Landing). A second reasonable cove turnout is beyond the first, 6.2 miles (0.1 mile after the road passes under a line of colored aircraft-warning balls).

Hiking Instructions: From the turnouts at both places the path down is steep.

Comments: Here on the backwaters of Brownlee Dam there is great openness among the sage and rabbitbrush. The first, larger cove has rock and gravel banks with some sand. The water is murky but quiet. At the second cove there is a powerline hum. Still, the place is nice, with a little wave action. The beach is gravel. Both places evoke a stark serenity.

Baker County Points of Interest

300. Gold Display •
U.S. Bank; Baker City; (503) 523-7791

Type: Mineral exhibit
Hours: Monday through Friday, 10 A.M. to 5 P.M.
Fee: No

Driving Instructions: From I-84 Exit 304 in Baker City, head west on Campbell Street to Main Street, 0.9 mile. Turn left and drive to Washington Street, 0.3 miles. Look for the U. S. Bank on the left. Park wherever parking spaces are available on the street.

Comments: The display is in the lobby. It is the largest display of gold in the state, including the 80.4-ounce Armstrong Nugget.

301. Gold Dredge ••••••••••••••••••••••••••
Sumpter

> **Type:** Historic site
> **Hours:** Daily
> **Fee:** No

Driving Instructions: Gold Dredge is 29.9 miles west of Baker City. From I-84 Exit 304 in Baker City, head west on Highway 7 to Main Street, 0.9 mile. Turn left, still on Highway 7, and drive to the turnoff for Sumpter, 26.2 miles, between mileposts 25 and 26 (follow signs for Sumpter and Highway 7 at the south end of Baker City). Turn right and go to the dredge, which is just past the town entry sign, 2.8 miles. Turn left into parking.

Comments: Sumpter Valley presents an illustration of prospecting gone amok. Dredge tailings, the piles of rock dug and left by the dredge, are throughout the valley (as well as tailings from other placer-mining operations). The dredge, which operated twenty-four hours daily from 1935 to 1954, is now closed to tours, but it is still possible to eyeball it and get an idea of its destructive power. Recently the dredge was purchased by the state to be converted into the centerpiece of a future state park.

302. National Historic Oregon Trail Interpretive Center
Bureau of Land Management; (503) 523-1843

> **Type:** History museum
> **Hours:** Daily, 9 A.M. to 4 P.M. (to 6 P.M. from May to September)
> **Fee:** No

Driving Instructions: National Historic Oregon Trail Interpretive Center is 7.3 miles northeast of Baker City. Follow the driving instructions for Swimming Hole #299 onto Highway 86 and drive up Flagstaff Hill, to the center turnoff, 5.0 miles, between mileposts 7 and 8. Turn left and go to parking, 0.9 mile.

Comments: The center is a tastefully done display, both graphic and oral, of the hardships of the westward migration of pioneers and of the forced mixing of cultural traditions.

303. Oregon Trail Regional Museum •••••••••••
2490 Grove Street, Baker City; (503) 523-9308

> **Type:** History museum
> **Hours:** Daily, 9 A.M. to 4 P.M. from mid-May-late October
> **Fee:** No; donation requested

Driving Instructions: From I-84 Exit 304 in Baker City, head west on Campbell Street to Grove Street, 0.7 mile. Turn left and park. The museum is immediately on the left.

Comments: Located in a natatorium that once housed an indoor swimming pool and dance floors, the museum emphasizes the pioneer roots of the region. It was a focal point of social interaction until it was filled with concrete and converted to use as an armory in response to the demands of World War II.

304. Sumpter Valley Railroad Steam Train • • • • • • •
Highway 7, Sumpter

Type: Train ride
Hours: Weekends and holidays, 11 A.M. to 5 P.M. from Memorial Day through the last weekend in September
Fee: Yes

Driving Instructions: Sumpter Valley Railroad Steam Train is 24.8 miles west of Baker City. From I-84 Exit 304 in Baker City, head west on Highway 7 to Main Street, 0.9 mile. Turn left, still on Highway 7, and drive to the turnoff for the Sumpter Valley Railroad Depot, 23.9 miles (follow signs for Sumpter and Highway 7 at the south end of Baker City), between mileposts 27 and 28. Turn left and then immediately right to parking.

Comments: Have a great ride through a comely valley, partly ruined by mining, on an old-fashioned train. Look for larch trees, a deciduous conifer, in the surrounding hills.

Gilliam County
(County Seat: Condon)

Swimming in Gilliam County is limited to a pleasing place next to the freeway. Driving instructions begin in Condon at the junction of Highways 19 and 206 (Walnut and Main).

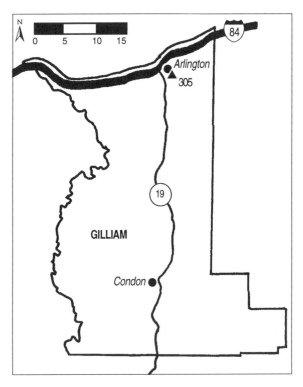

Gilliam County Swimming Hole

305. Arlington Park/Snell Memorial Park on Columbia River

Gilliam County Swimming Hole

305. Arlington Park/Snell Memorial Park •••••••
on Columbia River

           Rating: 6
       Location: Arlington City Park
  Water quality: Fair; 5′ transparency
 Vital statistics: 300′ wide; at least 15′ deep; 72° F (July); light algae; sand bottom; moderate use

Setting:	Scrub valley at 260'; light litter
Swim. skills:	Low to moderate
Amenities:	Drinking water; flush toilets
Entry fee:	No
Topo:	Arlington 7½'

Driving Instructions: Arlington Park/Snell Memorial Park is 38.0 miles north of Condon. From Condon at the junction of Highways 19 and 206, head north on Highway 19 to a stop sign at Cottonwood Street in Arlington, 37.8 miles. Turn right and drive to another stop, 0.2 mile. Turn left and then immediately right into parking next to the park. (Or take Exit 137, the I-84 exit for Arlington.)

Comments: This lagoon is a backwater of Umatilla Lake on the Columbia River. It is next to the freeway, so it is noisy. The swimming area is adjacent to a 200-foot sandy beach. The rest of the park, back from the sand, is grass.

Grant County
(County Seat: Canyon City)

Well-used but acceptable places to cool off are the rule in Grant County.
All driving instructions begin in Canyon City on Highway 395, adjacent
to the city hall and park.

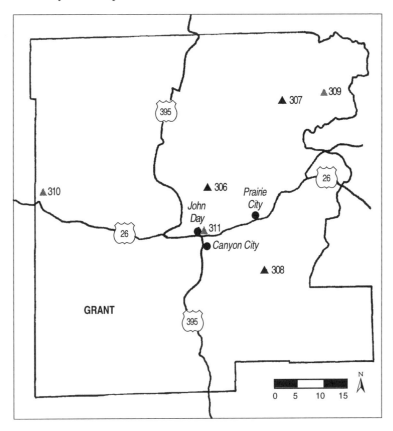

Grant County Swimming Holes

306. Magone Lake
307. Olive Lake
308. Strawberry Lake

Grant County Points of Interest

309. Granite
310. John Day Fossil Beds National Monument
311. Kam Wah Chung and Company Museum

Grant County Swimming Holes

306. Magone Lake •••••••••••••••••••••••

Rating:	6
Location:	Malheur National Forest
Water quality:	Good; 15′ transparency
Vital statistics:	30 acres; 98′ deep; 66° F (July); heavy bottom weeds; sand and silt bottom; heavy use
Setting:	Forested mountains at 4990′; light litter
Swim. skills:	Low to moderate
Amenities:	For-fee camping; drinking water; pit toilets
Entry fee:	No
Topo:	Magone Lake 7½′

Driving Instructions: Magone Lake is 26.8 miles north of Canyon City. From Highway 395, adjacent to the city hall and park in Canyon City, head north on Highway 395 to John Day at Highway 26, 2.0 miles. Turn right, heading east, and drive to Bear Creek Road, 9.5 miles, between mileposts 171 and 172. Turn left and drive to the end of the pavement at Four Corners, 9.7 miles. Continue straight, on gravel, to Forest Road 3620, 2.8 miles. Turn left and go to the junction with Forest Road 3618, 1.4 miles. Bear right and drive to the lake entrance sign, 0.8 mile. From there, follow open-air picnic table and swimming signs to parking by the beach, 0.6 mile. (See detail map on next page.)

Comments: A 190-foot beach has been created with hauled-in sand and gravel. The rest of the shoreline has a number of fallen logs and is composed of dirt.

307. Olive Lake •••••••••••••••••••••••••

Rating:	6
Location:	Umatilla National Forest
Water quality:	Excellent; 24′ transparency
Vital statistics:	153 acres; 90′ deep; 64° F (July); light algae; rock and silt bottom; moderate use
Setting:	Forested mountains at 5999′; light litter
Swim. skills:	Moderate
Amenities:	No-fee camping; drinking water; pit toilets
Entry fee:	No
Topo:	Olive Lake 7½′

Driving Instructions: Olive Lake is 88.0 miles northeast of Canyon City. Follow the driving instructions for Swimming Hole #306 onto Highway 26, heading east, and drive to its junction with Highway 7, 28.6

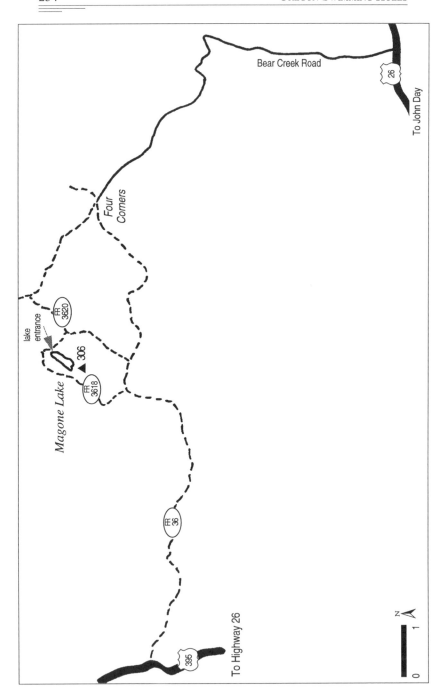

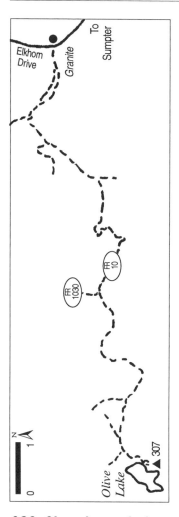

miles, between mileposts 190 and 191. Turn left and drive to the Sumpter turnoff, 25.1 miles. Turn left, onto Elkhorn Drive, and go to the junction at Granite with Forest Road 10, 19.4 miles. Turn left and drive on gravel to the Olive Lake turnoff, 12.0 miles (stay straight at 1.5 miles). Turn left and then bear left to parking above the lake, 0.9 mile. (See detail map.)

Hiking Instructions: It is a short climb down to the lake from the parking area.

Comments: This natural lake with a dam is not flashy but is comfortable and accessible. The shoreline is unremarkable rock and dirt. There are a few stumps. A small island is at the northeast end of the lake, near the boat ramp.

308. Strawberry Lake •

Rating:	7
Location:	Malheur National Forest
Water quality:	Good; 12′ transparency
Vital statistics:	36 acres; 27′ deep; 65° F (July); moderate to heavy bottom weeds; silt and mud bottom; moderate use
Setting:	Forested mountains at 6263′; light litter
Swim. skills:	Moderate
Amenities:	No-fee camping; drinking water; pit toilets—all at trailhead

Entry fee: No
Topo: Strawberry Mountain 7½'

Driving Instructions:
Strawberry Lake is 26.9 miles
southeast of Canyon City. Follow the driving instructions for Swimming Hole #306 onto Highway 26, heading east, and drive to Main Street in Prairie City, 13.2 miles. Turn right and go to Bridge Street, 0.4 mile. Curve to the left, then immediately turn right onto Strawberry Road (which becomes Forest Road 6001) and drive to the end of the pavement, 3.2 miles. Continue on gravel to where the road deteriorates badly, 5.5 miles. The last stretch of the route to parking at the lake trailhead (near a campground) is on horrendous gravel, 2.6 miles. (See detail map.)

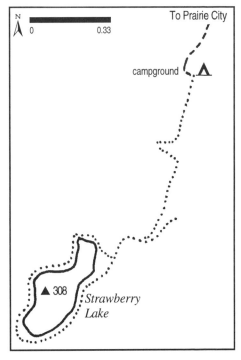

Hiking Instructions: It is a gradually ascending hike to the lake on a well-worn path, 1.4 miles.

Comments: This place, in the Strawberry Mountain Wilderness, is scenic. But as a place to swim, it may vary, depending on the water level. When the level is low there may be a tall, thick carpeting of aquatic weeds on much of the lake floor. When the level is high, the weeds pretty much die out. A good place for a rapid drop to depth is 0.3 mile clockwise around the lake at a rock outcrop. Between the outcrop and the trail entry are a couple of reasonable dirt/coarse sand beaches. A trail circles the lake.

Grant County Points of Interest

309. Granite •
Elkhorn Drive

Type: Historic town
Hours: Daily
Fee: No

Driving Instructions: Granite is 75.1 miles northeast of Canyon City. Follow the driving instructions for Swimming Hole #306 onto Highway 26, heading east, and continue as for Swimming Hole #307 to the Elkhorn Drive/Forest Road 10 junction. Turn right into the townsite.

Comments: Built shortly after gold was discovered in 1862, several historic community buildings have weathered a lot. They are identified by function.

310. John Day Fossil Beds National Monument • • •
National Park Service; (503) 575-0721

> **Type:** Geologic site
> **Hours:** Daily; the visitor center is open Monday through Friday, 8 A.M. to 4 P.M.
> **Fee:** No

Driving Instructions: John Day Fossil Beds National Monument is 42.3 miles west of Canyon City. Follow the driving instructions for Swimming Hole #306 to Highway 26, turn left, heading west, and drive to the turnoff for the Fossil Beds and Highway 19, 38.2 miles, between mileposts 124 and 125. Turn right and go to the Cant Ranch Visitor's Center in the Sheep Rock Unit, 2.1 miles, between mileposts 121 and 122, on the right.

Comments: Cant Ranch Visitor's Center is the main information center in the monument. There is a nice exhibit of fossils, and nearby Sheep Rock is interesting. The layered, colorful sediments and eroded formations are sights to behold. (See Point of Interest #325 for the Painted Hills and Clarno units in Wheeler County.)

311. Kam Wah Chung and Company Museum • • •
Northwest Canton Street, John Day; (503) 575-0028

> **Type:** Historic site
> **Hours:** Monday through Thursday, 9 A.M. to noon and 1–5 P.M.; Saturday and Sunday, 1–5 P.M.; open from May 1 to October 31
> **Fee:** Yes

Driving Instructions: Kam Wah Chung and Company Museum is 2.3 miles north of Canyon City. Follow the driving instructions for Swimming Hole #306 to Highway 26, turn left, heading west, and drive to Canton Street, 0.2 mile. Turn right and then bear left to parking, 0.1 mile.

Comments: This museum celebrates the contribution of the Chinese who worked the region's gold mines during the late 1800s.

Morrow County
(County Seat: Heppner)

Morrow County can be hot and dry, but the Columbia River furnishes pleasant relief. Driving instructions begin in Heppner at the joining of Highways 207 and 74.

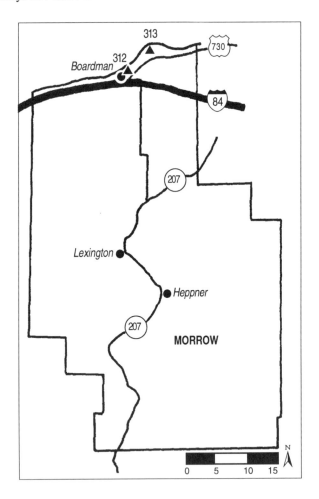

Morrow County Swimming Holes

312. Boardman Park on Columbia River
313. Umatilla National Wildlife Refuge on Columbia River

Morrow County Swimming Holes

312. Boardman Park on Columbia River ●●●●●●●

Rating: 6
Location: Boardman City Park and Army Corp of Engineers
Water quality: Fair; 5′ transparency
Vital statistics: 0.4 mile wide; at least 12′ deep; 70° F (July); moderate algae and bottom weeds; sand and pebble bottom; moderate use
Setting: Scrub valley at 270′; light litter
Swim. skills: Low to moderate
Amenities: For-fee camping; drinking water; flush toilets
Entry fee: No
Topo: Boardman 7½′

Driving Instructions: Boardman Park is 44.4 miles north of Heppner. From the joining of Highways 207 and 74 in Heppner, head northwest on Highways 207 and 74 to Lexington, where the highways split, 9.4 miles. Turn off to the right, staying on Highway 207 when Highway 74 splits away, and drive to the Boardman turnoff, 9.9 miles. Turn left and drive to a stop sign at I-84, the Exit 168 interchange, 19.7 miles. Turn right and drive to the freeway entrance, 0.2 mile. Get on I-84, heading west, and drive to Exit 164, the exit for Boardman, 3.9 miles, between mileposts 164 and 165. Take the exit and go to a stop, 0.3 mile. Turn right and head toward the river to another stop sign, 0.7 mile. Follow the swimming sign straight ahead, 0.1 mile. Then bear left, following another swimming sign to parking, 0.2 mile.

Comments: This is a cooperative City of Boardman and Army Corps of Engineers park on Lake Umatilla, the upper Columbia River backwaters of the John Day Dam. The park has a large grassy bank next to a 275-foot sandy beach. Two swimming areas are roped, both with docks. There is a playground. Boat and freeway noises are a bother.

313. Umatilla National Wildlife Refuge ●●●●●●●●● on Columbia River

Rating: 7
Location: National Wildlife Refuge; (503) 922-3232
Water quality: Fair; 4′ transparency
Vital statistics: 2.2 miles wide; at least 8′ deep; 80° F (July); light bottom weeds; sand bottom; light use
Setting: Wooded valley at 270′; moderate litter

Swim. skills: Moderate
Amenities: Drinking water; pit toilets—both at information display
Entry fee: No
Topo: Paterson 7½'

Driving Instructions: Umatilla National Wildlife Refuge is 48.0 miles north of Heppner. Follow the driving instructions for Swimming Hole #312 to the Exit 168 interchange, 19.7 miles. Turn right onto Highway 730, crossing under the freeway, and drive to Paterson Ferry Road, 4.0 miles, between mileposts 171 and 172. Turn left and go to the refuge information display, on the left, 1.8 miles. Continue beyond the information display to the turnoff

for Parking Area M, 0.9 mile. Turn left and drive on gravel to Parking Area M, 2.3 miles. (See detail map.)

Hiking Instructions: The trail to take is past the gate alongside the parking lot, next to water on both sides. It is 420 feet to the point where a tree line along the slough to the right is passed. At times there seems to be a trail system which allows following the tree line. At other times, trails are virtually nonexistent. On those occasions, backtrack and follow the bank of the slough to the river. In any event, the objective is to arrive at a beach spot at the end of the tree line, less than 0.2 mile.

Comments: On the backwaters of Lake Umatilla, the refuge in this locale is scrub-covered sand dunes. Try to stay on the paths in order to avoid getting scratched up and getting spiked grass seeds in clothing. The beach is sand and pebbles. It is a long way to deep water. The journey out to depth gives an arousing and solitary sense of being surrounded by water and far from shore. This part of the refuge is open from July 1 to September 30.

Umatilla County
(County Seat: Pendleton)

There is an interesting cowboy tradition to be discovered in the Pendleton area, along with perhaps the best swimming spot on the Columbia River. Driving instructions begin in Pendleton at the intersection of Main Street and Highway 30 (Court Avenue, heading west; Dorion Avenue, heading east).

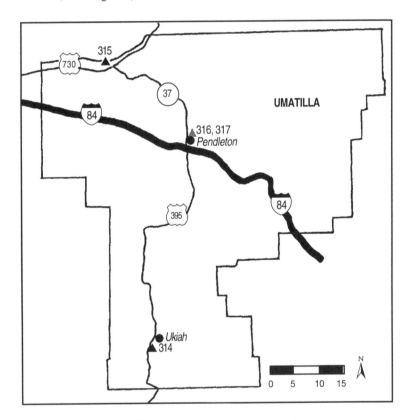

Umatilla County Swimming Holes

314. Camas Creek
315. Warehouse Beach on Columbia River

Umatilla County Points of Interest

316. Pendleton Underground
317. Pendleton Woolen Mills

Umatilla County Swimming Holes

314. Camas Creek •

Rating: 5
Location: Private
Water quality: Good; transparent to bottom
Vital statistics: 60' wide; at least 8' deep; 67° F (July); light algae; bedrock and gravel bottom; light to moderate use
Setting: Wooded valley at 3240'; moderate to heavy litter
Swim. skills: Moderate
Amenities: None
Entry fee: No
Topo: Bridge Creek 7½'

Driving Instructions: Camas Creek is 51.4 miles south of Pendleton. From the intersection of Main Street and Highway 30 in Pendleton, head southeast on Main Street to Emigrant Avenue, 0.1 mile. Turn right onto Emigrant Avenue, which becomes Highway 395, and go to I-84 at Exit 209, 1.1 miles. Proceed past the freeway and drive to Highway 244, 47.9 miles. Continue straight on Highway 395 to a large turnout on the left, 2.3 miles, between mileposts 51 and 52.

Hiking Instructions: Look for the pool over the bank from the turnout and locate the short, well-used trail down to the creek.

Comments: The water is sometimes burdened with a little foam. There is a nice gravel beach, and rock formations are on the opposite bank.

315. Warehouse Beach on Columbia River • • • • •

Rating: 9
Location: Army Corp of Engineers
Water quality: Fair; 4' transparency
Vital statistics: 1.2 miles wide; at least 18' deep; light current; 71° F (July); light algae; sand bottom; heavy use
Setting: Scrub valley at 340'; moderate to heavy litter
Swim. skills: Low to moderate
Amenities: No-fee, primitive camping; no drinking water; pit toilets
Entry fee: No
Topo: Hat Rock 7½'

Driving Instructions: Warehouse Beach is 31.5 miles northwest of Pendleton. From the intersection of Main Street and Highway 30 in Pendleton, head southwest on Court Avenue to its junction with Highway

37, 1.4 miles. Turn right and drive to milepost 1, 29.4 miles. Shortly after milepost 1 the road divides. The left fork is signed for Umatilla, Hermiston and Highway 730 heading west; the right fork curves to Highway 730 heading east. At the fork, bear left and then immediately, just past the sign, turn right onto one of two crummy asphalt roadways, less than 0.1 mile. Drive onto either one of these roadways and follow it under an overpass to the point where the pavement ends, 0.1 mile. Proceed to a four-way split in the road, 0.3 mile. Turn onto the farthest left fork to get to the most developed and spectacular portion of the beach, 0.2 mile. The other sandy roads all lead to less populated extensions of the beach. Take care to avoid getting stuck in loose sand. (See detail map.)

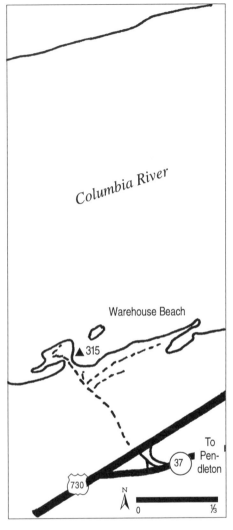

Comments: Located in sand dunes along the Lake Walulla backwater of McNary Dam on the Columbia River, this would be a 10 but for the heavy use, noise and litter pollution. Despite loud radios and motorboats, it is a truly extraordinary place. Sand dunes drop off into the water around a beautiful bay. The shoreline is irregular and interesting. A swimming area is marked. A small island is close by.

Umatilla County Points of Interest

316. Pendleton Underground • • • • • • • • • • • • • • • • •
37 Southwest Emigrant Avenue, Pendleton; (503) 276-0730

Type: Historic site
Hours: Office hours are Monday through Saturday, 9 A.M. to 5 P.M.; call for tour times
Fee: Yes

Driving Instructions: From the intersection of Main Street and Highway 30 in Pendleton, head southeast on Main Street to Emigrant Avenue, 0.1 mile. Turn right. The tours office is on the right.

Comments: A fascinating world of bordellos and underground speakeasies, dating from before the turn of the 19th Century through Prohibition, is exposed through entertaining guided tours.

317. Pendleton Woolen Mills ••••••••••••••••
1307 Southeast Court Place, Pendleton; (503) 276-6911

Type: Wool-processing factory
Hours: Monday through Friday, 8 A.M. to 4:45 P.M.; Saturday, 9 A.M. to 1 P.M. (Saturday, 8 A.M. to 2 P.M. from May to September)
Fee: No

Driving Instructions: From the intersection of Main Street and Highway 30 in Pendleton, head northeast on Dorion Avenue to a turn lane for Court Place, 0.5 mile (this is just before an overpass, after the road becomes two-way). Bear left and drive to the turnoff for parking at the woolen mills, 0.2 mile, on the left.

Comments: Don earphones and take a tour through a working factory to see wool coats and blankets spring from yarn. The tour is free, but beware of the gift shop.

Union County
(County Seat: LaGrande)

Waters in Union County are generally too shallow or too cold to be very enticing as swimming holes, but there are a couple of reasonable spots. Driving instructions begin in LaGrande at the intersection of I-84 and Highway 82.

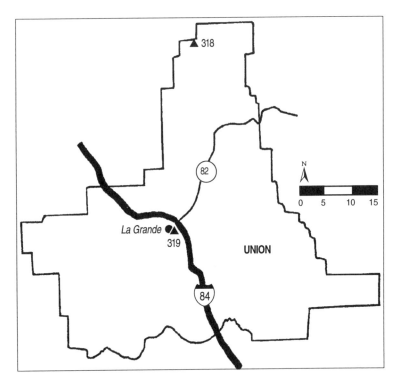

Union County Swimming Holes

318. Jubilee Lake
319. Riverside Park on Grande Ronde River

Union County Swimming Holes

318. Jubilee Lake

       Rating: 6
     Location: Umatilla National Forest
Water quality: Excellent; 16′ transparency
 Vital statistics: 90 acres; 45′ deep; 66° F (July); moderate bottom and

light shoreline weeds; silt bottom; moderate use

Setting: Forested mountains at 4696'; light litter
Swim. skills: Moderate
Amenities: For-fee camping; drinking water; pit toilets
Entry fee: No
Topo: Jubilee Lake 7½'

Driving Instructions: Jubilee Lake is 51.8 miles north of LaGrande. From Exit 261 in LaGrande at the intersection of I-84 and Highway 82, head northeast on Highway 82 to its junction with Highway 204 (10th Street) in Elgin, 19.1 miles. Turn left and drive to Forest Road 64, the Jubilee Lake turnoff, approximately 21 miles. Turn right and drive on gravel to the Jubilee Lake Campground turnoff, 11.0 miles. Turn right and go to parking by the boat ramp, 0.7 mile. (See detail map.)

Comments: An artificial lake, Jubilee is over-maintained but attractive. There is a wide gravel path all around it. Starting counterclockwise from the boat ramp, there are several clay entries to the water and also some small gravel beach spots. The lake is open and accessible.

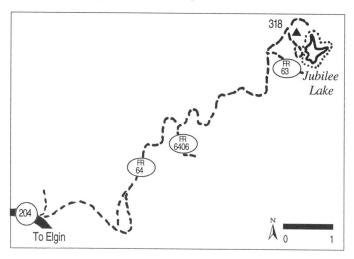

319. Riverside Park on Grande Ronde River •••••

Rating: 5
Location: LaGrande City Park
Water quality: Fair; 4' transparency
Vital statistics: 50' wide; at least 8' deep; moderate current; 67° F (July); light algae and bottom weeds; mud and rock bottom; moderate to heavy use
Setting: Wooded valley at 2780'; moderate litter

Swim. skills: Moderate
Amenities: Drinking water; flush toilets
Entry fee: No
Topo: LaGrande 7½'

Driving Instructions: From Exit 261 in LaGrande at the intersection of I-84 and Highway 82 (Island Avenue, toward town), head southwest on Island Avenue to Monroe Avenue, at the second light, 0.7 mile. Turn right and go to Spruce Street, 0.1 mile. Turn right and drive to the park entrance, just past a bridge, 1.1 miles. Turn right, bear to the right on the park road, and park, 0.1 mile.

Hiking Instructions: From parking, walk across the grass to the river.

Comments: The river has some decent holes downstream of a small boulder jumble. The bank is mud and gravel. Traffic noise is present. The park is equipped with a playground and grass. The DEQ 305(b) Report says this stretch of the river is partially water-quality limited.

Wallowa County
(County Seat: Enterprise)

Blessed with a share of Hells Canyon, Wallowa County has one of the best river locations for swimming in Eastern Oregon. Driving instructions begin in Enterprise at the junction of Highway 82 (North Street) and Highway 3 (1st Street).

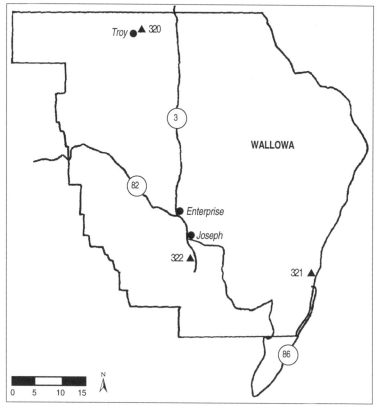

Wallowa County Swimming Holes

320. Grande Ronde River
321. Hells Canyon on Snake River
322. Wallowa Lake

Wallowa County Swimming Holes

320. Grande Ronde River • • • • • • • • • • • • • • • • • •

Rating: 7
Location: State Wildlife Area

Water quality: Excellent; transparent to bottom
Vital statistics: 170' wide; at least 12' deep; moderate current; 61°
(June); light algae; sand and pebble bottom; moderate
use
Setting: Wooded valley at 1600'; moderate use
Swim. skills: Moderate
Amenities: No-fee, primitive camping; no drinking water; pit toilets
Entry fee: No
Topo: Troy 7½'

Driving Instructions: Grande Ronde River is 48.6 miles north of
Enterprise. From the junction of Highways 82 and 3 in Enterprise, head
north on Highway 3 to the Troy turnoff, 33.7 miles, between mileposts 9
and 10. Turn left and drive to the end of the pavement, 7.8 miles. Continue
onto steep gravel and drive to the turnoff for Wenaha Wildlife Management
Area, 7.0 miles (give full attention to the road; do not look at the
dramatic scenery unless stopped at a turnout). Turn right and go to parking
near the river, 0.1 mile.

Comments: Along the river is a 125-foot fine-sand beach area. This
is a stop for driftboaters. A slack water area lies close to the beach, with
swifter current farther out. Upstream is a rapid.

321. Hells Canyon on Snake River ●●●●●●●●●●●

Rating: 10
Location: Wallowa-Whitman National Forest
Water quality: Good; 8' transparency
Vital statistics: 350' wide; at least 13' deep; swift current outside of
coves; 67° F (July); moderate algae and bottom
weeds; rock and boulder bottom; light to moderate
use
Setting: Scrub valley at 1520'; light litter
Swim. skills: Moderate to strong
Amenities: No drinking water; pit toilets at trailhead
Entry fee: No
Topo: Squirrel Prairie 7½'

Driving Instructions: Hells Canyon is 96.0 miles southeast of Enterprise. From the junction of Highways 82 and 3 in Enterprise, head
southeast on Highway 82 to the turnoff for Imnaha and Little Sheep Creek
Highway in Joseph, 6.5 miles. Turn left and drive to Forest Road 39/
Wallowa Mountain Loop, 8.0 miles. Turn right and drive to Highway 86,
approximately 52 miles. Turn left and go to the bridge across the Snake
River just below Oxbow Dam, about 6.5 miles.

It is possible to take a relatively shorter, easier route to the bridge across the Snake River from the freeway. From I-84 Exit 304, the exit for Baker City, at the intersection with Highway 7, head north on I-84 to Exit 302, the exit for Richland and Hells Canyon, 1.1 miles. Take the exit to a stop sign, 0.3 mile. Turn right onto Highway 86 and drive to the bridge across the Snake River just below Oxbow Dam, 68.3 miles.

From the bridge across the Snake River, cross the river, turn left (northeast) and drive along the Idaho side of the river to the Hells Canyon Dam, where the road crosses back to the Oregon side, then continue to parking next to the visitor center, 23.0 miles.

Hiking Instructions: Walk downriver from parking to the trailhead near pit toilets, 450 feet. The trail ends at sheer gorge walls, 1.4 miles. Along the trail are several delightful backwater coves, the best ones for swimming at 0.4, 1.1 and 1.2 miles. The cove at 1.1 miles is reached by a spur trail down to the river just after encountering sets of steps through notches in the rock. It is visible from ledges as one nears it, and is at the upstream end of the beach. The cove at 1.2 miles is near the end of the trail, shortly after crossing a log bridge. Be sure to note the appearance of poison ivy where it is identified at the trailhead.

Comments: The gorge, in the Hells Canyon National Recreation Area, is awe-inspiring. The Snake River is a National Wild and Scenic River. The cove at 0.4 mile has a rock-and-boulder beach with a long slack water stretch. The current is smooth beyond the slack water area, ending in a rapid. The cove at 1.1 miles has a gravel-and-boulder beach. It extends about 450 feet along the river. The cove at 1.2 miles has a gravel beach. The whole place is a spirit-lifter. There are occasional jet boats and numerous driftboats which cruise through this, the deepest gorge in North America. While they blemish, they cannot dim the beauty of the experience. If any place should have the protections of national-park designation, this is it. Be careful to stay in the slackwater of the coves when swimming. The water in the main stream is swift and unpredictable. Watch for schools of salmon.

322. Wallowa Lake ●

Rating:	5
Location:	State Park and Private
Water quality:	Excellent; 48′ transparency
Vital statistics:	1508 acres; 299′ deep; 72° F (August); light shoreline weeds; silt and gravel bottom; heavy use
Setting:	Forested foothills at 4372′; light litter
Swim. skills:	Low to moderate
Amenities:	For-fee camping; drinking water; flush toilets and pit toilets

Entry fee: Yes, at state park during summer

Topo: Joseph 7½'

Driving Instructions: Wallowa Lake is 13.2 miles southeast of Enterprise. From the junction of Highways 82 and 3 in Enterprise, head southeast on Highway 82 to the state park turnoff, 13.0 miles. Turn right and follow signs to camping, then go past the campground to parking next to the marked swimming area, about 0.2 mile. The entry to a privately owned swimming area, at the north end of the lake, is 4.8 miles back.

Comments: At the southern extreme of the lake, the marked swimming area is fronted by gravel beach with some sand. The setting is very nice on this natural lake with a dam, but the place is heavily congested with people, boats and noise. The privately owned spot is a little less crowded.

Wheeler County
(County Seat: Fossil)

The John Day River is at its finest in Wheeler County, and it offers a welcome, if murky, respite from the relentlessness of the desert. Driving instructions begin in Fossil at the intersection of Highways 19 and 218.

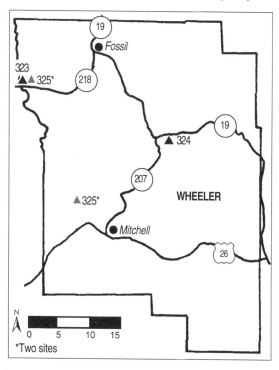

Wheeler County Swimming Holes

323. Clarno Park on John Day River
324. Muleshoe on John Day River

Wheeler County Point of Interest

325. John Day Fossil Beds National Monument

Wheeler County Swimming Holes

323. Clarno Park on John Day River • • • • • • • • •

      Rating: 6
     Location: State Park
Water quality: Fair; 5′ transparency

Vital statistics: 210' wide; at least 8' deep; light current; 78° F (July); moderate bottom weeds; pebble and mud bottom; light to moderate use
Setting: Scrub valley at 1300'; moderate litter
Swim. skills: Moderate
Amenities: No drinking water; pit toilets
Entry fee: No
Topo: Clarno 7½'

Driving Instructions: Clarno Park is 19.2 miles southwest of Fossil. From the junction of Highways 19 and 218 in Fossil, head south on Highway 218 to the poorly marked park turnoff, just before the bridge over the river, 19.2 miles, between mileposts 23 and 24. Turn right, into the park.

Comments: A pebble beach runs along the river. The flow by the state-park frontage is shallow, 3 or 4 feet deep. But there is plenty of depth just upstream of the bridge. Note that the upstream banks are private land. There are some attractive cliffs upstream.

324. Muleshoe on John Day River ● ● ● ● ● ● ● ● ● ● ●

Rating: 8
Location: Bureau of Land Management
Water quality: Fair; 7' transparency
Vital statistics: 150' wide; at least 10' deep; moderate current; 76° F (July); moderate bottom weeds; sand and rock bottom; light use
Setting: Scrub valley at 1680'; light litter
Swim. skills: Moderate
Amenities: No-fee camping; no drinking water; pit toilets
Entry fee: No
Topo: Masiker Mountain 7½'

Driving Instructions: Muleshoe is 21.6 miles southeast of Fossil. From Fossil, at the junction of Highways 19 and 218, head southeast on Highway 19 to the Muleshoe turnoff, 21.6 miles, between mileposts 80 and 81. Turn right and, at a fork, either bear left to a small parking area just above the hole, or bear right to the main parking, less than 0.1 mile.

Comments: On a hot day in the desert this is the only place to be, with the celestial scent of sagebrush and juniper and an exquisite, sculpted landscape. A 30-foot sand beach is beside a mostly dirt and gravel shoreline. There is a circular current pattern so the water is moving upstream next to the beach.

Wheeler County Point of Interest

325. John Day Fossil Beds National Monument • • •
National Park Service; (503) 575-0721

> **Type:** Geologic site
> **Hours:** Daily
> **Fee:** No

Driving Instructions: There are two units of the John Day Fossil Beds National Monument in Wheeler County.

Painted Hills Unit (50.1 miles south of Fossil)—From the junction of Highways 19 and 218 in Fossil, head southeast on Highway 19 to its intersection with Highway 207, 19.5 miles. Turn right and drive to Mitchell and Highway 26, 24.4 miles. Turn right and go to the Painted Hills turnoff, 3.4 miles, between mileposts 62 and 63. Turn right and drive to the Painted Hills Unit entrance, 2.8 miles.

Clarno Unit (16.1 miles west of Fossil)—From the junction of Highways 19 and 218 in Fossil, head south and then west on Highway 218 to the turnoff to the Clarno Unit, 16.1 miles, on the right.

Comments: The Painted Hills Unit consists of weathered and mineral-colored rolling hills. The Painted Hills are particularly alluring. The Clarno Unit consists of a grand volcanic monolith. (See Point of Interest #310 for the Sheep Rock Unit in Grant County, where the main visitor center is located.)

Southeast

Southeastern Oregon is desert country, mostly covered with sage. Its vastness can be appalling. Swimming holes are few and far between, and getting to them requires extra precautions. Always carry plenty of water, for both people and vehicles. Be prepared for heat. Plan the trip in order to be at a swimming hole during the heat of the day. Oregon's only poisonous snake, the rattlesnake, is found east of the Cascades, though it generally makes itself scarce. There are ticks and hence the danger of Lyme disease, so check body and clothing after jaunts. Folks in many rural parts of Eastern Oregon are "wavers": they wave at passersby—a friendly habit to be encouraged by waving back. Be sure to watch for the graceful and raucous magpie and to listen for the sweet song of meadowlarks.

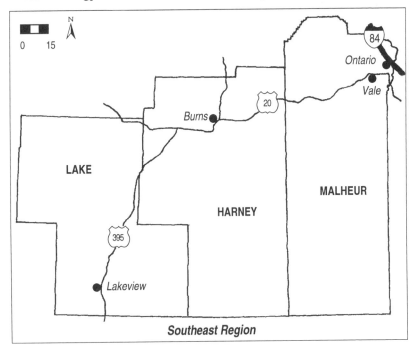

Southeast Region

Harney County
(County Seat: Burns)

There are a limited number of swimming spots in this dry country. Driving directions begin in Burns at the junction of Highways 20 and 395 with Highway 78.

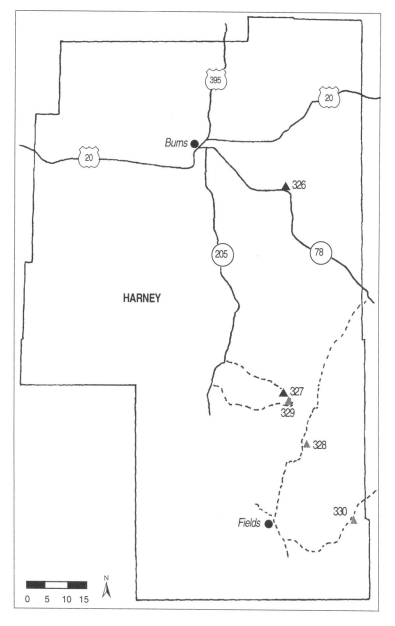

Harney County Swimming Holes

326. Crystal Crane Hot Springs
327. Fish Lake

Harney County Points of Interest

328. Alvord Hot Springs
329. Steens Mountain
330. Whitehorse Hot Springs

Harney County Swimming Holes

326. Crystal Crane Hot Springs • • • • • • • • • • • • • • •

Rating: 7
Location: Private; open daily, 7 A.M. to 10 P.M.; (503) 493-2312
Water quality: Good; 5' transparency
Vital statistics: 80' wide; 16' deep; maintained at 85–95° F, though may be higher during the heat of the day; moderate algae; gravel and silt bottom; moderate to heavy use
Setting: Scrub desert at 4120'; light litter
Swim skill: Moderate
Amenities: For-fee camping; drinking water; flush toilets
Entry fee: Yes
Topo: Warm Springs Butte 7½'

Driving Instructions: Crystal Crane Hot Springs is 25.5 miles southeast of Burns. From the junction of Highways 20 and 395 with Highway 78 in Burns, head east on Highway 78 to the hot springs turnoff, 25.4 miles, between mileposts 25 and 26. Turn left and find parking, 0.1 mile.

Comments: This is a commercial venture which does it right. A swim is available in a more-or-less natural pool with circulated water. A wooden platform gives access to the water from the gravel and grass shoreline. Hot tubs are also available.

327. Fish Lake •

Rating: 6
Location: Bureau of Land Management
Water quality: Excellent; 17' transparency
Vital statistics: 16 acres; 30' deep; 63° F (June); light bottom and moderate shoreline weeds; pebble and silt bottom; moderate to heavy use
Setting: Wooded mountains at 7371'; light litter

Swim skill: Moderate
Amenities: For-fee camping; drinking water; pit toilets
Entry fee: No
Topo: Fish Lake 7½′

Driving Instructions: Fish Lake is 77.3 miles south of Burns. From the junction of Highways 20 and 395 with Highway 78 in Burns, head east on Highway 78 to Highway 205, 1.7 miles. Turn right and drive south to the turnoff for Steens Mountain in Frenchglen, 58.7 miles, between mileposts 58 and 59. Turn left and drive on a gravel and dirt road to a fork that comes right after a double bridge crossing, 3.1 miles. Bear left onto Steens North Loop Road and go to the entrance for Fish Lake, 13.6 miles. Turn right and—bearing left, then right, at forks in the road along the way—go to parking next to the boat ramp, 0.2 mile.

Comments: A special oasis spot, complete with a stand of aspens, this glacially created lake is accessible except at a marshy area on the east end. The bank is grassy with occasional gravel spots.

Harney County Points of Interest

328. Alvord Hot Springs •
Alvord Desert

Type: Semi-developed hot springs
Hours: Daily
Fee: No

Driving Instructions: Alvord Hot Springs is 106.9 miles southeast of Burns. From the junction of Highways 20 and 395 with Highway 78 in Burns, head east on Highway 78 to the turnoff for Fields, 65.2 miles. Turn right onto the Fields-Denio Road and travel on gravel to the turnout for the hot springs, 41.7 miles, on the left.

Comments: On privately owned property, access to the springs is open to the public. At 4080 feet in elevation, the springs have been spiffed up recently. Half of the pool is enclosed by a corrugated wall above the ground. A wooden platform provides easy access. The pool is bounded by concrete walls with a concrete slab bottom. Expect nudity. The dimensions are 25 feet by 50 feet, with water 3 feet deep, and the temperature 102° F.

329. Steens Mountain •
Bureau of Land Management

Type: Scenic location
Hours: Daily
Fee: No

Driving Instructions: Steens Mountain is south of Burns. Follow the driving instructions for Swimming Hole #327 and then continue past the Fish Lake turnoff to viewpoints at the summit, about 4–5 miles beyond.

Comments: Steens Mountain presents great panoramas of Kiger Gorge, a classic U-shaped, glacially carved valley, to the north, and the Alvord Desert to the southeast.

330. Whitehorse Hot Springs
Bureau of Land Management

Type: Natural hot springs
Hours: Daily
Fee: No

Driving Instructions: Whitehorse Hot Springs is 139.6 miles southeast of Burns. From the junction of Highways 20 and 395 with Highway 78 in Burns, head east on Highway 78 to Highway 95, 91.7 miles. Turn right and drive to Whitehorse Ranch Road, 20.9 miles, between mileposts 87 and 88. Turn right and go on gravel to a dirt turnoff, past the ranch, 24.4 miles (Willow Creek is too far). Turn left and drive to where the road forks, 2.3 miles. Bear right and go to the hot springs, 0.3 mile. (See detail map.)

Comments: At 4520 feet in elevation, this is a wonderfully remote hot springs which has been dug out to be almost swimmable. There are two adjacent pools in a 45-foot by 10-foot space. The smaller is three feet deep with a sand and silt bottom and 104-degree water. The larger is four feet deep with a silt bottom and 95-degree water. Expect nudity.

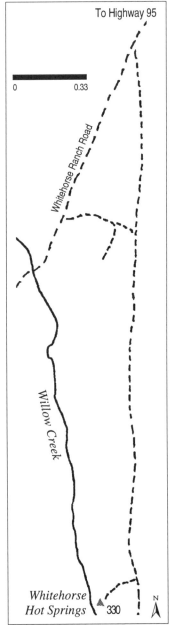

Lake County
(County Seat: Lakeview)

Much of the water in the county is unappealing, but there are nice exceptions to be found in this attractive Oregon backwater (so to speak). Driving directions begin in Lakeview at the junction of Highway 140 and Highway 395.

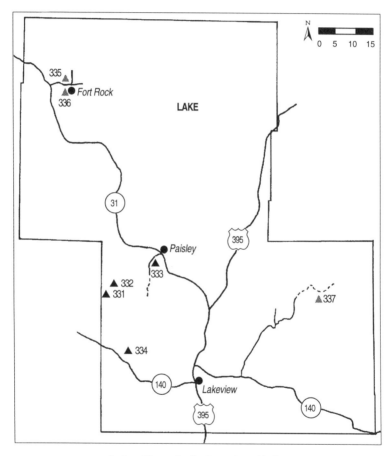

Lake County Swimming Holes

331. Blue Lake
332. Campbell Lake
333. Chewaucan River
334. Cottonwood Meadow Lake

Lake County Points of Interest

335. Fort Rock Park
336. Fort Rock Valley Homestead Village Museum
337. Hart Mountain National Antelope Refuge and Antelope Hot Springs

Lake County Swimming Holes

331. Blue Lake •

Rating: 8
Location: Fremont National Forest
Water quality: Excellent; transparent to bottom
Vital statistics: 0.3 mile wide; at least 26' deep; 64° F (June); light shoreline weeds; silt bottom; light use
Setting: Forested mountains at 7031'; light litter
Swim skill: Moderate
Amenities: No drinking water; pit toilet at trailhead
Entry fee: No
Topo: Lee Thomas Crossing 7½'

Driving Instructions: Blue Lake is 48.3 miles northwest of Lakeview. From the junction of Highway 140 and Highway 395 in Lakeview, head west on Highway 140 to Thomas Creek Road, 3.5 miles. Turn right and drive to the turnoff for Forest Road 28 and Campbell Lake, 5.5 miles. Turn left onto what becomes Forest Road 28 and go to the junction with Forest Road 3428, where the pavement ends, 22.3 miles. Continue straight onto Forest Road 3428 and drive on gravel to Forest Road 34, 7.5 miles. Cross Forest Road 34 to Forest Road 3372 on the other side and travel to the Blue Lake turnoff, 8.3 miles, between mileposts 13 and 14. Turn left and go to parking at the trailhead, 1.2 miles. (See detail map on next page.)

Hiking Instructions: From the trailhead, hike the well-trod, though occasionally steep, path to the lake, 2.7 miles.

Comments: The lake, in the Gearhart Mountain Wilderness, sparkles with remote beauty. There are several small, rocky areas along the shoreline, and occasional downed trees. The lake has a wonderful feeling of openness.

332. Campbell Lake •

Rating: 6
Location: Fremont National Forest
Water quality: Excellent; transparent to bottom
Vital statistics: 0.3 mile wide; at least 7' deep; 66° F (June); light bottom weeds; rock and silt bottom; moderate use
Setting: Forested mountains at 7195'; light litter

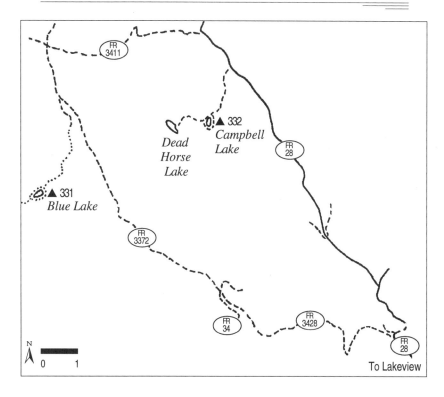

Swim skill: Moderate
Amenities: No-fee camping; drinking water; pit toilets
Entry fee: No
Topo: Lee Thomas Crossing 7½'

Driving Instructions: Campbell Lake is 44.0 miles northwest of Lakeview. Follow the driving instructions for Swimming Hole #331 to the junction with Forest Road 3428. Turn right, still on Forest Road 28, and drive to the Campbell Lake turnoff, 10.6 miles (the pavement is rough for the first couple of miles). Turn left and go to the entrance for the lake, 1.8 miles. Turn left. (See detail map for Swimming Hole #331.)

Comments: A gravel road encircles this otherwise pretty lake. Good access to the lake and its mostly gravel banks is from the east shore, next to the campground.

333. Chewaucan River • • • • • • • • • • • • • • • • • • •

Rating: 6
Location: Private
Water quality: Fair; 5' transparency

Vital statistics: 30' wide; at least 10' deep; moderate to swift current; 71° F (July); light algae; rock and bedrock bottom; moderate use

Setting: Scrub valley at 4440'; moderate litter

Swim skill: Moderate

Amenities: None

Entry fee: No

Topo: Paisley 7½'

Driving Instructions: Chewaucan River is 46.0 miles north of Lakeview. From the junction of Highway 140 and Highway 395 in Lakeview, head north on Highway 395 to Valley Falls and Highway 31, 22.4 miles, between mileposts 120 and 121. Continue straight onto Highway 31 (Highway 395 angles to the right) and proceed to Paisley at Mill Street, 22.3 miles, between mileposts 98 and 99. Turn left and drive to parking on a wide asphalt apron, on the right, 1.3 miles.

Hiking Instructions: Walk across the road from parking. A short, fairly steep scramble over the bank of formation rock and gravel leads to the spot.

Comments: There is a large rock formation along the river. The river trenches around it and then flows to a downstream rapid. Upstream is a nice string of rocky cascades.

334. Cottonwood Meadow Lake • • • • • • • • • • • • •

Rating: 5

Location: Fremont National Forest

Water quality: Fair; 9' transparency

Vital statistics: 39 acres; 12' deep; 61° F (June); moderate to heavy bottom weeds; rock and mud bottom; moderate use

Setting: Wooded mountains at 6128'; light litter

Swim skill: Moderate

Amenities: No-fee camping; drinking water; pit toilets

Entry fee: No

Topo: Cougar Peak 7½'

Driving Instructions: Cottonwood Meadow Lake is 29.2 miles west of Lakeview. From the junction of Highway 140 and Highway 395 in Lakeview, head west on Highway 140 to the lake turnoff at Forest Road 3870, 22.6 miles, between mileposts 73 and 74. Turn right and drive to the gravel road that nearly circles the lake, 5.9 miles. Bear left and go to the turnoff for picnic parking, 0.7 mile, on the right.

Comments: This artificial lake is not to be confused with Cottonwood Reservoir to the east. The surroundings are nice, and the bank is grass and gravel. Cattle share the place.

Lake County Points of Interest

335. Fort Rock Park •••••••••••••••••••••••
State Park

> **Type:** Scenic location
> **Hours:** Daily
> **Fee:** No

Driving Instructions: Fort Rock Park is 122.0 miles northwest of Lakeview. From the junction of Highways 140 and 395 in Lakeview, head north on Highway 395 to Valley Falls and Highway 31, 22.4 miles, between mileposts 120 and 121. Continue straight onto Highway 31 (Highway 395 angles to the right) and proceed to the turnoff for Fort Rock, 91.5 miles, between mileposts 29 and 30. Turn right and drive to Cabin Lake Road, 6.3 miles. Turn left and drive to the park turnoff, 1.0 mile. Turn left and go to the park entrance, 0.6 mile. Turn right and find parking, 0.1 mile.

Comments: This is a huge, circular-walled, spatter cone remnant. There are primitive roads inside the structure, but it is best to walk.

336. Fort Rock Valley Homestead Village Museum
Fort Rock; (503) 576-2388

> **Type:** History exhibit
> **Hours:** Friday through Sunday, 10 A.M. to 4 P.M. from Memorial Day through October hunting season
> **Fee:** No; donation requested

Driving Instructions: Fort Rock Valley Homestead Village Museum is 120.1 miles northwest of Lakeview. Follow the driving instructions for Swimming Hole #335 to the turnoff for Fort Rock. Turn right and drive to Fort Rock, just before the state park turn, 6.2 miles. The museum is on the right.

Comments: Homestead-era buildings are clustered on the grounds of the museum.

337. Hart Mountain National Antelope Refuge and Antelope Hot Springs
National Antelope Refuge; (503) 947-3315

> **Type:** Wildlife habitat
> **Hours:** Daily
> **Fee:** No

Driving Instructions: Hart Mountain National Antelope Refuge and Antelope Hot Springs are 67.4 miles northeast of Lakeview. From the junction of Highway 140 and Highway 395 in Lakeview, head north to the point where they diverge and Highway 140 continues east, 4.6 miles. Turn right and drive to the turnoff for Hart Mountain and Plush, 15.8 miles, between mileposts 15 and 16. Turn left, onto County Road 313, and drive to a crossroads in Plush, 18.8 miles. Turn left and continue to County Road 3-12, signed for Hart Mountain, 0.9 mile. Turn right and drive generally east to the end of the pavement, 13.4 miles (do not get sidetracked by another county road). Now on gravel, drive to the refuge headquarters, 9.6 miles (the last 3 miles are steep). Bear right at the junction just beyond the headquarters and drive to the turnoff for the bathhouse at the hot springs, 4.1 miles (go right when the road forks). Turn right and drive on a rough dirt road to parking near a cinder-block building, 0.2 mile.

Comments: There really are antelope to be seen. Ask at the headquarters for best times and places for sighting. The refuge is a wonderfully scenic place. The hot spring, at 5980 feet elevation, is basically maintained in its natural state, surrounded by unsightly concrete. Expect nudity. Be careful of the slippery wooden steps into the pool. The pool measures 10 feet by 15 feet, is 5 feet deep and has water that is 100° F. There is some sand on a bedrock bottom.

Malheur County
(County Seat: Vale)

It is tough to find good swimming in this part of the desert. The reservoirs are remote, and as unappealing as anywhere else in the state. But there are attractions, and the Owyhee River furnishes a couple of good ones for the swimmer. Driving instructions begin in Vale at the intersection of Highway 20 and Glenn Street.

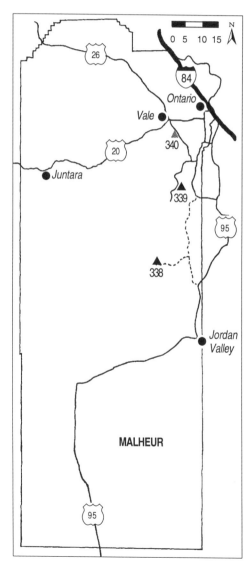

Malheur County Swimming Holes

338. Leslie Gulch on Owyhee Reservoir
339. Owyhee River and Snively Hot Springs

Malheur County Point of Interest

340. Keeney Pass

Malheur County Swimming Holes

338. Leslie Gulch on Owyhee Reservoir • • • • • • •

Rating: 6
Location: Bureau of Land Management
Water quality: Fair; 7' transparency
Vital statistics: 13,900 acres; 117' deep; 78° F (July); moderate bottom weeds and suspended algae; gravel and mud bottom; moderate use
Setting: Scrub valley at 2670'; light litter
Swim skill: Moderate
Amenities: No-fee camping; no drinking water; pit toilets
Entry fee: No
Topo: Rooster Comb 7½'

Driving Instructions: Leslie Gulch is 70.1 miles south of Vale. From the intersection of Highway 20 and Glenn Street in Vale, head south on Glenn Street to a stop sign on Owyhee Avenue, 16.4 miles (Glenn Street becomes Lytle Boulevard, which in turn becomes Janeta Avenue and Jefferson Drive). Turn left and drive to Owyhee Junction, 1.9 miles. Turn right onto Highway 201.

Alternatively, from Ontario to this point, take I-84 Exit 376 and head west on Idaho Avenue to 2nd Street, 0.6 mile. Turn left onto 2nd Street and drive to 4th Street/Highway 201, 0.2 mile. Turn right onto Highway 201 and go to Owyhee Junction, 20.3 miles. Owyhee Junction is between mileposts 7 and 8.

From Owyhee Junction, follow Highway 201 through Adrian, to the turnoff for Succor Creek Recreation Area and Succor Creek Road, 12.2 miles, between mileposts 19 and 20. Turn right and travel on dirt and gravel to Succor Creek Recreation Area, 15.8 miles. Continue past Succor Creek Recreation Area to the turnoff for Leslie Gulch, 9.9 miles. Turn right and follow the sometimes steep route down to parking, 13.9 miles.

Comments: The last 7 miles to parking are outstanding, with huge blocks and ridges of colorful rock, formed from volcanic sediments, rising to the sky. Take care to watch the road while enjoying the view. Handel's

Water Music, or something else with brass, would be appropriate on the descent into the gulch. This is more a fantastic desert spectacle than a place to swim. When the river is in its traditional bed, the water may reach only 5 feet deep, so it is not swimmable in the ordinary sense, but it does provide the opportunity for a very enjoyable float, looking up at the most scenic spot in the county. During high water times, since it is at the upper reaches of the Owyhee Reservoir, the largest reservoir in Oregon, the characteristics of the place are totally different. Then, the water is deep, languid and swimmable, with nice gravel beach spots 0.1 mile upstream.

339. Owyhee River and Snively Hot Springs •••••

Rating: 7
Location: Bureau of Land Management
Water quality: Fair; 2' transparency
Vital statistics: 100' wide; at least 10' deep; moderate current; 67° F (July); moderate algae; rock and boulder bottom; moderate use
Setting: Scrub valley at 2280'; moderate litter
Swim skill: Moderate to strong
Amenities: No-fee, primitive camping; no drinking water; pit toilets at the hot springs
Entry fee: No
Topo: Owyhee Dam 7½'

Driving Instructions: Owyhee River and Snively Hot Springs are 25.0 miles south of Vale. From the intersection in Vale of Highway 20 and Glenn Street, which becomes Lytle Boulevard, head south on Glenn Street to Janeta Avenue, 14.1 miles. There is a market on the right. Turn right and drive to the continuation of Lytle Boulevard, 0.2 mile. Turn left and drive to Owyhee Avenue, 1.7 miles. Turn right and go to Lake Owyhee Road (unmarked), 1.4 miles.

Alternatively, from Ontario to this point, take I-84 Exit 376 and head west on Idaho Avenue to 2nd Street, 0.6 mile. Turn left and drive to 4th Street/Highway 201, 0.2 mile. Turn right and go to Owyhee Junction, 20.3 miles, between mileposts 7 and 8. Turn right onto Owyhee Avenue and drive to Lake Owyhee Road, 3.9 miles.

From the Owyhee Avenue/Lake Owyhee Road junction, turn left onto Lake Owyhee Road and go to the turnout next to the source of the hot springs, 6.6 miles (this is 1.4 miles past the point where huge siphon pipes V up both sides of the canyon). To get to the swimming hole, continue on the road to a dirt turnoff beyond the hot springs, 1.0 mile. Turn left, bear to the left where the road forks, and drive on a rough road to the river, 0.1 mile. Turn right onto a rough-rock, primitive roadway alongside the river and look for the opening in the shrub willow, immediately to the left. (See detail map, next page, which does not show the unpaved roads to the swimming hole.)

Comments: Access to the river is partially blocked by the shrubbery along the bank at this place, 11 miles below a dam. At the in the shrub willow, look downstream to locate three large boulders which roughly mark the deep water. A rapid is farther downstream. There is some foam. Scenic volcanic monoliths rise overhead. The nearby hot springs are an added attraction. The springs come out of the ground near the road, encircled by a concrete barrier, two feet across. The temperature well exceeds 120° F. The water flows 300 feet down to the river, where a circular pocket of rock, about 20 feet in diameter, has been constructed (the shape changes with change of builders). The water within is 2–3 feet deep, while the adjacent river is 3–4 feet deep. Temperatures within the pool vary from 98 to 108° F, and are much hotter than that where the flow enters the pool.

Another hot spring, Mitchell Butte Hot Springs, is 4.0 miles back from Snively. It is a much smaller, hotter and more trashed spot. The turnoff is west of Lake Owyhee Road, and the spring is immediately to the right after the turn. The spring is walled with concrete and has concrete chunks for a bottom. It is a 12-foot by 12-foot enclosure, 2 feet deep and 117° F.

Malheur County Point of Interest

340. Keeney Pass •
Bureau of Land Management

        Type: Historic site
       Hours: Daily
         Fee: No

Driving Instructions: Keeney Pass is 6.5 miles south of Vale. From the intersection in Vale of Highway 20 and Glenn Street, which becomes Lytle Boulevard, head south on Glenn Street to the turnoff for the pass, 6.4 miles. Turn right and go to parking, 0.1 mile.

Comments: Fifteen percent of the 2,000-mile Oregon Trail remains. Here is part of it. Over 50,000 people went by Keeney Pass from 1843 to 1860, and the deep double ruts they left are plainly visible.

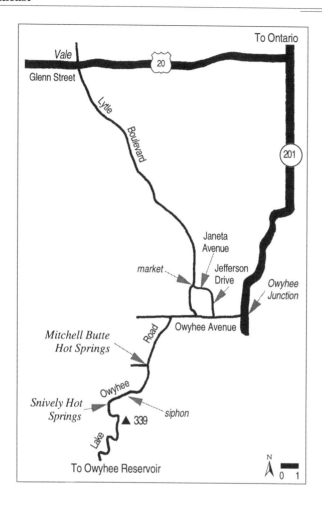

To Ontario

Vale

20

Glenn Street

Lytle
Boulevard

201

Janeta
Avenue

market

Jefferson
Drive

Owyhee
Junction

Owyhee Avenue

Road

*Mitchell Butte
Hot Springs*

Owyhee

*Snively Hot
Springs*

siphon

▲ 339

Lake

To Owyhee Reservoir

N

0   1

References

Atkeson, Ray, *Oregon I, II and III*, Graphic Arts Center Publishing Co.: Portland, Oregon, 1968–87. Here is Oregon in photographs.

DeLorme Mapping, *Oregon Atlas and Gazetteer*, Freeport, Maine, 1991. This is a good complement to the State Highway map and Forest Service maps, despite its sometimes difficult legibility.

Friedman, Ralph, *In Search of Western Oregon*, Caxton Printers: Caldwell, Idaho, 1990. This is an expansive treatment of the nooks and crannies of the western part of the state.

Jackson, Philip and Jon Kimerling, editors, *Atlas of the Pacific Northwest*, Oregon State University Press: Corvallis, Oregon, 1993. This is a nice coverage of the Northwest's physical and demographic features.

Johnson, Daniel and Richard Petersen, et al., *Atlas of Oregon Lakes*, Oregon State University Press: Corvallis, Oregon, 1985. This is a compendium description of 202 lakes or reservoirs, including physical characteristics and water-quality data.

Litton, Evie, *Hiker's Guide to Hot Springs in the Pacific Northwest*, Falcon Press: Helena, Montana, 1990. Here is a collection of hot springs with adjacent hikes.

Loam, Jayson and Marjorie Gersh, *Hot Springs and Hot Pools of the Northwest*, Aqua Thermal Access: Santa Cruz, California, 1993. This is an ample work on hot springs in the Northwest.

Loy, William, et al., *Atlas of Oregon*, University of Oregon Books: Eugene, Oregon, 1985. This is the comprehensive, if outdated, description of the state's human and natural features.

McLean, Cheryl and Clint Brown, *Oregon's Quiet Waters, A Guide to Lakes for Canoeists and Other Paddlers*, Jackson Creek Press: Corvallis, Oregon, 1987. This is a fun guide for folks who do not necessarily want to get wet. The lakes in the book are clustered primarily in the state's central and northern Cascades.

Oceanographic Institute of Washington, *Summary of Knowledge of the Oregon and Washington Coastal Zone and Offshore Areas*, in three volumes, prepared for United States Department of Interior, 1977. This thick compendium contains everything most folks would want to know about the coast.

Oregon Department of Environmental Quality (DEQ), *Oregon's 1992 Water Quality Status Assessment Report, "305(b) Report"*. This publication was submitted to the United States Environmental Protection Agency (EPA) to satisfy requirements of the federal Clean Water Act.

Oregon State Marine Board, *Oregon Boating Synopsis*, Salem, Oregon, October 1992. Frequently updated, the *Synopsis* capsulizes Oregon laws and regulations with respect to use of motors on Oregon waters.

Oregon Tourism Division, *Oregon Campground Guide*, available free at 1-800-547-7842, 775 Summer Street NE, Salem, Oregon 97310. This is a map guide to developed and semi-developed campgrounds under various agency management. It is a must for locating no-fee stays in established campgrounds.

Secretary of State, *Oregon Blue Book*, a biennial publication, Salem, Oregon. This is the definitive current trivia compilation of Oregon facts and figures.

United States Department of Interior Geological Survey, *Lakes of Oregon*, 1973–79. This is a six-pamphlet detailed survey of lakes in 13 Oregon counties.

United States Geological Survey, *Water Resources Data, 1990–91 and 1991–92*. This is a source of stream-flow information.

Willamette Kayak and Canoe Club, *Soggy Sneakers, Guide to Oregon Rivers*, Second Edition, Corvallis, Oregon, 1986. This is a wonderful collection of river runs throughout the state.

Appendix A. Useful Phone Numbers and Addresses

Oregon Department of Forestry
2600 State Street
Salem, OR 97310
(503) 945-7422 or (503) 945-7200
(Can provide closure information for state, municipal and private lands, and for BLM land west of the Cascades.)

Oregon State Parks
525 Trade Street SE
Salem, OR 97310
Camp Information 1-800-452-5687 or (503) 378-6305

Oregon Tourism Division
775 Summer Street NE
Salem, OR 97310
1-800-547-7842 or (503) 378-3451

US Department of Agriculture—Forest Service
(Forest Service lands are rarely closed, though there may be use restrictions.)

Pacific Northwest Regional Office
333 SW First Avenue, PO Box 3623
Portland, OR 97208
(503) 326-2877

Deschutes National Forest
1654 Highway 20 E
Bend, OR 97701
(503) 388-2715

Fremont National Forest
524 North G Street, PO Box 551
Lakeview, OR 97630
(503) 947-2151

Malheur National Forest
139 NE Dayton Street
John Day, OR 97845
(503) 575-1731

Mount Hood National Forest
2955 NW Division
Gresham, OR 97030
(503) 666-0700

Ochoco National Forest
3000 E Third, PO Box 490
Prineville, OR 97754
(503) 447-6247

Rogue River National Forest
333 W 8th Street, PO Box 520
Medford, OR 97501
(503) 776-3600

Siskiyou National Forest
200 NE Greenfield Road, PO Box 440
Grants Pass, OR 97526
(503) 479-6516

Siuslaw National Forest
4077 Research Way, PO Box 1148
Corvallis, OR 97339
(503) 750-7000

Umatilla National Forest
2517 SW Hailey Avenue
Pendleton, 97801
(503) 276-3811

Umpqua National Forest
2900 NW Stewart Parkway,
  PO Box 1008
Roseburg, OR 97470
(503) 672-6601

Wallowa-Whitman National Forest
1550 Dewey Avenue, PO Box 907
Baker City, OR 97814
(503) 523-6391

Willamette National Forest
211 E 7th Avenue, PO Box 10607
Eugene, OR 97440
(503) 465-6561

Winema National Forest
2519 Dahlia Street
Klamath Falls, OR 97601
(503) 883-6714

US Department of the Interior—Bureau of Land Management (BLM)

(For districts east of the Cascades it is necessary to call individual districts for closure information, etc. BLM now operates more like the Forest Service than the State Department of Forestry, with a preference for public rather than commercial use, so closures to the public are infrequent.)

Oregon State Office
1300 NE 44th Avenue, PO Box 2965
Portland, OR 97208
(503) 280-7001

Burns District
HC 74 - 12533 Highway 20 W
Hines, OR 97738
(503) 573-5241

Coos Bay District
1300 Airport Lane
North Bend, OR 97456
(503) 756-0100

Eugene District
2090 Chad Drive, PO Box 10226
Eugene, OR 97440
(503) 683-6600

Lakeview District
1000 Ninth Street S, PO Box 151
Lakeview, OR 97630
(503) 947-2177

Medford District
3040 Biddle Road
Medford, OR 97504
(503) 770-2200

Prineville District
185 E Fourth Street, PO Box 550
Prineville, OR 97754
(503) 447-4115

Roseburg District
777 NW Garden Valley Boulevard
Roseburg, OR 97470
(503) 440-4930

Salem District
1717 Fabry Road, SE
Salem, OR 97306
(503) 375-5646

Vale District
100 Oregon Street
Vale, OR 97918
(503) 473-3144

Appendix B. Hot Springs

Following is a list of hot springs that are or have been available in Oregon. Where a place is closed or restricted to public use, that is indicated.

Alvord Hot Springs—Harney—#328
Antelope (Hart Mountain) Hot Springs—Lake—#337
Austin Hot Springs (closed)—Clackamas
Bagby Hot Springs—Clackamas—#13
Baker's Bar M Ranch (commercial, guests only)—Umatilla
Belknap Hot Springs (commercial)—Lane
Blue Mountain Hot Springs (closed)—Grant
Breitenbush Hot Springs (commercial)—Marion—#150
Cove Hot Springs (commercial)—Union
Crystal Crane Hot Springs (commercial)—Harney—#326
Hot Lake Hotel (closed)—Union
Hunter's Hot Springs (commercial)—Lake
Jackson Hot Springs (commercial)—Jackson
Kahneeta Resort (commercial)—Wasco—#295
Kitson Hot Springs (Boy Scouts only)—Lane
Lehman Hot Springs (commercial)—Umatilla
McCredie Springs—Lane—#97
McKenzie River Hot Springs—Lane—#99
Medical Springs (closed)—Union
Mitchell Hot Springs—Malheur—#339
Radium Hot Springs (closed)—Baker
Ritter Hot Springs (closed)—Grant
Snively Hot Springs—Malheur—#339
Summer Lake Hot Springs (commercial)—Lake
Terwilliger Hot Springs—Lane—90
Umpqua Hot Springs—Douglas—#229
Wall Creek (Meditation Pool) Hot Springs—Lane—#104
Whitehorse Hot Springs—Harney—#330

Note: All the hot springs designated "commercial," with the exception of Crystal Crane and Breitenbush, have concrete pools.

Appendix C. Conversions to Metric

feet x 0.3048 = meters
(327 feet equals about 100 meters)

miles x 1.609344 = kilometers
(6 miles equals about 10 kilometers)

acres x 0.404686 = hectares
(25 acres equals about 10 hectares)

(degrees F - 32) x $\frac{5}{9}$ = degrees C

C	F*
0	32
1	34
2	36
3	37
4	39
5	41
6	43
7	45
8	46
9	48
10	50
11	52
12	54
13	55
14	57
15	59
16	61
17	63
18	64
19	66
20	68
21	70
22	72
23	73
24	74
25	77
26	79
27	81
28	82
29	84

* Rounded off

Index

298